SOCIAL RIGHTS AND HUMAN WELFARE

An essential overview of rights-based approaches in social policy, this text critically explores how social rights underpin human wellbeing. It discusses social rights as rights of citizenship in developed welfare states and as an essential component within the international human rights and human development agenda. It provides a valuable introduction for students and researchers in social policy and related applied social science, public policy, sociology, socio-legal studies and social development fields.

Taking an international perspective, the first part of the book considers how social rights can be understood and critiqued in theory – discussing ideas around citizenship, human needs and human rights, collective responsibility and ethical imperatives. The second part of the book looks at social rights in practice, providing a comparative examination of their development globally, before looking more specifically at rights to livelihood, human services and housing as well as ways in which these rights can be implemented and enforced. The final section re-evaluates prevailing debates about rights-based approaches to poverty alleviation and outlines possible future directions.

The book provides a comprehensive overview of social rights in theory and practice. It questions recent developments in social policy. It challenges certain dominant ideas concerning the basis of human rights. It seeks to re-frame our understanding of social rights as the articulation of human needs and presents a radical new 'post-Marshallian' theory of social rights.

Hartley Dean is professor of social policy at the London School of Economics. His 30 years in academia were preceded by a 12-year career as a welfare rights worker in one of London's most deprived multicultural neighbourhoods. His principal teaching and research interests stem from concerns with poverty, social justice and welfare rights. Among his more recently published books are *Welfare Rights and Social Policy* (2002), *Social Policy* (2006 & 2012) and *Understanding Human Need* (2010).

SOCIAL RIGHTS AND HUMAN WELFARE

Hartley Dean

Routledge
Taylor & Francis Group

LONDON AND NEW YORK

First published 2015
By Routledge
2 Park Square, Milton Park, Abingdon, Oxon OX14 4RN

and by Routledge
711 Third Avenue, New York, NY 10017

Routledge is an imprint of the Taylor & Francis Group, an informa business

British Library Cataloguing-in-Publication Data
A catalogue record for this book is available from the British Library

Library of Congress Cataloging-in-Publication Data
Dean, Hartley, 1949–
  Social rights and human welfare / written by Hartley Dean.
    pages cm
  1. Social rights.   2. Social policy.   3. Public welfare.   4. Social rights—Great Britain.   5. Great Britain—Social policy.   6. Public welfare—Great Britain.   I. Title.
  HM671.D384 2015
  361.6'14—dc23
  2014037849

ISBN: 978-1-138-01310-0 (hbk)
ISBN: 978-1-138-01312-4 (pbk)
ISBN: 978-1-315-79542-3 (ebk)

Typeset in Bembo
by Apex CoVantage, LLC

MIX
Paper from
responsible sources
FSC
www.fsc.org   FSC® C013604

Printed and bound by CPI Group (UK) Ltd, Croydon, CR0 4YY

To Pam, with love and gratitude

CONTENTS

ILLUSTRATIONS

Figures

Tables

Boxes

ACRONYMS

BNA	Basic Needs Approach
CESCR	Committee on Economic, Social and Cultural Rights
DRtD	Declaration on the Right to Development
ECOSOC	Economic and Social Council (of the United Nations)
ICCPR	International Covenant on Civil and Political Rights
ICESCR	International Covenant on Economic, Social and Cultural Rights
ILO	International Labour Organisation
IMF	International Monetary Fund
MDGs	Millennium Development Goals
NGO	Non-Governmental Organisation
NHS	National Health Service
NICE	National Institute for Health and Care Excellence (in England)
OECD	Organisation for Economic Co-operation and Development
OHCHR	Office of the High Commissioner for Human Rights
SDGs	Sustainable Development Goals
UDHR	Universal Declaration of Human Rights
UK	United Kingdom (of Great Britain and Northern Ireland)
UN	United Nations
UNCRC	United Nations Convention on the Rights of the Child
UNDP	United Nations Development Programme
UNESCO	United Nations Educational, Scientific and Cultural Organisation
UN-HABITAT	United Nations Human Settlements Programme
UNHRC	United Nations Human Rights Council
US	United States (of America)
WHO	World Health Organisation
WTO	World Trade Organisation

PREFACE

To readers interested in human rights and/or citizenship rights this book offers an introduction to social policy, and for readers interested in social policy it provides an introduction to rights-based approaches. It is a book about connections: the connections between social rights and human welfare; between theory and practice; between debate and reality.

This is a book that has evolved over a period of some 20 years. It began life as a volume entitled *Welfare, Law and Citizenship,* published in 1996 by Harvester Wheatsheaf/Prentice Hall. A second, but differently titled edition, *Welfare Rights and Social Policy* was published in 2002 by Pearson Education/Prentice Hall. This iteration of the book is not so much a third edition as a successor to the previous versions. It is in some ways a radically different book. The nature of its evolution reflects elements of the author's own intellectual journey and is captured in part through the changes in title. *Social Rights and Human Welfare* captures a specific range of rights – to livelihood and social security, to health and social care, to education and cultural participation, to housing and a safe environment – while the term 'human welfare' captures the essence of the wellbeing that may be fulfilled through the realisation of such rights. Though the terms welfare and wellbeing have accrued and can convey different meanings and each is liable to different challenges and misinterpretations, their origins are closely inter-related. For the purposes of this particular book they can be regarded as being if not quite synonymous, as in many contexts virtually interchangeable, and I shall use them accordingly.

The book has expanded to consider the human rights agenda as much as citizenship rights. While still embracing the role of law and policy making, it is more focused on matters of generic principle. Some of the material from the earlier books has been retained and either developed or updated, but detailed illustrations based on the British context have been pared back. This volume looks to expanded horizons and is addressed to an international readership. It aims, so far as possible, to be relevant to emerging welfare systems of the global South as well as to established welfare states of the global North. It will touch on deep-seated questions to do with the fundamental nature of human need and the ethical foundations of social policy.

In some ways, therefore, the book is more complex than its predecessors. But I make no apology for this, since I believe it to be necessary to a critical understanding of social rights.

Most fundamentally, I seek to understand social rights as articulations of human need; as rights that are defined not exclusively by welfare state citizenship or human rights frameworks, but through the practices by which we socially negotiate the means for achieving human welfare or wellbeing. In this book, I go further than I have previously in presenting a new theoretical perspective on social rights.

Structure of the book

The book is in three parts.

Part One is concerned with social rights in theory and consists of four chapters. The first considers the origins of social rights in the creation of modern capitalist states. The second brings in the human rights agenda and explores competing ideas about the ways in which human needs can be defined and translated into rights. The third discusses the ethical foundations of social rights claims and ideas about collective responsibility. Finally in Part One, Chapter 4 presents a range of ideological and theoretical critiques of the social rights concept and of social rights-based approaches to social policy.

Part Two is concerned with social rights in practice and also consists of four chapters. Chapter 5 considers the different ways in which social rights have developed and are understood around the world, both in the global North and the global South. Chapter 6 is concerned with rights to work and to subsistence, focusing on generic issues and principles of relevance wherever social rights are developed. Chapter 7 addresses rights to human services, including housing, education, health, and social care provision, once again focusing on generic issues and principles. Chapter 8 provides a discussion of the mechanisms by which social rights may be enforced, including legal and administrative processes at both national and international levels.

Part Three contains two chapters, which concern themselves with how we might re-think social rights. Chapter 9 re-evaluates prevailing debates about rights-based approaches to poverty alleviation. Finally, Chapter 10 reflects on alternative future scenarios and radical new ways of conceptualising social rights.

Acknowledgements

It is difficult, if not invidious, for any author to single out even a few of the legions of people who have influenced her/his thinking and, in this instance, all I can do is to acknowledge a few of those whose role has been especially important. My perspective on social rights and human welfare was forged in the years between 1973 and 1985 when I worked as a welfare rights advice worker in Brixton, South London. From among the colleagues with whom I shared that experience it is the influence of Maureen Boyle and Paul Vercruyssen that has been for me, perhaps, the most enduring. The seeds of the idea for the original book from which this volume evolved were sown by my erstwhile PhD supervisor, Vic George, and my first attempts to improve that text were driven by the constructive criticisms of Mike Adler. My more recent conceptual reappraisal of social rights owes much to my engagement with the 'Road to Global Social Citizenship' research co-operation group which deliberated during the spring of 2011 at the Center for Interdisciplinary Research (ZiF) in Bielefeld. I owe a significant debt to my collaborators in that venture – Ulrike and Ben Davy, Lutz Leisering, Armando Barrientos, Sony Pellisery and Harvey Jacobs. I am also grateful to

Virginia Mantouvalou, Engin Isin and Nick Ellison for insightful comments on my subsequent attempts to develop my ideas following that experience.

Additionally, several people have provided valuable comments on early drafts of chapters for this book, including James Midgley, Gemma Wright, Mike Noble, Polly Vizard and Kinglun Ngok. But many more people have contributed to my understanding, most notably all those master's students from around the world who studied between 2005 and 2013 on the course entitled *Social Rights and Human Welfare* that I am still teaching at the London School of Economics: I believe I learnt as much from their insights and feedback as I was able to impart to them.

I indicated above that this book represents the latest offering to emerge from my own often fumbling and misguided intellectual journey. It draws upon, develops, revises and corrects past work. It has benefited immensely from the insight and assistance of those I have identified above, but responsibility for the undoubted errors and inadequacies in the finished product is solely mine.

PART ONE
Social rights in theory

1

THE SOCIAL RIGHTS OF CITIZENSHIP

The term, 'social rights', is subject to a variety of interpretations, depending on the context. It may be applied to specialised individual entitlements specifically created by social legislation in the context of a 'welfare state'. As such they are rights relating to social security, employment protection, housing, education, health and social care. These are rights that originated largely in the course of the twentieth century in industrialised capitalist states, but which are now also emerging in various forms and to varying degrees in developing countries. However, the term social rights may also be used in a normative sense to refer more generally to societal objectives and the levels of social protection that are, or perhaps ought to be, mutually guaranteed within all human societies. Social rights can emerge, arguably, at an informal local level through the customary expectations that people have of one another within the communities in which they live, or at a formal global level as the subject of internationally negotiated treaties, such as the UN's Universal Declaration of Human Rights (UDHR). Finally, the terms social rights and welfare rights may be used to refer to an arena of vocational or professional practice in which activists, development workers, advice workers and welfare lawyers engage. Such rights can be more than technical phenomena or abstract principles, but practical tools and discursive resources for campaigning, negotiation and advocacy – particularly by or on behalf of vulnerable, poor or disadvantaged people.

Inevitably, these meanings intersect and overlap, and this book will be concerned with all of them. Rights are central to social policy not only because they relate to the substantive entitlements to which the policy making process gives rise, but because they provide the basis of the principled claims that drive social policy debates and practices. Lawyers sometimes define the first kind of rights as 'positive' or 'black-letter' rights and the latter as 'moral' rights. Social scientists tend to recognise that all our rights are in one way or another socially or ideologically constructed. We shall be concerned throughout this book with interactions between competing conceptions of social rights and the effects of these interactions on how social rights are framed and how they work in practice.

In this introductory chapter, however, we shall start with a conceptual discussion of the social rights of *citizenship*. I shall discuss the way in which the concept of social rights emerged explicitly, as a defining feature of citizenship under welfare state capitalism, before reflecting on the prior origins of citizenship rights and finally, analysing recent developments affecting the nature of social rights in the welfare states of the global North. We shall broaden the discussion in later chapters to consider the place of social rights within the international human rights agenda and to reflect on the deeper origins of social rights.

The coming of welfare capitalism

Social rights according to the sociologist T. H. Marshall (1950) were the unique achievement of the twentieth-century capitalist welfare state. His exemplar was the British case. In Britain the struggle to achieve civil rights (i.e. civil liberties and property and legal rights) had by and large succeeded by the eighteenth century, and the struggle to achieve political rights (i.e. voting and democratic rights) took major strides in the nineteenth century. The establishment of social rights – that is entitlement to basic standards of education, health and social care and housing and income maintenance – was completed with the formation of the 'modern' welfare state after the end of the Second World War. Marshall may be accused of overgeneralisation, particularly in his characterisation of different historical periods, but this ought not to obscure the importance of his argument and the idea that the coming of the capitalist welfare state – in Britain and elsewhere – had ushered in a new form of rights for a new economic and social order. His contentions were first, that social conflicts and inequalities based on class divisions had been or could be 'ameliorated' through the development of citizenship, and second, that full citizenship required three components – not just civil and political rights, but social rights as well.

Beyond class society?

The first of these points finds support among many commentators and supporters of the welfare state, including those on the social democratic left (George & Wilding, 1994: ch. 4). However, T. H. Marshall was a social liberal rather than a social democrat. His use of the term amelioration had been directly drawn from the works of the nineteenth-century economist Alfred Marshall. It was in a series of lectures in memory of Alfred Marshall that T. H. Marshall advanced the proposition that the post–Second World War welfare state as founded in Britain represented the 'latest phase in an evolution of citizenship which has been in continuous progress for some 250 years' (1950: 7). In so doing, he claimed he was addressing a question raised by his erstwhile namesake some seven decades before, namely 'whether the amelioration of the working classes has limits beyond which it cannot pass [or] whether progress may not go on steadily, if slowly, till by occupation at least, every man is a gentleman' (Alfred Marshall 1873, cited in T. H. Marshall, 1950: 4–5).

The equality foreseen by Marshall, the nineteenth-century economist, was an equality of opportunities and status rather than a material equality of incomes or wealth. Technological advances he believed would ameliorate the arduous nature of manual labour, while compulsory elementary education would civilise the manners of the working classes. Marshall, the twentieth-century sociologist, similarly believed that 'equality of status is more important than equality of income' (1950: 33). The development of a range of social services and cash benefits financed through taxation clearly did involve an equalisation of incomes, but this was not its only or even its primary achievement:

> What matters is that there is a general enrichment of the concrete substance of civilised life, a general reduction of risk and insecurity, an equalisation between the more and the less fortunate at all levels − between the healthy and the sick, the employed and the unemployed, the old and the active, the bachelor and the father of a large family. Equalisation is not so much between classes as between individuals within a population which is now treated for this purpose as though it were one class.
>
> (Marshall, 1950: 33)

The argument then is that social rights could abolish inequality based on class difference. Social policy scholars, such as Titmuss (1958, 1968), agreed that the development and maintenance of state welfare provision constituted a moral imperative insofar as it represented the peaceful means of mitigating the unacceptable consequences of class inequality; social rights were a civilising force which compensated for the diswelfares of the industrialised capitalist system.

One British Labour politician, Anthony Crosland (1956), went so far as to argue that the development of social legislation and the rise of labour and trade union power could together shift the balance so far against the old capitalist class system as to promise the imminent realisation of a democratic form of socialism. In reality, however, T. H. Marshall's concept of citizenship was not at all consistent with socialist pretensions. Marshall saw citizenship, particularly through the effects of a truly meritocratic state education system, as an alternative instrument of social stratification (1950: 39). Certainly, he believed the emergence of social rights signalled the extent to which *laissez faire* capitalism had been superseded. But the result would be a society based on status and desert, rather than contract and mere good fortune: 'Social rights in their modern form imply an invasion of contract by status, the subordination of market price to social justice, the replacement of the free bargain by the declaration of rights' (1950: 40). Paradoxically, shorn of any commitment to economic equality, this liberal view of social rights can be rendered consistent or can at least cohabit with a form of one-nation conservatism and its ideal of a non-conflictual or stable social order.

Unstable citizenship?

Capitalism of course never did achieve a non-conflictual social order. David Lockwood has argued that the structuring of life chances in capitalist welfare states was 'the direct result of the institutionalisation of citizenship under conditions of social and economic inequality' (1996: 532) and that the tension between state and market was managed by 'the fine-tuning of social rights' (1996: 535). The result he called a process of 'civic stratification', which depends on the one hand on the extent to which citizenship rights are allowed to develop and on the other the nature of the relative gains and deficits citizens might experience depending on their social status. We shall see in Chapter 4 that the administrative power of the capitalist welfare state can be implicated in the perpetuation or shaping of social divisions. Class structures have been changing, but despite the welfare state, socio-economic class status still strongly correlates with an unequal distribution of life chances (Crompton, 2008). Social inequality has lately accelerated throughout much of the developed world (OECD, 2011).

Elements of the instability of post-industrial capitalist societies can be said now to stem from consequences of individual risks, rather than active class conflict (Beck, 1992). The predominant fault line in the occupational structures of post-industrial capitalist societies is now passive in nature and lies not between 'workers' and 'bosses' or even between manual and non-manual workers, but between securely employed, highly trained and well paid 'core' workers on the one hand and precariously employed, low skilled and poorly paid 'peripheral' workers on the other (Standing, 2009, 2011). Changes in class structure have been driven by changes in the nature of capitalism itself, rather than by any direct influence of the welfare state (Esping-Andersen, 1999).

For the moment, however, let us return to the second limb of T. H. Marshall's argument, which was that civil, political and social rights are all necessary to a mature form of citizenship. Marshall recognised the sense in which citizenship based on a broad equality of rights might potentially conflict with the workings of a capitalist market economy. Nevertheless, he stressed that full citizenship need not inhibit a market economy, provided a state of equilibrium can be sustained between political, social and civil rights in what he characterised as a 'hyphenated' society, 'democratic-welfare-capitalism'. The hyphens in this formulation symbolise the interconnectedness of a democratic polity, a welfare state and a mixed economy, all functioning in harmony (1981). The maintenance of a flourishing 'hyphenated' society is therefore a matter of achieving the right balance between the constituent components of citizenship. Upon this premise, if too much emphasis is being placed in capitalist societies on our rights as producers and consumers and not enough upon our rights to participate in democratic decision making and our rights to guaranteed living standards and social provision, in as much as this creates an imbalance between the civil, political and social aspects of citizenship, it poses a potential threat to stability. Similarly, social upheavals in post-communist regimes, such as the former Soviet Union, might be regarded as a consequence of violent shifts in the equilibrium of citizenship. Under former Stalinist regimes, social rights had been guaranteed, while civil and political rights were either suppressed or neglected, but subsequently political rights were promoted at the expense of social rights and without an adequate framework of civil rights (Deacon, 1993).

Marshall's sociological model of citizenship, though highly influential, has attracted criticism on a number of counts. First, feminists in particular have complained that his analysis failed to address social divisions other than class: his 'image of an ideal citizenship' (1950: 29) did not ostensibly or necessarily include women, disabled people or migrants on equal terms as indigenous, able-bodied male citizens (e.g. Lister, 2003). These are issues to which I shall return in Chapter 4. Second, though Marshall theorised the functional role of social citizenship in relation to the amelioration of social class, he failed to account for the impact which social classes have had on the development of citizenship (Bottomore, 1992). The development of civil rights and the beginnings of political rights resulted, as we shall see, from the struggles of an emerging capitalist class to wrest power from the feudal aristocracy. The more recent development of political rights and aspects of the beginnings of social rights owed much to the struggles of working-class organisations – the Chartists, the trade unions and socialist and social democratic parties. Marshall expressed the conflicts from which citizenship has emerged in terms of clashes between opposing principles rather than between opposing classes. The development and maintenance of capitalist welfare states has been analysed, from differing perspectives, by other commentators (e.g. Esping-Andersen, 1990; Korpi, 1983; Offe, 1984) with reference on the one hand to political pressures applied directly through the democratic process and on the other to the influence of corporatism. Corporatism, in this context, is the process of tri-partite negotiation between the representatives of capital, labour and the state (customarily referred to as 'social partners'). What is often involved in the development of social rights is not an impersonally established equilibrium between formal principles, but a directly negotiated compromise between substantive class interests.

A third objection is that Marshall's account of state and market was, at best, reductionist. It may be observed that the antagonism between state and market to which social citizenship can supposedly bring equilibrium is not a simple opposition, since in some circumstances responsive market systems can and do fulfil social needs, while in others authoritarian state welfare systems can frustrate them (Hindess, 1987). What is more, there are many places on Earth where effective markets and legitimate state apparatuses upon which Marshall's citizenship ideal depend simply do not exist (Gough *et al.,* 2004). Finally, Marshall, at the time he presented his theory of social rights, was strangely silent with regard the contemporaneous emergence of an international human rights regime (U. Davy, 2013) and the idea of rights that are universal. And six decades later in a 'Globalizing World' (Fraser, 2010), his nation-based approach to social rights has, arguably been superseded (Dean, 2013).

This last argument is one to which we shall return in later chapters. But rather than look to future global trends, we need for a moment to consider where conceptions of and assumptions about 'citizenship' and 'rights' first came from and how they have evolved and changed in the capitalist welfare states where they originated.

The origins and species of rights

Rights and citizenship are intimately linked and the orthodox assumption is that their common origins lie in antiquity and the creation in the fifth century BCE of the Athenian city state, where rights of citizenship were implied through rules of self-governance adopted by a patrician male elite (Held, 1987: ch. 1). Such rights did not extend beyond the city. Nor for that matter did they extend to women and slaves within the city. Citizenship entailed membership of a distinctly exclusive political community, but also a practice based on principles and procedures. Later forms of citizenship similarly invoke principles or *doctrines* on the one hand and provide procedures for the making and resolution of *claims* on the other. Through the dialectical engagement between doctrines and claims emerge competing understandings of rights, both *formal* and *substantive*. Our rights may be determined by abstract or constitutional *doctrines,* or they may arise from *claims* or political demands. They may be framed in terms of *formal* freedoms or in terms of *substantive* entitlements.

The significance of these distinctions – between doctrinal and claims-based rights and between formal and substantive rights – may be considered in both historical and jurisprudential contexts.

Doctrines and claims: The emerging significance of property

It is important to recognise that what might once have been successfully demanded from below as claims-based rights may through processes of compromise and acceptance assume the character of doctrinal orthodoxies handed down from above, while conversely rights that are conferred by doctrinal decree may establish themselves or be adapted as a basis for formulating or articulating new claims-based demands. Historically speaking, the form of rights in 'hyphenated' democratic-welfare-capitalist societies is inescapably traceable to Western 'Enlightenment' attempts in the seventeenth and eighteenth centuries to achieve a formal separation between market (the economy) and state (politics), but just as fundamentally to establish the inalienability (or 'freedom') of property.

Prior to this, in pre-Enlightenment feudal Europe, classical Greco-Roman conceptions of citizenship had lapsed into obscurity and there had been no rights other than the right to govern: a natural right supposedly bestowed by God upon the sovereign and the nobility. To the extent that there were paternalistic duties attached to such rights, then privileges and gratuities might be conferred from time to time upon the common people (Kamenka & Tay, 1975), but they enjoyed no rights in the modern legal sense. Though lauded for having prefigured the modern concept of rights, England's Magna Carta of 1215 was no more than a concession of restricted liberties by the Crown to the nobility; it was not until the English Petition of Rights in 1628 that the process that would lead to the modern concept would unfold (Perry, 1964). A necessary precondition was the invention throughout Europe of the sovereign nation state (partially attributable to the Treaty of Westphalia of 1648) and conceptions of citizenship that now applied beyond the narrow sphere of the city state.

The doctrines of 'natural' law upon which feudal beliefs and practices had been founded afforded absolute power to a potentially capricious Crown and aristocracy, while imposing constraints upon property ownership. Natural law frustrated the market freedoms necessary to the economic foundation of capitalist society. Belief in natural law had therefore to be replaced over time by liberal beliefs in 'man-made' laws (women continued at that time to have no legal status). Bob Fine (1984) has contended that the doctrines which laid the foundations for man-made laws were inseparable from the doctrines of political economy. In the philosophical writings of Locke (1690) and the political writings of Paine (1791), we see reflected a moral discourse by which 'natural' rights were first recast as inalienable individual rights to 'life, liberty and estate [i.e. property]' and then exchanged, as it were, to become civil rights under doctrines of liberal governance (Raphael, 1989). This in essence was the discourse of rights that informed the English Bill of Rights of 1689 and a century later the American Declaration of Independence of 1776, the USA Constitution of 1787 and the French Declaration of Rights of 1789. By these constitutional instruments it was not the claims of ordinary people that were ascendant over governments, so much as the interests of incipient property-owning middle classes over those of old aristocracies.

Nevertheless, the subsequent interpretation and influence of these various instruments would differ significantly. The celebrated French Revolutionary slogan, *Liberté, Egalité, Fraternité,* embodied a set of potential contradictions: the objectives of Freedom, Equality and Solidarity are not easy companions (Hobsbawm, 1962). Equality is capable of competing interpretations – a point to which we shall shortly return – while, at root, Freedom and Solidarity are conflicting principles. Hegel (1821) clearly understood this. He asserted that the ultimate freedom is the right of personal as opposed to common ownership, but he also acknowledged that citizens are mutually interdependent, such that public provision should be made for poor relief, health, education and public works:

> The state will flourish, if it has good laws, of which free property is the fundamental condition. But since I am wholly environed by my particularity, I have a right to

demand that in connecting myself with others I shall further my special happiness. . . . [That right] contains the two following factors. It asks firstly that person and property should be secured by the removal of all fortuitous hindrances, and secondly that the security of the individual's subsistence and happiness, his particular well-being, should be regarded and actualized as a right.

(§§229–230)

This he recognised to be controversial. The notion of property was as contestable as it was essential. For heuristic purposes we can draw a broad distinction between the liberal citizenship tradition that came to characterise the Anglophone world and the civic-republican tradition that came to characterise the Western continental European world. The former prioritised individual Freedom; the latter acknowledged Solidarity. The liberal tradition reflected Locke's view of property rights as individual prepositive rights (1690); the civic-republican tradition reflected Rousseau's (1762) view of property rights as possessive claims upon common assets, legitimised only through the collective will (see Davy, 2012).

The origin of rights in ownership leads to competing understandings of social rights. Rights and equality before the law are universal only in the formal and abstract sense that in an ordered (capitalist) society everybody has to relate to and respect everybody else as proprietors. Even people without land or goods at their disposal may 'own' (and therefore sell) their labour power. It has been suggested that social rights are or ought to be directly analogous to property rights, and that 'government largesse' (such as welfare benefits, subsidies, grants, education, etc.) constitute a kind of property which may be subject to the same legal rules and categories as other property forms (Reich, 1964). This is one way of looking at social rights: as an expression in legal form of the logic of individual ownership. Such benefits – provided all the conditions of eligibility are met – are available as an entitlement rather than as a gift, and the principles which give rise to that entitlement are supposed to operate with indifference to the personality and status of the recipient. They can be rights within the liberal definition of the rule of law. In contrast, the rhetoric of social rights campaigners and activists is more usually cast in terms of a very different doctrinal understanding of property. For example, opposition by nineteenth-century Owenites and Chartists to the tightening of the English Poor Laws was founded upon solidaristically conceived 'birth rights', that is to say:

the right to have a living out of the land of our birth in exchange for labour duly and honestly performed; the right in case we fell into distress, to have our wants sufficiently relieved out of the produce of the land, whether that distress arose from sickness, from decrepitude, from old age, or from inability to find employment.

(William Cobbett, cited in E. P. Thompson, 1968: 836)

The claim here – the right to work, the right to a living wage, the right to an adequate income in the event of incapacity, unemployment or retirement – is premised on the idea of common ownership through birth, yet it speaks nonetheless to the significance of property for social rights.

The doctrines that informed the coming of the twentieth-century human rights agenda, which we shall discuss in Chapter 2, centred neither upon the ordinances of God (Klug, 2000), nor necessarily upon principles of property ownership (Jacobs, 2013), but upon the potentially problematic idea of humanity's inherent 'dignity'. Nevertheless, as Clarke (1996) has argued, it was citizen rights that provided the model for human rights and not the other way round. The history of the rights-bearing subject as 'citizen', as 'proprietor' and (more recently) as 'human' is a narrative of social construction: it is a continuing story of shifting doctrinal orthodoxies and innovative claims-making.

The formal and the substantive: Meanings of equality

The language or 'discourse' of rights, as should be evident, is shot through with ambiguities. Not only is there a distinction to be drawn between the kinds of rights that are prescribed from above by established doctrine and the kinds of rights that are framed and claimed from below, there are also competing understandings of what it means for citizens, proprietors or humans to have *equal* rights. The liberal citizenship tradition has tended towards a formal or procedural approach to equality – the civic-republican tradition to a more substantive approach. The liberal tradition embraces the ideal of equality under the law. At its meanest this is captured by Anatol France's celebrated aphorism: 'The law, in its majestic equality, forbids the rich as well as the poor to sleep under bridges, to beg in the streets, and to steal bread' (1849). More inclusive understandings of liberalism recognise that free markets can perpetuate social disadvantage and so favour equality of opportunity and the idea that every citizen should be allowed to succeed on the basis of her ability. Communitarian versions of the civic-republican tradition emphasize equality of belonging, inclusion and respect rather than strict material equality, though social democratic derivations of the tradition support broad equality of material outcomes.

These are issues to which we shall repeatedly return. But for the moment we shall remain focused on rights of citizenship. I mentioned at the beginning of this chapter the distinction lawyers make between 'black letter' rights that are written down and enforceable as opposed to 'moral' rights that are extolled and debated but have no necessary effect. The utilitarian philosopher Jeremy Bentham (1789) dismissed as 'nonsense on stilts' the very idea that there can be basic moral rights that naturally belong to every individual citizen: what matters, he believed, are the laws we might make to ensure the greatest good of the greatest number of citizens. This represents a legal positivist tradition, which refers to any right that is legally defined as a 'positive' right as distinct from a mere 'moral' right, which is unspecified and unenforceable.

Other legal scholars, however, have debated a quite different distinction between 'negative' rights, which formally protect the individual from external interference, and 'positive' rights, which substantively guarantee state intervention. Here the term positive is being used with a different meaning. The distinction between negative and positive 'liberties' was drawn by Isiah Berlin to mark the difference between a 'right' to forbearance by others, as opposed to 'the freedom which consists in being one's own master' (1967: 149). The words 'liberty' and 'right' are not necessarily synonymous but they can refer to different species of rights. Hohfeld (1946) identified four kinds of rights: liberties, claims, immunities and powers. Liberties and immunities are what might be called species of negative rights because they signal a *freedom from* something, whereas claims and powers are positive rights because they signal an *entitlement to* something. In practice, if one takes, for example, what might be regarded as the most elemental of social rights, the right to be free from hunger, this would imply a right to food or, at least, to the means of subsistence. To be positive in this sense the right must have substance: it requires someone or somebody not merely to refrain from action, but to act.

The distinction between formal and substantive can be expressed not only in terms of negative and positive rights, but in terms of different theories of rights: the *will* or *choice* theory on the one hand and the *interest* or *benefit* theory on the other (e.g. Campbell, 1988, 2006; P. Jones, 1994). The former is premised on the idea that every human individual with a free will must necessarily have the right to exercise choice in relation to her dealings with others. The latter is premised on the idea that rights are created by rules which benefit the human individual by imposing obligations on other individuals to protect or further her interests. The theories resonate respectively with liberal and civic-republican citizenship traditions and neither alone can account for the ways in which social rights necessarily have both procedural form (through the way they are established) and material substance (in terms of what they actually deliver). An attempt to do this has been made by Ronald Dworkin (1977), who draws a different kind of distinction – between *background* rights and *institutional* rights. Background rights embody the fundamental formal principles that justify political and judicial decision making, while institutional rights are policy- or goal-directed and impose substantive duties on people or the government. The background rights that inform institutional rights imply not an empty morality of the kind dismissed by Bentham, but a notion of social justice, such as that espoused by Rawls (1972). However, background rights may be translated into more or less substantively generous institutional rights, depending on just how they are framed. For instance, Dworkin's background rights would seem to equate to what Michael Walzer (1994) has described as 'thin' or minimalist moralities: they represent, as it were, the lowest common denominator in terms of the principles upon which policy actors might agree, rather than a 'thick' or maximalist moral understanding of the substantive rights of citizenship. (This distinction between thin and thick understandings will become important in our discussion of human needs in Chapter 2.)

We may conclude first, that rights are ideological constructions, albeit that they have real consequences, and second, that their nature and meaning are inevitably fluid and change over time.

Post-industrial capitalism and the privatisation of social rights

The final set of preliminary debates that this chapter must address relates to the distinctive nature of social rights as demands upon resources and the extent to which, having been invented as creatures of capitalism, they will survive in the capitalist world as capitalism itself evolves. I shall be concerned: first, with the way in which social rights entailed or enabled a partial de-commodification of both labour power and human services; and second, with the crisis of the modern welfare state and the resulting processes of re-commodification or 'privatisation'. We shall see that in the welfare states where they were first created the nature of social rights is changing.

Social rights and de-commodification

The development of twentieth-century capitalist welfare states was achieved through bodies of social legislation that extended the 'positive' or substantive rights of citizenship by expanding public services. Whereas civil and political rights primarily entail 'negative' or formal rights (e.g. freedoms of movement and opinion), social rights entail substantive rights to the provision of goods and services necessary for human wellbeing. Social rights came onto the agenda when the state began to adopt a role in relation to such goods and services rather than leaving their provision entirely to the mechanisms of the market: in other words when through social policy intervention certain goods and services were to some extent 'de-commodified'. It is a process that had actually begun in many countries before or during the early years of the twentieth century with partial reforms to nineteenth-century systems of poor relief. We have seen that, according to T. H. Marshall, social rights developed only after certain 'negative' or formal rights had successfully secured the legal and economic infrastructure necessary for a free-market economy – an economy in which not only land, but goods and services, and even labour power, were instituted as alienable property that could be traded as commodities. However, Karl Polanyi (1944) has contended that labour power is in reality only a 'fictitious commodity'. Unlike ordinary commodities, labour power cannot be separated from its owners and is uniquely dependent for its existence upon the health and wellbeing of those owners. While it is possible for the owners of ordinary commodities to withhold them from sale until the price is right, the owners of labour power cannot do so unless they can secure an alternative means of subsistence. If labour power is to be traded as if it were a commodity, certain conditions must be met, including certain non-commodified support systems (Offe, 1984), including social security, healthcare and education. Marshall's analysis is arguably misleading, since the development of substantive social rights was as necessary to the effective development of capitalism as the development of formal civil and political rights.

The development of social rights has been messier and more complex than Marshall suggested, and Esping-Andersen has elaborated the concept of de-commodification in order to explain the emergence of different kinds of welfare states in different capitalist regimes. He makes clear that:

> . . . de-commodification should not be confused with the complete eradication of labour as a commodity; it is not an issue of all or nothing. Rather the concept refers to the degree to which individuals, or families, can uphold a socially acceptable standard of living independently of market participation.
>
> (Esping-Andersen, 1990: 37)

I shall return to Esping-Andersen's work in Chapter 3, which will examine how social rights can differ between countries, but this chapter will consider a particular element of his argument about the development of social rights. Esping-Andersen suggests that historically there were three kinds of response to the commodification process, reflecting in effect three different ways of thinking about social rights. He defines these in terms of the classical paradigms of conservatism, liberalism and social democracy, while seeking to demonstrate that all welfare state regimes are in fact compromises between these competing notions of what social rights should achieve.

- The conservative approach is suspicious of commodification because it undermines traditional authority. Characteristically, therefore, this approach favours 'rights' in a paternalistic sense: the kind of rights which come from imposing obligations on employers to look after their workers; from encouraging corporatist guilds and mutual self-help societies; or from state intervention in a paternal-authoritarian mode (e.g. compulsory national insurance schemes).

- The liberal approach embraces commodification and seeks to intervene only to the extent that intervention will assist the commodification process or correct 'market failures'. Characteristically, this approach favours 'rights' of a conditional nature (such as means-tested social assistance schemes).
- The social democratic approach is inclined to resist commodification because it is the basis of social alienation and class exploitation. Characteristically, this approach favours 'rights' which are emancipatory, and which minimise stigmatising conditions and maximise equality.

Since the 1970s a combination of forces – economic globalisation, the ascendancy of neo-liberal ideological orthodoxies and concerted social and demographic pressures – have provoked continuing crises for the capitalist welfare states of the world (Esping-Andersen, 2002; Mishra, 1984; Pierson, 1998; Taylor-Gooby, 2013). Writing in the 1980s, Claus Offe suggested that advanced capitalist societies were facing a paralysis of the commodity form, precisely because of the competing tendencies towards commodification and de-commodification. In the face of this, neither inaction, a return to economic *laissez faire,* nor further development of an extensive and fiscally unviable welfare state was tenable. The alternative, presciently identified by Offe as the underlying basis of emerging policies in welfare state societies, was 'administrative re-commodification' (1984: 125). What Offe anticipated was the use of the administrative power of government to sustain the commodity form. This may be achieved by regulating the self-destructive tendencies of market competition; by investing in the 'supply side' of the economy (in education, training, research and development, transport and communications systems, etc.); or by introducing new forms of joint public/private decision making and financing. The concept of re-commodification captures the sense in which the social rights of citizenship in capitalist welfare states are being or have been transformed. It is not that social rights are being extinguished, rather that they are being made less democratic and more akin to the property rights of classical jurisprudence. Social rights are now less about enabling people to exist independently of the market, and rather more about requiring them to participate in markets, including 'quasi-markets' within the public sector. Paradoxically, however, social rights are no less administrative in nature; it is simply that administrative power has been made more technical than political in character (cf. Barry *et al.,* 1996; Foucault, 1991). This has been primarily manifested through two processes: a shift to welfare pluralism and the introduction of new public managerialism – processes that have played out in different ways and have varied in their significance in different welfare state regimes.

Re-commodification and privatisation

The capitalist welfare state can protect, promote or secure the fulfilment of social rights by a variety of means: not only by directly providing services, but by financing and/or regulating services delivered by non-state providers (Burchardt, 1997, 2013). Re-commodification or privatisation (which – as we shall see – are not necessarily the same thing) can be contrived through a restructuring of public spending and a transition to what is widely termed the 'mixed economy of welfare' or 'welfare pluralism' (e.g. Johnson, 1987; Le Grand & Robinson, 1984; M. Powell, 2007). The concept of welfare pluralism rests on the idea that, instead of the public sector (the state) being the dominant or principal provider of welfare goods and services, an increasingly significant level of provision should also come from the 'informal' sector (families and communities), the 'voluntary' sector (independent, self-help or not-for-profit organisations) and the 'commercial' or private sector. The suggestion is not that the state should cease to guarantee the social rights of the citizen, but that that guarantee need not necessarily be honoured through the direct provision of services by public sector organisations. The state might instead fund the provision of services by other agencies, or it might do no more than regulate the standards of provision made by such agencies.

- The very idea of an *informal sector* amounts in one sense to an oxymoron: it refers to the ostensibly 'unorganised' everyday care and support that people provide for one another within households and neighbourhoods (Rose, 1988) – services expected and provided not by way of formally negotiated rights and responsibilities but in terms of common understandings (Finch & Mason, 1993). Nevertheless, households and communities are the original source of personal welfare and the elemental resource on which people the world over to varying degrees depend. Indeed, some developing countries with ineffectual state provision, but strong kinship and community traditions, have been defined as 'informal welfare regimes' (Gough *et al.,* 2004; and see Chapter 5, this volume). In economically developed countries, however, social and demographic changes have diminished the scope for informal care, and some governments have been seeking to counter this trend by re-harnessing and supporting the kind of care that can be provided, for example, to disabled and frail elderly people in their own homes by family members, sometimes as an alternative to publicly provided or financed care (Balloch & Hill, 2007).
- The *voluntary sector* is also known as the Third Sector or the civil society sector (to distinguish it from the public and the private sectors) or sometime the NGO (non-governmental organisation) sector. It has been dubbed a 'loose and baggy monster' (Kendall & Knapp, 1995) on account of the number and diversity of the forms, functions and purposes of the local groups, mutual societies and national and international bodies by which it is constituted. Historically speaking, it is the sector from which all organised social welfare provision once stemmed and from which, during the twentieth century, welfare states to a large extent took over. Provisions for poor relief, education and healthcare were once primarily the preserve of charitable or religious organisations and were provided not as of right, but out of calculated beneficence. Many welfare state governments in seeking to re-commodify a range of human services are now seeking to revitalise the voluntary sector as a source of unpaid time and commitment in the service of the wider community or to engage voluntary sector organisations contractually as independent providers (Billis & Glennerster, 1998). Where voluntary sector provision represents a return to the feudal charitable principle of *noblesse oblige,* it amounts, according to Ruth Lister (1990), to a 'privatisation' of citizenship and a negation of social rights. Where voluntary sector provision amounts to a direct substitution for public sector provision, the implications for social rights can be ambiguous and may depend on by whom and on what terms provision may be accessed (Ishkanian & Szrerter, 2012).
- The *commercial sector* consists of organisations that sell social or human services as commodities. They differ from some public and voluntary sector providers primarily because they do so competitively and for profit. The commercial sector can trade in the open market in pension plans, employment services, unemployment and health insurance,

healthcare, education, housing, residential and domiciliary care services, and so on. Controversy surrounds the extent to which the World Trade Organisation's (WTO's) Global Agreement on Trade in Services (GATS) may ultimately open all forms of public services to worldwide competition from commercial providers (Deacon, 2007). There is a clear trend among welfare state governments on the one hand to admit such competition and to allow commercial organisations to provide a range of state-funded services and on the other to promote private alternatives or additions to public sector pensions, healthcare and educational provision (Drakeford, 2000; Papadakis & Taylor-Gooby, 1987). Once again, the implications for social rights are ambiguous and clearly depend on whether and on what terms citizens can access commercially provided services. And, as we shall see, even if no payment is required at the point of delivery of a privately provided public service, the rights of the service user are likely to be more akin to the civil rights of a customer than the social rights of a citizen.

Even where the provision of services remains within the public sector, provision can be made for services to function according to market principles and/or in a more 'business like' way. This was the purpose informing the doctrines of new public managerialism (Clarke & Newman, 1997; Hood, 1991). The application of such doctrines may entail the introduction of quasi-markets (Le Grand, 1990), whether by creating purchaser-provider splits within public sector organisations (such that some parts of the organisation commission services from others) or by generating funding mechanisms that require providers, such as schools or hospitals, to compete with one another for pupils or patients by improving the standards or the accessibility of their services. New managerialism also challenged the efficacy of the public service ethos, by seeking to incentivise service providers through the imposition of performance targets and, for example, by instituting public service user or customer charters. Such charters amounted to symbolic contracts between social security claimants and administrators, pupils (or their parents) and schools, patients and healthcare professionals. Perhaps the most iconic example was Britain's overarching Citizen's Charter, which aimed to make public services more open and accountable, by offering 'more privatisation; wider competition; further contracting out; more performance-related pay; published performance targets – local and national; comprehensive publication of information on standards achieved; more effective complaints procedures; tougher and more independent inspectorates; better redress for the citizen when things go badly wrong' (Prime Minister's Office, 1991: 5). Central to the idea of the Citizen's Charter is the link between payment for services (whether directly or through taxes) and the quality of those services. The competent citizen is therefore the successful consumer, able to get the best out of the services. The users and providers of services are cast as opponents of each other's interests. What is more, the 'business' of service provision is uncoupled from the politics of welfare: policy makers may evade responsibility for policy failures (because customers are encouraged to blame the providers of services), and the collectivist ethos of the welfare state is diluted (because service provision is driven by individualised incentives rather than policy, or vocational or professional commitment). In T. H. Marshall's terms, the Citizen's Charter strengthened civil rights (the kind of rights 'customers' enjoy in the market place) at the expense of political rights and social rights.

Re-commodification, therefore, involves more than simple privatization – the selling off or transfer of public services from one sector to another (cf. Starr, 1988). It is also about the framing of the citizen and her rights. One aspect of privatisation relates to the way in which decisions are transferred from public agencies to private individuals (Burchardt, 2013). The key mantra of new managerialism is the importance of choice: customers, however vulnerable or confused, must choose their service provider or have the opportunity to do so. Services provided by a private or third sector supplier need not be financed by way of direct transactions between the state and the provider, but by the medium of state financed tax-reliefs, allowances or vouchers provided to citizens to enable them to purchase services in the market place and compelling them to choose between providers and so driving competition. Service user charters may guarantee or even require service users to choose between schools, hospitals, pension funds, etc. Citizens are thereby accorded formal rights of choice above their substantive rights of benefit. Substantive benefits may be constrained or conditional, especially if resources are scarce and must be rationed. Re-commodification amounts to privatisation in the sense that the fulfilment of social rights must be individually sought through personal transactions. T. H. Marshall's conception of social rights – as the 'invasion of contract by status [and] the replacement of the free bargain by the declaration of rights' (see above) is displaced, or at best qualified, through the application of principles based on economic as opposed to social liberalism – principles primarily premised on the ownership and exchange of property, rather than considerations of social justice.

Summary/conclusion

All our rights are ideological constructions. When we speak of social rights we are dealing with abstract, if powerful, ideas rather than concrete realities. Nonetheless, it is social rights which give expression to the effects (though not always the intentions) of social legislation and the substantive exercise of state power. This chapter has examined a range of theoretical explanations concerning the basis of social rights.

We have been concerned first with the extent to which social rights were initially founded in a settled form of citizenship which displaced class as a basis for processes of social organisation in developed capitalist societies. If this view were to be accepted, in place of a society founded on class antagonisms and inequalities, we would now have a society based on a broad equality of citizenship. It is difficult, however, to reconcile this view with the realities of contemporary welfare state societies, although there is a sense in which the idea of social rights represents only a part of a wider project in which property (or civil) rights and democratic (or political) rights must also play a part if capitalism is to work.

We have also considered the extent to which the concept of rights under capitalism is problematic. Essentially, the basis of individual 'rights' stems from the definition of private property. Social rights, however, are bestowed by the collective authority of the state. Whilst it is possible to speak of social rights as if they are property rights, in practice they are defined with reference to obligations imposed both on those who administer and those who benefit from such rights. To this extent, social rights are also political in character because they may represent negotiable claims made by or on behalf of groups in society.

Clearly, therefore, social rights are not static attributes of citizenship. They change over time and we have considered how recent welfare state reforms have resulted in sometimes subtle transformations to the nature of social rights. In particular, we have examined how the privatisation of certain aspects of social provision and changes to the way in which public services are administered have been reflected in a more consumer-oriented form of rights. Following from this, we have discussed commodification, de-commodification and re-commodification – concepts which provide a particular perspective upon the development of social rights in capitalist societies, and an explanation, both of the contradictory potential of social rights (as rights to an existence independent of the market) and their ambiguous status (when deflected into the form of consumer rights).

The next chapter will move on from definitions of social rights as a component of citizenship to a discussion of human need and, specifically, the extent to which social rights may be more broadly construed as responses to human need.

2

HUMAN NEED AND HUMAN RIGHTS

The last chapter discussed social rights as a component of citizenship within a democratic-welfare-capitalist state. Just as citizens of such a state are supposedly guaranteed rights to legal protection and political participation, they are also entitled to have their needs for certain essential goods and services met. But which needs and to what extent? Understandings of need are not only a part of everyday life but are also central to social policy. And yet need is a deeply contested concept with an extraordinary array of meanings (Dean, 2010).

I would argue that social rights may be understood as articulations of human need. Citizenship, as we have seen, entails a more or less inclusive process by which needs can be named and claimed, and by which claims may be recognised and rules for the distribution of resources can be made. Citizenship has been the principal arena in which rights have been formulated. And what we have identified as social rights were first specifically formulated at a particular point in the development of industrial capitalism, when a particular set of social ills warranted a particular kind of state intervention. We considered T. H. Marshall's account of this process in Chapter 1. His was an account premised on the British example and on a welfare state whose foundations had been consolidated at the end of the Second World War. It was an era in which it was believed that the administrative power of the warfare state could be turned, like a sword into a plough shear, into a peacetime welfare state that would engage and defeat what were characterised in a report by Sir William Beveridge (1942) as five metaphorical 'giants': Disease, Idleness, Ignorance, Squalor and Want. Each giant represented an unmet human need: the need for health, for work, for education, for decent housing and for a means of subsistence.

Meanwhile, on the other side of the Atlantic, the US president, Franklin D. Roosevelt (1941) was propounding Four Freedoms: the freedom *of* Speech and Worship and the freedom *from* Fear and Want. Roosevelt elaborated explicitly on freedom from Want when he declared, 'Necessitous men are not free men. People who are hungry and out of a job are the stuff of which dictatorships are made.' (1944). When it came to developing its post-war welfare state, the USA would later be regarded as something of a 'laggard' compared to Western European countries (e.g. Offe, 1972), but the legacy of Roosevelt's Four Freedoms declaration (in part through the role played by his widow, Eleanor, as chair of the United

Nations [UN] Commission on Human Rights) is nonetheless to be found in the preamble to the UDHR of 1948. This proclaims 'the advent of a world in which human beings shall enjoy freedom of speech and belief and freedom from fear and want [to be] the highest aspiration of the common people'. The rhetoric of mid-twentieth-century social liberalism was implicated not only in promoting rights of welfare state citizenship, but also in the social rights component of the international human rights agenda. The idea of freedom from want – of needs as a basis for the construction of rights – though potentially ambiguous, is conceptually compelling. It will lead us in this chapter to a broadening of the discussion, including an introduction to the international human rights agenda, but also to an evaluation of the extent to which the needs of humanity remain unequally or insufficiently satisfied. To begin, however, I shall turn to a discussion of human need.

Concepts of need

The word 'need', in English, is both a verb and a noun. The things we need, we call needs. Need may be defined in terms of that which we feel or experience, or in terms of things we must have or must do. Needs may be equated (though they are not necessarily synonymous) with wants, preferences or desires. Insofar as people may suffer for 'want' or lack of that which they find necessary, Agnes Heller has argued that 'all needs considered by humans to be real must be considered as real' (1980: 215). We may say that we need to eat, we need to work, we need a home, we need to rest, we need to love and be loved, we need to understand the world in which we live, or that we need to lead a 'good' or fulfilling life. To unpack the many different ways in which we talk about need, we might distinguish needs according to (a) whether they are being defined from the top down or the bottom up, and (b) whether they derive from a 'thin' or a 'thick' understanding of human wellbeing.

Top down vs. bottom up

Top-down definitions of human need can be described as 'inherent' conceptions in that they are needs that have been adjudged to be inherent to the human person. They therefore require an implicit or explicit theory of personhood, whether this is scientifically, philosophically, ideologically or theologically derived. They are top down in the sense that they are needs that are prescribed for us on an *a priori* basis, which is not to say that we might not accept or embrace them as needs. Bottom-up definitions of human need can be described as 'interpreted' conceptions in that they are needs that we may name and claim for ourselves, albeit that our claims may be culturally shaped or else our claims may sometimes be named and claimed on our behalf by legitimate advocates or beneficent welfare professionals. They are pragmatically formulated and bottom up in the sense that they are articulated through demands people make on other people or on social institutions. In practice the distinction between top down and bottom up can be difficult to sustain (for the same sort of reason that it can be difficult to sustain the distinction made in Chapter 1 between doctrinal and claims-based rights): today's bottom-up definitions can become tomorrow's top-down definitions and *vice versa*. But the distinction is heuristically valuable. It helps us reflect upon and make sense of the dynamic way in which needs are defined.

Top-down definitions can be diversely informed by utilitarian assumptions that regard the person as an independent rational actor with objective interests (Thomson, 1987); by economistic beliefs that regard the person as a market actor with subjective preferences (e.g. Menger, 1871); by psychological theories that regard the person as a sentient being with inner drives (e.g. Maslow, 1943); or by Marxist philosophy that regards the person as a member of a unique species with distinctive constitutive characteristics (Marx, 1844). For social policy purposes, the most influential attempt to provide a theory of universal human need has been provided by Doyal and Gough (1991), who draw out a distinction between, on the one hand, basic or universal needs – for physical health and personal autonomy – and, on the other, the intermediate needs that must be met if basic needs are to be optimally satisfied in any given socio-economic or cultural context. Doyal and Gough's list of intermediate needs or needs satisfiers (see Box 2.1) can be, and sometimes are, read as if they are a list of social rights.

Bottom-up definitions of need can similarly be shaped through a diversity of processes – not only through active resistance to perceived injustices (Moore, 1978; Thompson, 1993), but through passive acceptance of the local customs by which a shared understanding of 'necessaries' is established (Smith, 1776: 691), or through everyday expectations fuelled by consumer culture (Bauman, 1998; Galbraith, 1992; Marcuse, 1964). From a social policy perspective, Jonathan Bradshaw (1972) has suggested that need may be not only 'normative' (as when it is determined by welfare professionals and experts), but also 'felt' (and revealed, for example, by opinion polling); 'expressed' (and voiced through democratic participation); or 'comparative' (as when it is evaluated through social research). Nancy Fraser (1989) has expressly advocated more active bottom-up processes of definition through a 'politics of needs interpretation', an idea to which we shall return in later chapters.

Both top-down and bottom-up understandings of need contribute to the construction of social rights. Social citizenship is the process that sets the parameters within which under-standings of need are negotiated (Dean, 2013) – within which the top down and the bottom up meet one another. The outcomes may vary. Bryan Turner (1990, 1991), when considering the emergence of different kinds of citizenship during the period of the Western Enlighten-ment (see Chapter 1, this volume), draws a broadly framed historical distinction, between a 'descending' and an 'ascending' view of citizenship: 'In the descending view, the king is all powerful and the subject is the recipient of privileges. In the ascending view a free man was a citizen, an active bearer of rights' (1990: 207). Turner suggests that the English outcome was a triumph for a descending constitutionalist view, whereby the rule of the sovereign-in-parliament was established over subjects-as-citizens. In contrast, the aspirations – but not necessarily the eventual outcome – of the French Revolution epitomised the ascending view. In the event, the post-absolutist settlement in France, as across much of continental Western

---

BOX 2.1 DOYAL AND GOUGH'S 'INTERMEDIATE' NEED SATISFIERS

- Adequate nutritional food and water
- Adequate protective housing
- A non-hazardous work environment
- A non-hazardous physical environment
- Appropriate healthcare
- Security in childhood
- Significant primary relationships
- Physical security
- Economic security
- Safe birth control and child-bearing
- Basic education

Europe, represented a brokered rather than a constitutionalist outcome and the kind of power-sharing arrangements that prefigured modern corporatism (Mann, 1987).

But this is a retrospective analysis of power struggles at a macro-level. The social rights of citizenship are about human needs and human encounters that are experienced at a micro-level. Citizenship encompasses both the systems in which power operates and living agents who exercise power. The distinction between top down and bottom up is also reflected in Jürgen Habermas's celebrated distinction between 'system' and 'life-world'. Habermas's (1987) characterisation of late Western 'modernity' is that it exhibits a separation and continuing tension between, on the one hand, the technical systems by which rights of citizenship are formulated and administered and, on the other, the life-world that gives meaning to social participation and in which the well-springs of behaviour and aspiration are located. Perhaps, however, there always has been a tension between systemic top-down prescriptions for meeting human needs and bottom-up agency through which voice is given to life-world needs. The enduring question is whether – and in what circumstances – this can be a creative tension, or a destructive one.

Thin vs. thick

In Chapter 1 I mentioned in passing Walzer's notions of thin and thick moralities. A similar distinction can be made between thin needs and thick needs (Soper, 1993). Both kinds of need are important, but whereas 'thin' needs relate to what is required for bare *survival,* 'thick' needs relate to what is required for true *fulfilment* (cf. Ignatieff, 1984). The distinction captures the relativity of need and different levels of necessity. Insofar as needs are articulated through rights, thin needs may in part be met through the protections offered by formal or procedural rights, which guarantee equality of access and opportunity. Thick needs may be met through substantive rights, which ensure universal protection or provision. But even when there is provision for substantive social rights, provision may be thin – a parsimonious safety-net against total destitution. A universal minimum level of social rights may be sufficient for some citizens, but provide too thinly for those with complex needs. Relatively generous levels of rights-based social provision may meet the thick needs of some citizens, but not the needs of others.

Doyal and Gough's list of needs satisfiers in Box 2.1 was intended as an attainable standard to which even poorer countries might aspire, but arguably it implies a relatively thin definition of need. It refers only to 'adequate' food and housing, to 'appropriate' healthcare and to 'basic' education. Thicker definitions might insist on plentiful and palatable food, good standard housing, high quality healthcare, and secondary and even tertiary education. The terms thin and thick are, of course, metaphorical and though it is a banal analogy, it is often used in relation to soup. It may be seen, however, from Box 2.2 that deeper meaning can be read even into such an analogy. Human wellbeing necessarily depends on physical survival, but it has other – thicker – dimensions because human wellbeing depends on social context. This is plainly recognised by Doyal & Gough when they include such things as 'security in childhood' and 'significant primary relationships' as intermediate needs. We might quibble that it would be preferable to demand ontological security *throughout* the human life course and significant social relationships *beyond* the bounds of immediate family, but in fairness, Doyal & Gough's emphasis here is upon 'optimising' rather than maximising needs satisfaction (1991: ch. 7). Clearly, if one were to hold to a meanly Hobbesian view of human nature

---

BOX 2.2 THIN SOUP/THICK SOUP

All soup is made from ingredients taken from nature and gathered and prepared by human endeavour. But there is a distinction to be drawn – sometimes metaphorical but often literal – between 'thin' soup and 'thick' soup.

Thin soup may be perfectly nutritious, even wholesome, but it is characterised as thin because it is insipid, relatively flavourless and unappetising, if not unpleasant to taste. It is likely to have been prepared impersonally, in a factory or institutional kitchen, by anonymous people with little or no culinary skill. It relieves hunger or is minimally satisfying and it keeps you alive. The consumption of a thin soup is an act performed solely to ensure personal survival.

Thick soup may be equally nutritious, but it is characterised as rich because it is richer in texture and flavour. It is likely to have been prepared with care by a skilled chef or a loving parent, partner or companion. It provides enjoyment and can make you feel not just satiated, but fulfilled: good to be alive. The appreciation of a thick soup cements respect for others' skills and/or gratitude for their love.

---

and assume that human society entails nothing more than 'a war of all against all' (1651), one's view of human need is likely to be minimalistically thin. But as soon as one acknowledges human society to be an association of vulnerable and fundamentally interdependent beings (e.g. Turner, 2006), one's view of human need begins to take on thicker dimensions.

Thin and thick conceptions of need equate directly with competing understandings of human wellbeing, the provenance of which may be traced back to classical philosophy and, in particular, Aristotle (c. 350 BCE). What we are referring to as thin needs equate with a *hedonic* understanding, which associates wellbeing with the pursuit of pleasure and the avoidance of pain. Thick needs equate with a *eudaimonic* understanding, which associates wellbeing with leading a good life: with civic virtue and spiritual fulfilment (in the sense of fully realising one's human personality). I shall develop the idea of eudaimonic wellbeing in Chapter 3, but it should by now be evident that the term 'wellbeing', though widely used, is ambiguous and, like the term 'welfare' (Daly, 2011), conceals significant controversies with regard to the nature and meaning of human need.

Competing understandings of human need lead to radically different debates about the role of policy. A distinctly thin, if not explicitly hedonic, approach to human need has driven a recent global preoccupation with subjective wellbeing or 'happiness', which now widely figures as a measure of human progress and as a metric to inform social policy (Helliwell *et al.*, 2012; OECD, 2013; Stiglitz *et al.*, 2009; UNDP, 2011). It is a trend informed by the so-called Easterlin Paradox (Easterlin, 2005), which observes that economic growth does not necessarily correlate with increased subjective wellbeing. The implication that it is time for humanity to rein in its destructive pursuit of wealth is one that finds favour with some (e.g. NEF, 2012), but the alternative implication – that the wellbeing of poor and disadvantaged people may be addressed other than by policies for wealth redistribution – would seem to be the more dominant assumption. By contrast, a thicker approach to wellbeing is evident, for example, in scholarly work around concepts such as 'social quality' (Beck *et al.*, 1997) and 'social value' (Jordan, 2008), concepts that challenge the essentially individualist-utilitarian premises of the subjective wellbeing agenda and seek to re-establish a notion of wellbeing premised on the 'centrality of the *social* human being' (McGregor, 2007: 321).

The international human rights agenda

There is no global consensus as to the definition of human need. Indeed in some languages there is no single word that directly corresponds with the ambiguous and encompassing English word 'need' (Lederer, 1980). And yet we do have an internationally agreed UDHR – a declaration that defines certain substantive social rights and by implication accords recognition to certain agreed human needs (Freeman, 2002; Woodiwiss, 2005).

The UN organisation, founded at the end of the Second World War in 1945, established a Human Rights Commission to draft a universal declaration which was eventually adopted and proclaimed by the UN General Assembly in 1948. The declaration explicitly included well-established 'first generation' civil and political rights (to life, liberty, property, equality before the law, privacy, fair trial, religious freedom, free speech and assembly, to participate in government, to political asylum and an absolute right not to be tortured); it also included, more controversially, a 'second generation' of economic, social and cultural rights. Though distinctions can be and are drawn between 'economic', 'social' and 'cultural' rights, they may and shall for our purposes be encompassed within a single expanded concept of 'social' rights and they specifically included rights to work, education and even leisure. Most particularly, Article 24 states:

> Everyone has the right to a standard of living adequate for the health and wellbeing of himself[/herself] and his[/her] family, including food, clothing, housing and medical care and necessary social services, and the right to security in the event of unemployment, sickness, disability, widowhood, old age or other lack of livelihood in circumstances beyond his[/her] control.

First- and second-generation rights were declared to be inalienable and indivisible, but for the purposes of preparing legally binding international covenants, they were in fact separated. The resulting covenants – the International Covenant on Civil and Political Rights (ICCPR) and the International Covenant on Economic, Social and Cultural Rights (ICESCR) – were presented to the UN General Assembly in 1954 and eventually adopted in 1966. Unlike the ICCPR, the ICESCR admits a principle of 'progressive realisation' (Article 2), requiring states parties unable immediately to fulfil rights prescribed by the covenant to 'take steps' towards achieving the full realisation of such rights. Monitoring and reporting arrangements under the ICESCR require states parties to report periodically on their progress to a committee – the Committee on Economic, Social and Cultural Rights (CESCR).

The discussion between states parties' representatives on the Commission on Human Rights as to the drafting of the UDHR and the ICESCR and their subsequent reports to, and discussions with, the Economic and Social Council (ECOSOC) of the UN reveal that there were at that time significant divergences of interpretation as to the substantive nature of social rights (U. Davy, 2013). What clearly emerges is the extent to which, initially, the social rights framed by the UDHR and the ICESCR represented an uneasy compromise between different understandings of social rights: between a social citizenship ideal espoused by the US and Western European nations; a developmental approach espoused especially by Latin American nations; and a state socialist approach espoused by Eastern European nations (which, in practice, abstained from much of the debate). The liberal social citizenship ideal was focused on individual freedom from want; the developmental approach on collective need for economic and thereby social development; and the state socialist approach on state duties for the meeting of needs. Social rights or social rights–related clauses were subsequently written into a variety of supranational treaties and instruments (see Box 2.3) and, in various forms, into many national constitutions (Jung *et al.,* 2013). While generally replicating or borrowing features of the UDHR, these clauses would appear to have had quite different and in some instances limited substantive effects. However, the apparent convergence mentioned above, following the collapse of communism in Eastern Europe and the development of new forms of social assistance provision in the emerging economies of the global South (Leisering & Barrientos, 2013), suggests elements of a global shift in favour of the liberal social citizenship ideal, with its focus on individual freedom from want.

By the turn of the millennium, the United Nations Development Programme (UNDP) declared that the rhetoric of human rights, having been reduced during the Cold War years 'to a weapon in the propaganda for geopolitical interests' (UNDP, 2000: 3), should henceforth be harnessed to a common vision and a common purpose for the respective concepts of human rights and human development. The framing of this vision was significantly

---

BOX 2.3 SUPRANATIONAL TREATIES CONTAINING SOCIAL RIGHTS OR SOCIAL RIGHTS–RELATED CLAUSES BEARING UPON PARTICULAR GROUPS OR GLOBAL REGIONS

UN conventions

- International Convention on the Elimination of all Forms of Racial Discrimination (1966)
- Convention on the Elimination of All Forms of Discrimination Against Women (1979)
- Convention on the Rights of the Child (1989)
- International Convention on the Protection of the Rights of All Migrant Workers and Members of Their Families (1990)
- Convention on the Rights of Persons with Disabilities (2006)

UN declarations

- Declaration on the Right to Development (1986)
- United Nations Principles for Older Persons (1991)

Regional charters

- European Social Charter (1961 – amended 1996)
- American Convention on Human Rights (1969) and the Additional Protocol of San Salvador (1988)
- African Charter on Human and People's Rights (1981)

influenced by Nobel laureate Amartya Sen, who argues that human rights guarantee the basic freedoms necessary for 'human development'. They are, therefore, primarily means to an end, namely the realisation of human *capabilities* (Sen, 1999, 2004; UNDP, 2000: ch. 1). By capabilities, Sen was alluding to the freedom of the human individual to be and do in her life that which she values and has reason to value. What has come widely to be known as the 'capabilities approach' (Deneulin, 2006; Nussbaum, 2011) had some direct impact in the framing of the Millennium Development Goals (MDGs) (UNDP, 2003; UN General Assembly, 2000). It served in some respects to re-inflect the international human rights agenda and to reframe the distinction that may be drawn between social rights development and human development. The capabilities approach was regarded as a palatable alternative, first, to the 'Basic Needs Approach' (BNA) – that had informed the broadly social democratic conception of social development that was initially promoted by the International Labour Organisation (ILO) in the 1970s and fleetingly adopted within the World Bank (Reader, 2006; Streeten *et al.,* 1981) – and more immediately, to the widely discredited neo-liberal Washington Consensus that had displaced the BNA in the 1980s and '90s (see Chapter 5, this volume).

In essence, the capabilities approach is fundamentally liberal-individualist in the sense that individual fulfilment is constituted through the capacity to exercise choice (Dean, 2009). The implication for human rights is that they may be seen (contrary to the protestations of Jeremy Bentham mentioned in Chapter 1, this volume) to be consistent with a utilitarian ethic (Sen, 2004). Human development is about maximising individual freedom and therefore:

> human rights can include significant and influenceable economic and social freedoms. If they cannot be realized because of inadequate institutionalization, then, to work for institutional expansion or reform can be a part of the obligations generated by the recognition of these rights. The current unrealizability of any accepted human right, which can be promoted through institutional or political change, does not, by itself, convert that claim into a *non*-right.
>
> (Sen, 2004: 320)

According to this view, the social rights component of human rights may for the time being (and perhaps unavoidably) be violated for want of individual freedom. But freedom, not needs satisfaction, is the paramount consideration.

This draws us back to the question of the relationship between social rights and human need. The UDHR came into existence in the aftermath of the horrors of two world wars. It was a time of deep concern about the consequences of totalitarianism and 'rightlessness', and human rights offered us the 'right to have rights', independently of any nation state or government (Arendt, 1978). There is a sense in which 'social rights' is a term that might be used to refer to all rights created by sovereign nation states, whereas human rights are the innate or imprescriptible rights of human beings (Turner, 2006: 2). This is not a terminology I would adopt (since there are important distinctions to be drawn between different species of citizenship rights), but the argument points us to a different vein of reasoning wherein the most fundamental of rights relate at least as much to human *sociality* as to individual *autonomy* – as much to solidarity as to freedom. Contemporary claims to cosmopolitanism of a human rights approach are suspect: 'Because [human rights discourse] very clearly privileges autonomy over reciprocity, it also allows some individuals to be more autonomous than others' (Woodiwiss, 2005: 123). In fact, long before the current era, Hannah Arendt, mindful of the ontological essence of human existence, had warned that:

> the concept of human rights can again be meaningful only if they are redefined as the right to the human condition itself, which depends on belonging to some human community, the right never to be dependent on some inborn human dignity which de facto, aside from its guarantee by fellow men, not only does not exist but is the last and possibly most arrogant myth we have invented in our long history.
>
> (Arendt, 1951: 439)

Social rights – whether they are considered as citizenship rights or human rights – are social. While writing about social rights of citizenship, rather than human rights, Fred Twine (1994) located social rights in relation to the 'interdependence of self and society'. Similarly, in pursuit of a theory of human rights, Bryan Turner has argued that 'it is from a collectively held recognition of individual frailty that rights as a system of mutual protection gain their emotive force' (1993: 507). Social rights are located in relation to the shared vulnerability that characterises the human condition. Such approaches at present stand, at best, as a 'minor tradition' within human rights discourse (Woodiwiss, 2005: 134). While the major hegemonic tradition attributes violations of human rights to the lack of *freedom,* the minor tradition attributes violations to failures of *solidarity.* But it is to the deficits and failures in *equality* and equality of needs satisfaction to which we now turn. The 'myth' against which Arendt railed was the premise contained in Article 1 of the UDHR, that 'All human beings are born free and *equal* in dignity and *rights*' (emphasis added). Leaving aside the hollowness of the concept of dignity in this context, this begs the question – what is the relationship between equality and rights?

The failures of social rights

The survival of social inequality and poverty, even within developed welfare state nations suggests that their approach to social rights has failed. At best, it would seem citizens' needs are unequally satisfied. At worst, their needs remain unsatisfied. The problems of inequality and poverty in the richer countries of the world imply a failure of the social liberal citizenship ideal (Lister, 1990, 2010). Among the Organisation for Economic Co-operation and Development (OECD) countries, according to recent data, the ratio of the average income of the richest decile to that of the poorest was 9:1. Even in egalitarian countries (e.g. Sweden and Denmark) it had risen to 6:1, and in countries where inequality had been falling (e.g. Chile and Mexico) the ratio was still 25:1 (OECD, 2011). And across the world as a whole, within the last three decades, for every country in which inequality got better, there were more than two where it got worse (UNDP, 2010); and, while global per capita income grew and that of the richest rose, that of the poorest fell (Milanovic, 2007).

The persistence of extreme poverty – despite interventions by a variety of UN agencies – and growing inequalities between and within poorer countries amount to a continuing global violation of human rights (Pogge, 2002, 2007). Despite improvements, the UNDP has estimated that globally around 1.3 billion people are living on the equivalent of less than $1.25 a day and *at least* 1.7 billion are living in poverty according to a newly developed non-income-related multidimensional measure (UNDP, 2010; and see Alkire & Santos, 2010).

Even in the richest parts of the world, in countries such as the UK, around a quarter of the population in practice experience what a majority of Britons would consider to be an unacceptably low standard of living (PSE UK, 2013).

Inequality

We have seen in Chapter 1 that equality is a fiercely contested concept when it comes to the distinction between formal equality under the law and substantive equalities of entitlement to social protection or provision. There are related contests between arguments for equality of outcome as opposed to equality of income; equality of opportunity as opposed to equality of reward; equality of dignity as opposed to equality of power; and equality of status as opposed to equality of condition. As we might expect, when Amartya Sen contentiously posed the question 'Equality of What?' (1982a), he concluded that his preferred concept – equality of capabilities – could effectively settle such arguments. The concept of capabilities entails both formal and substantive freedom: freedom of choice as to the life one leads. But this doesn't necessarily deal with the question of just how free human beings can 'really' be when in the course of their lives they are so necessarily interdependent with and upon one another; when they live in a world so dominated by an economic system (capitalism) founded on the exploitation of human labour power; and when they may be systemically subordinated by relations of power that oppress, control or simply exclude them (Dean, 2009).

Inequality, as the negation of equality, provides tangible evidence of when and where needs are not fully met. It is when attempts are made to identify inequality that connections between needs and rights may be rendered explicit. In Britain, for example, an independent review, set up in preparation for the creation of an Equality and Human Rights Commission (EHRC), made recommendations for a measurement tool by which to evaluate dimensions of inequality across Britain. The review identified and operationalised a framework of ten 'domains of valuable capabilities' (see Table 2.1) quite explicitly distilled from the international human rights framework (Equalities Review, 2007; Vizard & Burchardt, 2007). A rather different approach has been taken by Baker *et al.,* (2004) who, in an attempt to forge a substantive multidimensional egalitarianism reaching beyond that implied by Article 1 of the UDHR, have proposed five 'dimensions of equality' (also set out in Table 2.1). Their dimensions, they claim, establish a framework 'that helps to map the differences between

TABLE 2.1 Equality and need

Vizard and Burchardt's *'domains of valuable capabilities'*	*Baker* et al.'s *'dimensions of equality'*
• life • physical security • health • education • standard of living • productive and valued activities • individual, family and social life • participation, influence and voice • identity, expression and self-respect • legal security	• respect and recognition • resources • love, care and solidarity • power • working and learning

liberal egalitarians and equality of condition' (2004: 25). What may be seen in Table 2.1 are two contrasting ways of reflecting on equality and human need. Using the notions of 'thin' and 'thick' we might say that Baker *et al.*'s dimensions are thicker than Vizard and Burchardt's domains. But important connections can be made between the two lists. What is clear is that discussions about equality and equal rights lead back to definitions of need.

This book began with a discussion of T.H. Marshall's theory of social rights, which explicitly claimed that social rights would and should ameliorate class inequality, which they have not. What has happened is that the structural dynamics of class and inequality have changed. Karl Marx had claimed that 'the history of all hitherto existing society is the history of class struggles' (1848: 16), and under capitalism, inequality of needs satisfaction stems from the fact that workers are unequally and inequitably rewarded for their labour. Under classic industrial capitalism the boundaries between bosses and workers and between relatively privileged non-manual and manual workers were reasonably clear. But fundamental changes in the nature of labour processes associated with shifts towards post-industrial service and information economies have resulted in, on the one hand, increasing labour diversification and associated income inequalities and, on the other, the fragmentation of traditional classes. Paradoxically, while socio-economic and occupational status continue to be a key determinant of life chances across the capitalist world (e.g. Goldthorpe *et al.,* 1982; Marshall, 1997; Meiksins-Wood, 1995), the transparency of class relations evaporated. The phenomenon is conventionally captured by dual labour market theory (e.g. Watson, 1995: ch. 5) and the idea that labour markets are now polarised between a securely employed, highly skilled and well paid 'core' and a chronically precariously employed, lower skilled and badly paid 'periphery'. Guy Standing (2009, 2011) has recently attempted an alternative global class analysis (see Figure 2.1), focusing on seven groups of actors in the globalised economy and hypothesising the emergence within this fluid structure of a new class, the 'precariat', situated between a diminishing traditional working class and a reserve pool of unemployed workers. The precariat is a class ill-served by social rights, as will be further discussed in Chapter 6.

Classic Weberian class analysis (Scaff, 1998; Weber, 1978) has focused more upon the interrelationship between socio-economic and socio-cultural differences in society: it considers life-styles as much as living standards. Sociologists have presented us with insights into how it is not only a person's standing in relation to the means of production, but her engagement with relations of consumption that characterise and give meaning to inequalities in needs satisfaction. Social divisions may depend not so much on people's occupational status as upon whether they are able to meet their needs for housing, healthcare and education independently in the market place, as opposed to having to depend on inferior or stigmatised forms of state provision (Saunders, 1984). In consumer societies people's sense of subjective sufficiency and social inclusion depends on their capacity to comply with a prevailing

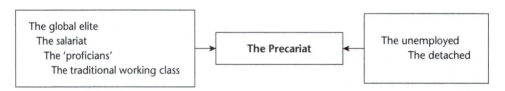

FIGURE 2.1 Standing's global classes

'aesthetic of consumption' (Bauman, 1998) – for example, the ability of children to have 'the right trainers' (Ridge, 2002).

Recent analyses of inequality have moved beyond class analysis to consider how the substantive differences in human experience and life chances may result from other dimensions of human diversity. This has resulted, in part at least, from the 'cultural turn' that occurred in the global North with the advent of the post-industrial era (Clarke, 1999), the significance of which can, paradoxically, be linked as much to the maturity of capitalist welfare states as to the crisis that apparently befell them in the 1970s (Mishra, 1984, 1990). The welfare states of the post–Second World War era had developed to the point that they provided a degree of material security for a comfortable majority: indeed, there is evidence that it was the comfortable middle classes rather than the poorest in society who benefited most (Le Grand, 1982). This made way for more individualistic or introspective cultural concerns, as issues of personal identity took precedence over issues of material survival (Inglehart, 1990). At the same time, new social movements – the second-wave feminist movement in particular – and new forms of community activism began to challenge monolithic, inflexible and sometimes oppressive state welfare institutions (Lewis *et al.*, 2000; and see Chapter 4, this volume). There was a shift from a politics of class to a politics of identity – a new awareness of social diversity and difference and, in particular in the 1970s, the inequalities associated with gender, ethnicity and disability. Increasingly now, the focus is on multiple and intersecting inequalities – in the plural (e.g. Platt, 2011; and see Chapter 4, this volume).

Inequalities in human society are, perhaps, inevitable. Some would even say that inequality can be functional (Davis & Moore, 1945) – others that, within limits, it may be socially just (Rawls, 1972). What is becoming clear, however, from a burgeoning body of international evidence (Wilkinson, 1996, 2005; Wilkinson & Pickett, 2009; WHO, 2008) is that inequality has consequences for human wellbeing. Those countries in which material needs are more equally satisfied tend by and large to exhibit not only higher levels of subjective wellbeing, but less variation in health outcomes and life expectancy.

Poverty

Poverty has been defined as the 'unacceptable face of inequality' (Tawney, 1913), which begs the question, how do we define acceptability and unacceptability and the point at which something should be done about inequality or poverty – the point at which, perhaps, a right to poverty relief might kick in? Elements of this question will be addressed in the next chapter, but here I want to make a link between definitions of need and definitions of poverty.

There is an enduring debate as to whether poverty should be defined in absolute or relative terms. But beneath this distinction lies a question of the standard which should be applied in relation to some level of absolute need as opposed to a broader conception of relative need. What are generally identified as, or purport to be, 'absolute' definitions may in practice apply to a spectrum of quite different standards: a person may be adjudged poor only if they have insufficient resources to avoid *starvation,* or, more generously, if they have insufficient resources to achieve a sometimes arbitrarily defined minimum level of *subsistence.* And definitions that are explicitly acknowledged to be 'relative' may of course adopt different standards: a person may be adjudged to be poor if, though they have enough resources for bare subsistence, they are unable to *cope* in the context of prevailing social standards, or, more generously still, if they are unable fully to *participate* in the society of which they are a part (George & Howards, 1991). Associated with debates about definition are a host of underlying controversies:

- Technical controversies with regard to where to draw the 'poverty line'; how to set a 'budget standard' that defines an adequate standard of living; whether there can be a social consensus as to what is minimally necessary; whether there is a resource threshold below which people cannot socially participate? (Alcock, 2006: ch. 6);
- Explanatory controversies with regard to whether poverty is attributable to individual pathology, cultural malaise, policy failure or the structural consequences of capitalism (Alcock, 2006: ch. 3; Jordan, 1996; Novak, 1988);
- Political controversies with regard to whether governments should be responsible for minimally relieving poverty if and when it occurs, or whether they should attempt to prevent poverty from happening in the first place (Alcock, 2006: ch. 13; Townsend & Gordon, 2002);
- Sociological controversies with regard to whether, on the one hand, poverty is an objective phenomenon or social fact or whether, on the other, it is a symbolic process of subjection and a social construct (Dean with Melrose, 1999).

Just as Sen considers that his concept of human capabilities answers the question 'Equality of What?', he has also argued that it resolves the controversy about absolute and relative definitions of poverty. Poverty, Sen claims (1985), may be relative in the space of the commodities that human beings need, but it is absolute in the space of human capabilities. By this he means we all need different things in order to fulfil our personal life projects and achieve acceptable kinds of human functioning, but we each absolutely need the freedom to choose how we live. This claim was challenged by Peter Townsend (1993: ch.6), who feared that Sen's insistence on an 'absolutist core' of poverty could too easily perpetuate a narrow subsistence-standard conception of poverty. Sen, for his part, was alleging that Townsend's concept of relative deprivation was merely conflating poverty with inequality. Sen and Townsend each recognised that human needs have a social context, but they had different conceptions of social justice. Townsend (1979) had been seeking to define an objective material threshold beneath which relative deprivation leads to a person's exclusion from social participation. He was not conflating poverty and inequality: his quest was to determine a definitive relationship between them. It has been suggested from a very different quarter that such a quest could nevertheless miss the point. The sheer diversity of human beings' lifestyles and behaviour makes it difficult to pin down a threshold by which to define where poverty starts and ends. The term 'poverty', Piachaud points out, 'carries with it an implication and a moral imperative that something should be done about it' (1981: 119).

When the UN Copenhagen Summit (United Nations, 1995) appeared to declare poverty to be a violation of human rights, it pronounced a call to action. Sceptics may claim that when the problem is hunger and malnutrition, the victims don't need rights, just action: they need farmers and doctors, not lawyers or philosophers (O'Neill, 1986). But here I would return to my contention that social rights may be understood as the articulation of human need. Debates about the distinction between absolute and relative poverty or absolute and relative need can most certainly miss the point. The answers are on the one hand quite simple: we should seek optimally to satisfy people's needs. But on the other they are in some ways more complex, precisely because embodied and 'needy' human beings and the societies they have created are so diverse and complex. Human beings' needs differ in character (they may be prescribed from the top down or demanded from the bottom up) and extent (they may be thin or thick).

Summary/conclusion

Social rights, though first defined as rights of citizenship, are fundamentally constructed through the identification and articulation of human need. The inspiration in the twentieth century both for the capitalist welfare state and for the international human rights agenda was the crystallisation of an uncertain consensus centred on a social liberal concern to promote Freedom from Want. What is here referred to as social liberalism has also been termed 'reluctant collectivism' (George & Wilding, 1985) or 'liberal collectivism' (Cutler *et al.,* 1986) because it accommodated a measure of collective provision to meet individual human need. The primary motivation of social liberals was to promote the freedom of the individual on which liberal democracy depends – though, in the international context this was initially promoted on terms that obliquely acknowledged social development and state socialist perspectives.

This chapter has considered competing ways in which human need may be conceptualised. It examined first the dynamic tension between top-down prescriptions and bottom-up demands by which understandings of human needs are constructed. Secondly, it discussed the extent to which human needs and the essence of human wellbeing may be thought of as existing along a continuum, ranging from thin to thick – from the imperatives of individual survival to the cause of social fulfilment. Though understandings of human need are dynamic and diverse, it has been possible through the emergence of the international human rights agenda to achieve a modicum of consensus, not as to the nature and extent of human need, but in favour of a set of potentially realisable social rights that might secure provision for human need and from which some definitions of human need may be indirectly inferred. With the end of the Cold War and the gathering effects of economic globalisation, the extent of that hegemonic consensus appears to be solidifying.

The prevailing global reality, however, is that inequalities both within and between nation states are for the most part increasing, while poverty in its different manifestations persists. The failure to date of social rights to limit inequalities and prevent poverty may be understood from within the broadly prevailing progressive liberal consensus as stemming from a lack of freedom. From the critical 'minor tradition', however, it may be understood as a failure of solidarity, and it is to debates about the ethical foundations of social rights and the relationships between rights and responsibilities that the next chapter will turn.

3

ETHICS AND SOCIAL RIGHTS

We have considered social rights first, as creatures of welfare state citizenship and second, as articulations of human need. We turn now to consider what might be referred to as the 'ethical' foundations of social rights. We have, of course, already touched on ethics when discussing 'doctrinal' conceptions of rights in Chapter 2, but the particular focus of this chapter is on the relationship between rights and responsibilities; with whether and when social rights should be conditional on the individual acceptance of responsibilities; and with whether and when there can be collective responsibility for meeting individual human needs. Sen has defined rights as 'primarily ethical demands' (2004: 319). Discussions of ethics do not figure too prominently in academic social policy texts, other than in relation to 'applied' ethics (e.g. Bochel, 2005; Fitzpatrick, 2008), but issues relating to rights and responsibilities – to human welfare and interdependency – clearly have ethical connotations that bear fundamentally on our discussion of rights and needs (Dean, 2004). In this chapter, therefore, I aim very briefly to set the scene by explaining a distinction I would wish to emphasise between ethics and morality. I then return to the distinction I began to discuss in the last chapter between hegemonic and minor traditions in rights discourse in order to reflect on their ethical underpinnings. And I shall finally bring together elements of this discussion with the ideas presented in the preceding two chapters by presenting an overarching conceptual taxonomy of social rights-based perspectives.

Ethics and morality

Arguments about the difference between ethics and morals can be dismissed as mere pedantry. There is a tendency sometimes, even amongst philosophers, to treat the terms as if they were synonymous. Nevertheless, there is some purpose in my wishing to make a distinction between the two. It is a distinction directly analogous to that which I have drawn between the doctrinal and claims-based foundations of rights and between top-down and bottom-up definitions of needs. Ethics, as a branch of philosophy, is quite simply the study or the 'science' of morals: ethics is to morality what methodology is to methods in social science or what theology is to religion. (As to theology and religion, they too can have consequences for perspectives on social rights, but that would be a subject for another treatise!) Clearly, therefore, ethics and morality are intimately related, but that relationship is important. The two inform each other; they evolve in relation to each other over time; they have a dialectical relationship.

If one considers the etymological origins of the terms, ethics comes from the Greek, *ethos,* meaning 'character', while morality comes from the Latin, *mores,* meaning 'behaviour'. Contemporary English usage of the term ethos is concerned with cognitive awareness of the societal context in which a person acts. We speak of a 'public service ethos' as the shared understanding between public servants as to their vocation and purpose. Contemporary English usage of the term mores is concerned with cultural expectations as to the nature of acceptable behaviour; for example:

> The men, women and children who compose a society at any time are the unconscious depositories and transmitters of the mores. They inherited them without knowing it; they are molding them unconsciously; they will transmit them involuntarily. The people cannot make the mores. They are made by them.
>
> (Sumner, 1906: 477)

This is a jaundiced, if not misanthropic, interpretation of popular mores, but despite its exaggeration, the point it makes is that while ethics is concerned with values and that which should be regarded as 'right', morality is concerned with norms and that which is popularly accepted as 'good'. Ethics is concerned with abstract reasoning, principles and doctrines – morality with everyday codes and agreed or even implicit rules of conduct. There is once again a connection to be made with Habermas's (1987, 1996) distinction between 'system' and 'life-world': systemic ethics on the one hand; the morality of the life-world on the other, together framing the structure of communicative action. Ethical arguments dreamed up by philosophers may or may not have influence on everyday thinking in the real world of policy making where social rights may be named and claimed, but they do tell us something about what had once been, or is now, thinkable.

Hegemonic and minor traditions of rights discourse

In the last chapter I contrasted the hegemonic liberal-individualist conception that sees social rights as a condition precedent for personal freedom with what Woodiwiss (2005) has dubbed the 'minor' tradition that conceives of social rights as an intrinsic expression of human solidarity. These traditions embody competing ethical premises, drawn from a range of established schools of thought. The connections can be tenuous and are messy. The account that follows, therefore, is highly simplified, but it represents one way of telling an otherwise complicated story.

Consequentialist and utilitarian foundations

Consequentialism reasons that human beings should act in whichever way will have the best consequences. If the consequence of 'necessity' or 'Want' (i.e. unmet human need) is a limitation upon individual freedom, social rights that substantively provide for human need are, we might think, justified (see, for example, Sen, 1982b). However, this 'welfarist' and ostensibly beneficent interpretation of consequentialism can be heavily qualified by strictly utilitarian versions of the creed (e.g. Bentham, 1789), which would argue that the utility of freedom is surely the pursuit of self-contentment or happiness and, since we can't all be equally happy, the job of government is to maximise the happiness not of all citizens, but of the greatest number. The utilitarian ethic reflects a tradition that reaches back to a particular strand in classical philosophy beginning with Epicurus (see George, 2010: ch. 2), who appears to have first articulated a very particular contractarian view of the relationship between the individual and society – the idea that society exists not to provide for human need but to provide the security wherein individuals might peaceably provide for their own needs. The Epicurean view of the good life was distinctly hedonic, though not hedonistic: life's aim was to pursue pleasure – both physical and spiritual – and avoid pain, but to abjure wasteful luxuries or excess. Though Epicurus valued personal friendship, he insisted that human beings were essentially individualistic, self-interested and disinclined to community spirit or civic participation. Epicurean thinking was reflected in Stoicism, a philosophical movement which began in ancient Athens and achieved later prominence in classical Rome. Stoicism established an intellectual foundation for the principle of formal equality of rich and poor before the law, since rich and poor were deemed equally capable of leading a good life (though not necessarily equally comfortable lives). Towards the end of Europe's feudal era, this principle would eventually re-emerge in liberal Enlightenment thinking, most conspicuously in the work of Hobbes (1651), who clearly and influentially advocated a form of government based on a notional compact or contract, whereby the individual citizen would forgo or trade certain elements of his own freedom in return for the protection of the state against the predations and irresponsible tendencies of his fellow citizens. The initial object was to secure the minimum necessary level of social order.

The utilitarian ethic may be called upon in justification of policy interventions that inflict suffering on a minority of people so long as it is thought to benefit the majority. This was indeed what occurred in the more punitive kinds of Poor Law regimes that preceded the modern capitalist welfare state – regimes that incarcerated paupers in the workhouse. A utilitarian ethic justifies interventions that encourage or compel people to act in particular ways to ensure the greatest benefit to the greatest number in society. Such justification is premised on an assumption that all human beings are motivated primarily by self-interest and can be relied upon to respond to material incentives; they will be deterred by penalties and attracted by rewards. Social rights therefore can legitimately be made conditional on behaviour that is judged to be desirable and in the interests of society at large; social assistance claimants can be required to seek low paid or uncongenial employment; penalties can be imposed on parents who fail to send their children to school; public housing can be denied or withdrawn from families deemed guilty of anti-social behaviour.

The utilitarian tradition – though potentially authoritarian and therefore illiberal in many respects (King, 1999) – has clearly been an important component in the hegemonic liberal-individualist ethic. Its first priority is to secure social order for the benefit of the individual through the rule of law and, therefore, the maintenance of civil rights. Its second priority is to ensure some influence of the sovereign individual over the state and, therefore, the maintenance of political rights. Within this context the development of social rights, if it is supported at all, is likely to be a lower priority. And the framing of social rights is likely to entail elements of conditionality, a trend whose significance in the twenty-first century has been re-emerging across the world (Dwyer, 2000, 2004; Gaia *et al.*, 2011).

We have seen in previous chapters, however, that other strands of liberal thought were decisive to the development of social rights in the mid-twentieth century. There had been important precursors to the reluctant liberal collectivism of Beveridge and Roosevelt. Political liberals, such as Paine (1791) in the eighteenth century and early social liberals such as T.H. Green in the nineteenth century (see Carter, 2003; George, 2010: ch. 11), each had in their writing prefigured ideas of social rights. Fundamentally, however, all strands of liberalism are rooted in a belief in the autonomous individual as the bearer of rights. It was the economic liberalism of Adam Smith that most clearly captured the need for moral rules in the context of an amoral capitalist market system: the idea that though the free market could harness the pursuit of economic self-interest, a sense of selfless civic duty was necessary to the 'harmony of sentiments and passions' (1759: 72) on which human wellbeing depends.

Deontological and ontological elements

Deontological reasoning is concerned not with the consequences that follow from human actions, but with principles, rules and duties that apply prior to such actions. And it is reason itself that matters above feelings and emotions. Deontology – as the opposite of ontology – was the product of Cartesian dualism and the idea that the mind is separate from the body, and that thinking is more than being. The deontological thinking of Immanuel Kant holds a vital place within the broader spectrum of liberal thought insofar as it furnished the rational argument for exactly that which Adam Smith had in mind: it could temper the naked pursuit of self-interest and encourage selfless civic duty. Deontological thinking requires an understanding of the human subject, not only as a competitive self-seeking individual, but as a socially situated being who must recognise and respect the rationality of other human beings. From this flows the Kantian categorical imperative:

> Act in such a way that you always treat humanity, whether in your own person or in the person of any other, never simply as a means, but always at the same time as an end.
>
> (Kant, 1785: 91)

Kant's deontology is based, according to Fitzpatrick, 'on the freedom of rational beings who observe the laws and duties of universal reason in a moral and social system of mutual respect' (2008: 47). This is an understanding that clearly supports 'first-generation' rights, namely, the liberal Enlightenment conceptions of civil liberties and constitutional government. But its implications for 'second-generation' social rights are less clear. It is an understanding that can be developed in different directions.

One such direction – that is distinctly liberal – has been championed through Rawls's (1972) theory of social justice. This is a theory that is described as 'contractualist', as distinct from 'contractarian' (the term I applied above to the Hobbesian bargain between individual and state). It is contractualist in the sense that Rawls envisages a hypothetical negotiation between rational actors as to the rules that should apply not only in relation to the defence of liberty, but also with regard to the distribution of rewards in society. The parties to this hypothetical negotiation would not know what their own station in society would be, so would rationally determine principles of distribution that would be in the interests of everybody. This metaphysical proposition is capable (though not without difficulty) of political interpretation in relation to the construction of social rights and taxation policies in the real world (e.g. White, 2003).

The other direction in which Kantian deontology leads stems from the manner in which Kant himself opens the door to thinking about the nature and limits of individual autonomy and the ontological implications of human dependency and interdependency – of needs for care and recognition. Kant draws a firm distinction between 'perfect' duties that cannot rationally be ignored and 'imperfect' duties that may be feasible and morally desirable but cannot be universally demanded. Sen (2004) has alluded to this distinction in defence of the idea that certain social rights do not cease to be rights if they have not or cannot yet be realised. The idea that there is a realm of imperfect duties and correlative social rights that may yet be developed lies arguably at the heart of not only social liberal but also social democratic ideological aspirations. For Kant, however, the existence of imperfect as opposed to universal duties required a doctrine of virtue (Fitzpatrick, 2008: 48–51). Virtue had been a central feature of Aristotelian ethics, but Kant alludes to virtues not simply as characteristics of a good life, but as rationally contestable (and in that sense imperfect) moral duties.

Virtue ethics is sometimes presented as a third branch of moral philosophy – after consequentialism and deontology – though Nussbaum (1999) suggests its intersections with the other branches (including Kant's work) render it insufficiently distinctive. It is important, nevertheless, since it addresses ontological issues – issues to do with the fundamental nature of human interdependency and wellbeing. Virtue ethics is concerned not so much with effects or rules of action as with moral character and moral rationalities. In a sense it attenuates the distinction between ethics and morality. MacIntyre (2007), in particular, drawing from Aristotle, is profoundly critical of the values of the liberal Enlightenment and the construction of the 'liberal self'. Instead he advocates what he calls the 'narrative self', rooted not in abstract reasoning, but in the context of communal life and substantive social practices. The approach can be seen as essentially, even nostalgically, conservative, but it connects, for example, with important recent debates about ontological identity and the ethic of care.

In Chapter 2 mention was made of the recent shift towards a politics of identity, a shift that is consonant with liberal values of equality and tolerance. However, David Taylor (1998) has suggested that in addition to focusing on categorical identities and the importance of ensuring just treatment for women, ethnic minority groups, disabled people, young people, older people, gay people, etc., social rights must surely also ensure the maintenance of ontological identity and wellbeing. Ontological identity, irrespective of the multiplicity of our particular categorical identities, relates to our frailty and embodied-ness; our uniqueness as human beings; our inner or noumenal sense of 'self'; the integrity of our moral being. This is an aspect of human need ill-served by the dominant ethic lately informing social rights provision.

An ethic of care might be regarded as an alternative to the liberal ethic of justice (Slote, 2001). Caring for one another is a daily social practice and moral obligation (Finch & Mason, 1993). The motivation to care for others is a moral virtue, and feminist theorists (Sevenhuijsen, 1998; Tronto, 1994) have argued for an ethical approach premised on a construction of the individual not as an abstract individual rights holder, but as a self-in-relationship – an approach that recognises that 'vulnerability is part and parcel of ordinary human subjectivity' (Sevenhuijsen, 2000: 19). And here we have a direct connection to Bryan Turner's conception of human rights (see Chapter 2, this volume). An ethic of care might arguably provide an alternative basis for social rights – for the provision of not only intimate care, but the provision of 'asylum' in times of distress, or protection, for example, against exploitation by employers or landlords. Fiona Williams (1999) captures the sense in which an ethic of care, embracing concerns for interdependence, bodily integrity, ontological identity and voice, may be translated into 'good-enough' principles of welfare: 'good enough' in the sense portended by Winnicott's (1953) notion of good-enough parenting, since provision for social rights can never achieve some rational standard of perfection, but sustained by unconditional commitment, it will be good enough.

Dependency and responsibility

Whereas interdependency is an essential feature of the human life course and the human condition, the dominant ethic is implicitly premised on an assumption that dependency and responsibility are somehow inimical (Dean, 2004: ch. 10). Autonomy is conflated with self-sufficiency: sustaining oneself through dependency on an employer and/or within one's family is regarded, perversely, as independence. The tendency, especially in the Anglophone world, is towards a form of 'dependency fetishism', whereby protective social rights, rather than promoting citizens' autonomy or independence, are thought to promote an undesirable and stigmatising form of dependency. Dependency fetishism is analogous to commodity fetishism (Marx, 1887: ch. 1), a distorted perception that obscures true understanding of the nature of our human relationships and transactions. The hegemonic liberal-individualist conventions upon which the development of capitalist welfare states are in large part founded – whether they are justified in whole or in part by utilitarian or deontological ethical principles – have been implicated in sustaining this distorted understanding of dependency, and in constraining welfare state citizens' sense of interdependency and solidarity (Dean & Rodgers, 2004).

Economic globalisation and the ascendancy of neo-liberalism (Amin, 1997; Stiglitz, 2003) would appear to have accentuated this. In the late twentieth century, when capitalist welfare states were subject to economic pressures, this was accompanied and fuelled by a significant backlash against social rights (Roche, 1992). The extension of social rights, it was feared, could eclipse individual responsibilities and was literally 'de-moralising' (Himmelfarb, 1995). We shall consider such critiques in Chapter 4, but what is important for now is the extent to which a new preoccupation with 'responsibility' pervaded debates about social rights, not only in relation to established welfare states, but more globally. What Nikolas Rose (1996b) identified as a new form of 'advanced liberalism' seeks now to promote not social rights, but prudentialism, self-provisioning and the 'responsibilisation' of everyday life. However, it follows from our discussion above that responsibility is not a simple concept. Does responsibility equate with obedience, duty and moral obligation or can there be such a thing as collective responsibility – a form of responsibility to which social rights, far from negating, give expression?

Philosophers have a range of answers. James Griffin (2008), for example, argues that as human beings we each have ethical responsibility for everybody else and, insofar as minimum material provision is as constitutive of personhood as individual autonomy, that we should all contribute to collective provision for social rights. This is consistent with, on the one hand, Richard Titmuss's (1970: ch. 16) idea that welfare states enable their citizens to care not just for their family and neighbours, but also for strangers; on the other, it is consistent with Tom Campbell's (2007) case for a Global Humanitarian Levy whereby the citizens of richer countries might contribute to the relief of poverty in poorer countries. The logic of the argument is illustrated by the anecdote in Box 3.1. Karl Otto Apel (1980, 1991) has similarly developed a concept of 'co-responsibility': a form of responsibility that links individual duty and collective obligation, but which is premised on rational judgement, rather than moral tradition.

One of the most compelling ethical arguments that might indirectly be called upon in support of social rights has been advanced by Axel Honneth (1995). He contends that the requirements of an ethical life are constituted through the three ways in which human beings achieve mutual recognition: love, solidarity and rights. It is through *love* that we can achieve the most intimate kind of recognition, care and respect for another needy being; and so we discover our own being and self-identity. It is through *solidarity* that we can achieve shared recognition, accommodation and respect for members of a social group defined by their

---

BOX 3.1   THE RIGHTS OF STRANGERS: AN ANECDOTE

Philosophers will often employ vignettes – imaginary situations – in order to illustrate some important argument or conundrum. Though the anecdote that follows is redolent of one such widely used vignette, it is actually a true story. It concerns a long-standing friend of mine, with whom I grew up in South London in the 1960s. We'll call him Adam (not his real name).

Once upon a time, just a year or two ago, Adam was revisiting some of his childhood haunts and was strolling through a popular inner-city park, in the midst of which, he remembered, was a little visited and isolated ornamental pond. As he approached the pond he saw to his horror that lying motionless and face down in the middle of the pond was a child: a little boy of perhaps four years of age. There was nobody else in sight. The pond was shallow, and Adam, at no risk to himself other than the discomfort of getting his feet wet, was in a position to wade into the water and rescue the child. And this he did. The child, fortunately, was still alive and Adam was able to remove him from the water and resuscitate him. Some minutes later, the child's mother appeared, wholly unflustered. She had been unaware of her son's predicament and was angry with him for getting wet rather than concerned that he had very nearly drowned. She offered no word of thanks to Adam.

We might ask: in these circumstances, did that child (or his mother) have a right to expect Adam to save his life? The child had behaved irresponsibly: there is a fence around the pond over which he must have climbed. The mother had irresponsibly allowed her child to wander unsupervised. It was none of Adam's business. But most reasonable people would probably agree that the child's right to life placed an *accidental* responsibility upon Adam.

If we can any of us individually incur accidental responsibility to help even irresponsible strangers, can we not share collective responsibility (even at the cost of some modest sacrifice) to relieve or prevent the foreseeable suffering of strangers in need? Do systematically disadvantaged members of our society, or even other societies, have a right to collectively organised assistance, even if this is provided or funded by people who are not directly to blame for their disadvantage?

difference in unity; and so we establish our own human self-esteem. And it is through *rights* that we can achieve cognitive recognition, empathy and respect for distant strangers who may have legitimate claims for our assistance, as we may have claims for their assistance; and so we may consolidate our own self-respect. This is an insight combining ontological and deontological ethics. It re-situates rights in relation to human interdependency and notions of co-responsibility.

Taxonomising rights-based perspectives

I have sought to present an analysis that links rights, needs and responsibilities, each of which may be approached or understood from a variety of perspectives. One way of achieving a synthesis or overview of the story so far is through a three-in-one taxonomy or classification of these different perspectives. In one sense this simplifies the analysis, but in the process it undeniably entails some complexity. I have struggled over the years with the complexity of the component parts of this taxonomy. The struggle, I hope, is worth it. However, readers who find this kind of conceptual modelling unhelpful may prefer at this stage to move on to the next chapter! And though I shall occasionally refer back to the taxonomy in later chapters, readers who would prefer to do so should feel free to pass over such references, which though they may add insight, are not essential to my main argument.

It is a taxonomy or classification intended to serve as a heuristic device; it is not meant to provide a knock-down, all-inclusive explanation of reality. That is impossible. Despite its apparent complexity it is intentionally parsimonious: it deliberately oversimplifies some things in an attempt to understand the big picture. And, though the picture is big, not all of it will necessarily be equally or immediately relevant to everybody who reads this. Later in the book, however, we shall be thinking about whether we might move beyond the perspectives illustrated in the taxonomy. But to engage with that possibility, it helps to have some understanding of that from which we could or should be moving on. A diagrammatic representation of the taxonomy is provided in Figure 3.1.

The top part of Figure 3.1 is intended to summarise the arguments I have presented in relation to social constructions of social rights (Chapter 1), human needs (Chapter 2) and ethical responsibilities (see above). Each argument revolved around two distinctions, which are represented here as continua or dichotomies along two intersecting axes: one vertical and the other horizontal.

The vertical axes: Power relations

The three vertical axes are related. In Chapter 1 we discussed a distinction between doctrinal and claims-based conceptions of social rights; in Chapter 2 we discussed a distinction between top-down and bottom-up definitions of need; in this chapter we have discussed a distinction between ethical and moralistic understandings of responsibility. I have indicated above and readers may already have an intuitive sense that there is a relationship between these distinctions. They are each and together associated with communicative relations of power: the hierarchical relations within which rights, needs and responsibilities are negotiated. The tensions between doctrinal and claims-based social rights, top-down and bottom-up need and ethical and moralistic responsibility are all dialectically mutually constitutive: they feed off each other.

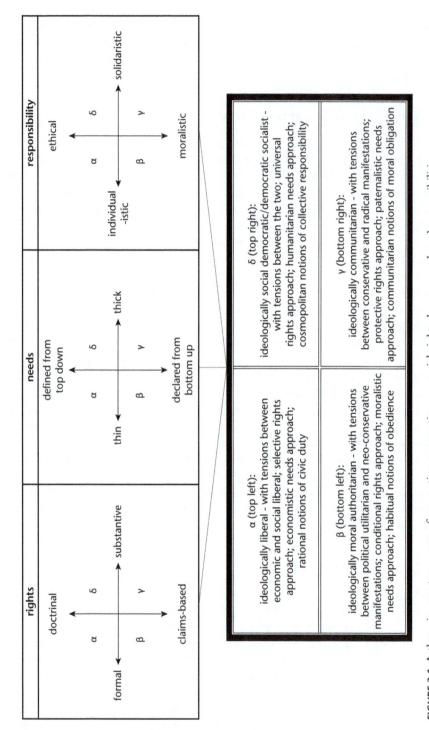

FIGURE 3.1 A three-in-one taxonomy of competing perspectives on social rights, human needs and responsibilities

Though not directly analogous, there is a resonance between all three axes and the 'grid' axis in Mary Douglas's (1977) highly influential cultural theory. Douglas's grid axis signified the extent to which individuals were free from or 'locked in' to a culturally dominant view of the world. However, our three axes are premised on the idea that hegemonic relations of power can lock people in in different ways, and that powerful people can be as constrained by elaborated ideological rationality as powerless people are constrained by simple customary mythology. And powerless people are not necessarily cultural dupes, but may be capable of artful compliance or counter-hegemonic resistance (Scott, 1985) as opposed to passive compliance. Power and communication can flow up as well as down.

So, who are the principal advocates of doctrinal rights, top-down needs and ethical responsibilities? They are promoted we might suppose by those in authority: by rulers, sages or priests. And who are the principal advocates of claims-based rights, bottom-up needs and moralistic responsibilities? They are promoted we might suppose by subaltern members of society or by their representatives: civil society organisations, trades unions and community activists. In practice, however, dissident politicians, radical scholars and liberation theologists may side with the subaltern, while civil society organisations, trades unions and community activists can be co-opted by the authorities (Piven & Cloward, 1977). And fundamentally, of course, systemic orthodoxies can 'colonise' the life-world (Habermas, 1987); they can shape and ossify the claims, the needs and the mores of the people. Conversely, yesterday's dissidents may sometimes become tomorrow's governors. It should be clear that rights, needs and responsibilities are dynamically negotiated and renegotiated at the point where competing perspectives engage with one another.

The horizontal axes: Social relations

The three horizontal axes are also related. In Chapter 1 we discussed a distinction between formal and substantive conceptions of social rights; in Chapter 2 we discussed a distinction between thin and thick definitions of need; in this chapter we have discussed a distinction between individualistic and solidaristic understandings of responsibility. Once again, readers may already have an intuitive sense that there is a relationship between these distinctions. They are each and together associated with social relations; with the social orientation within which rights, needs and responsibilities are constituted. Human sociality may be oriented to a person's freedom in, or her connectedness to, society. Formal and substantive social rights, thin and thick need and individualistic and solidaristic responsibility stand respectively in relation to each other as opposing ends of a spectrum of theories, discourses and practices upon which social actors may draw – in a variety of combinations.

Once again, there is a resonance between all three axes and in this instance the 'group' axis in Mary Douglas's cultural theory. Douglas's group axis signified the extent to which individuals were free from, or protectively bound by, social group membership. There is a clear correspondence between the distinctions captured by the group axis and the distinction between the principles of liberty and solidarity. These are competing principles by which different people in different societies will in different ways live out their lives.

We might suppose that the principal advocates of formal rights, thin needs and individualistic responsibilities would be found towards the right of the ideological spectrum, and that the principal advocates of substantive rights, thick needs and solidaristic responsibilities would be found towards the left. Reality, however, is more complex than that. These are not always distinctions that fit neatly into conventional ideological categories. What is more, people are perfectly capable of embracing more than one principle at a time and to combine them in complex and even ostensibly contradictory ways (Dean with Melrose, 1999).

The synthesis

The bottom part of Figure 3.1 brings together the rights, needs and responsibilities taxonomies into a single model that categorises just four perspectives. I have eschewed the temptation to assign a definitive name or discursive label to each perspective, since any name or label one might choose is liable to be at best reductive and at worst confusing. So, I have called them just α (alpha), β (beta), γ (gamma) and δ (delta) and I describe them as follows:

The α perspective (constructed at the intersection of the axes that delineate the top left quadrant in each of the three sections in the top part of Figure 3.1) might currently be regarded, as we have seen, as the *dominant* perspective. The perspective:

- Is ideologically liberal, though the spectrum of liberal beliefs is wide. There is an important divide between economic and social liberalism. Economic liberalism is rooted in 'classical' liberal-individualist egalitarianism, but variants of what is dubbed 'neo-liberalism' may share *some* ground with far-right neo-conservative authoritarianism. Social liberalism, as we have seen, has been dubbed 'reluctant collectivism' and can share *some* political centre ground with social democrats. All liberals, however, share a commitment to the autonomy of the individual.
- Adopts a selective approach to social rights. Rights are doctrinally conceived on the basis of a belief in the fundamental efficacy of a competitive market economy, an efficacy that depends, however, on formal equality of opportunity – on a 'level playing field' for all. A right to targeted social assistance is considered to be legitimate where – for example, through unemployment or infirmity – a citizen is excluded from economic participation. Or else there can be a right to provision at the basic minimum 'floor' necessary to ensure a person's readiness for economic participation. A right to education and/or healthcare is considered legitimate in circumstances where markets fail or are unable to maintain the skills and health of the labour force.
- Adopts an economistic approach to human need in the sense that the human subject is defined *a priori* as an economic actor who, as a producer of goods or services, should have freedom to compete and, as a consumer, should have freedom to choose. Needs reflect people's wants and preferences and are thin in the sense that they are particular to the individual.
- Conceives of responsibility as civic duty: an individual duty to be self-sufficient on the one hand (but respectful towards one's competitors and their freedoms on the other) and to act and to contribute in such a way as is commensurate with the maintenance of a functional market economy. The performance of duties should, ideally, be a self-regulating process.

The β perspective (constructed at the intersection of the axes that delineate the bottom left quadrant in each of the three sections in the top part of Figure 3.1) might currently be regarded as a *resurgent* perspective. Though redolent of the principles of social assistance that preceded the capitalist welfare state, elements of the perspective have endured and are evident, as we shall see in later chapters, within current policy innovations. The perspective:

- Is difficult to define in conventional ideological terms, but is best captured by the term 'moral authoritarian'. It has diverse elements: nineteenth-century Benthamite political utilitarianism on the one hand, twentieth-century neo-conservatism (Elliott & McCrone, 1987; Thompson & Brook, 2011) on the other. Its essence is individualist, yet anti-libertarian.
- Adopts a conditional approach to social rights (when and insofar as it recognises social rights at all). Rights are properly the conditions on which bilateral exchange between competitive individuals is conducted, but they may, under certain circumstances, be transposed to a multilateral context. An individual right to any form of social assistance, if claimed, will necessarily be conditional on the deservingness of the supplicant and/or her compliance with behavioural constraints.
- Adopts a circumstantial understanding of human need. Needs equate with that which is required for survival in a competitive and hazardous social environment.
- Conceives of responsibility in terms of compliance with authority. The baseness of human nature must necessarily be constrained. Irresponsible behaviour should be suppressed by the inculcation of habitual obedience or through the imposition of rules or conditions by which all are equally bound.

The γ perspective (constructed at the intersection of the axes that delineate the bottom right quadrant in each of the three sections in the top part of Figure 3.1) might currently be regarded as a *declining* perspective. Its influence on social rights development, though by no means exhausted, is arguably waning. The perspective:

- Is ideologically communitarian, though this covers a spectrum of beliefs. There is an important divide between the communitarianism of traditional conservatives – such as Burke (see Lock, 1999) or Bismark (see Steinberg, 2011) – and that of radical democrats – such as Rousseau (1762) or, in recent times, Michael Walzer (1983). In essence, however, whether the emphasis is on the traditions of *noblesse oblige* or the general will of the people, its commitment is to some version of social solidarity.
- Approaches social rights as rights to social protection. Such rights arise because the people share certain risks and vulnerabilities. Conceding the people's claims to protective rights serves to bind them together and to the social order; it guards against subversive influences and so protects the institutions of society.
- Adopts a paternalistic approach to human need. Human needs are needs held in common. They are thick in the sense that they encompass the ontological need to belong. They are responsively defined in accordance with principles of subsidiarity, with priority accorded to support for families and communities.
- Conceives of responsibility in terms of mutual moral obligation. Responsibility is constructed with reference to collective loyalties and traditions; to moral norms and social values; and to the expectations that arise from membership of a particular community. Failure to comply is seen as shameful.

The δ perspective (constructed at the intersection of the axes that delineate the top right quadrant in each of the three sections in the top part of Figure 3.1) might currently be regarded as a *potentiating* perspective. In describing it thus, I am anticipating discussions that will come in Chapter 10 as to the future of social rights. The perspective:

- May be defined in ideological terms as social democratic or as democratic socialist. The ideological integrity of social democracy, some would argue, has been compromised by an ever closer association through the so-called Third Way with neo-liberalism (Pierson, 2001), but the principles of democratic socialism still offer a vision that is both solidaristic and informed by what might be described as a social humanistic ethic (Fromm, 1965) or 'social humanism' (Fitzpatrick, 2008: 21–26 & 91–93) .
- Has a preference for universal social rights: rights that should as a matter of principle attach to every citizen, or even to every human being; that are comprehensive and should extend to substantive and appropriate support during every stage of the human life course; and that should be unconditional.
- Adopts a humanitarian approach to human need, in the sense that the human individual is regarded as a social actor, defined inherently by her humanity. Its focus is on people's need not merely to survive, but to participate socially and to be personally fulfilled.
- Conceives of responsibility as collective: a form of co-responsibility that is cosmopolitan in nature, in that it is as inclusive as possible.

Summary/conclusion

This chapter has rounded off a story about the development of social rights to date, and it has done so through a discussion of ethics. As its title portends, this book is about social rights and human welfare. And a concern for human welfare is axiomatically ethical. But we have seen that different ethical values might lead us in the direction of different understandings of what constitutes 'welfare'. In recent times in the Anglophone world the term 'welfare' has taken on a pejorative connotation, since it is widely used by politicians and the press to refer not to the full range of social benefits and human services provided by the welfare state, but to social assistance benefits provided to economically inactive people of working age. In that context, 'welfare' has become a code word for idleness, personal irresponsibility and moral degeneration. The ethics of social rights provision have been reinterpreted, or 'spun', so as to give social rights a different moral meaning. This is an illustration of why it is necessary to draw the distinction made at the start of this chapter between ethics (systemic reasoning about what is right) as opposed to morality (prevailing judgements about what is acceptable).

Though the terms are for most purposes synonymous, we can argue as to whether in present circumstances we might speak about 'wellbeing' as opposed to 'welfare', though this raises its own problems (Dean, 2012b: 9–12). However, it is hard to disagree with Mary Daly (2011) when she suggests that the original meanings of 'welfare' need to be restored. The philosophical distinction between hedonic and eudaimonic wellbeing or welfare (that we explored both in this chapter and the last) demonstrates the extent to which ethics presents a spectrum of definitions. The chapter has teased out the connections between the main schools of ethical reasoning and the dominant tradition in social rights, and it has discussed ethical theories of moral duty and how these relate to the minority tradition in social rights discourse. Key to these discussions has been a focus on the relationship between human interdependence and the ethics of responsibility. If we cannot dissociate a discussion of social rights from a discussion of human needs, neither can we dissociate it from a discussion of responsibilities.

Finally, the chapter has presented a taxonomy of four principal perspectives on social rights, considering their ideological foundations in relation to the manner in which their understandings of social rights, human need and ethical responsibility are constructed. The account of the taxonomy enables us to grasp the sense in which the development of social rights has been:

- largely dominated by a liberal tradition;
- underpinned, nonetheless, by a moral authoritarian tradition that is increasingly resurgent;
- significantly informed by a communitarian tradition that is now in decline;
- embraced by a social democratic tradition, which though faltering, may yet potentiate an understanding of social rights premised on an ethic of collective responsibility for human welfare.

4

CRITIQUES OF SOCIAL RIGHTS

Challenges to the idea that citizens can, or should, enjoy social rights have issued from several quarters and this chapter will explore certain of these. It should by now already be clear that social rights are an ambiguous phenomenon, capable of dichotomous interpretations (see Box 4.1). First, therefore, we shall briefly consider just how the fragile ideological consensus that permitted the original development of the capitalist welfare state was possible. We shall then consider the critiques of that consensus that emerged from the extremes of the ideological spectrum, before turning to a range of newer critiques that have emerged in the late or post-modern era.

An uneasy consensus

We have already seen that the social rights agenda, whether framed in terms of welfare state citizenship or the international human rights framework, was driven by a social liberal consensus (the α perspective in Figure 3.1). In part this was an uneasy consensus between factions within liberalism: right-leaning economic liberals who broadly favoured 'negative' rights (which demand *freedoms from* things) had to concede to left-leaning social liberals who were prepared, reluctantly perhaps, to countenance 'positive' rights (which demand *entitlements to* things). However, the consensus had also to embrace traditional conservative and moderate socialist opinions (elements of the γ and δ perspectives in Figure 3.1) and to temper the authoritarian excesses of political utilitarianism (an element of the β perspective in Figure 3.1).

Giving people rights is ostensibly one way of protecting their liberties, of safeguarding them from arbitrary power. This was fundamental to the historic strategy by which the property-owning bourgeoisie, in their bid to wrest power from the Crown and the feudal aristocracy, had sought to displace conceptions of 'natural' rights with laws which were 'man-made' (Thompson, 1975). For precisely this reason, conservatives in the mould of Edmund Burke (see, for example, Lock, 1999) were mistrustful of any extension of rights, since the only common right that they would recognise was the 'right to adjudication', that is the right to be governed by the decisions of established authority with the power to translate imagined rights into realities (see Scruton, 1991: 16–18). Rights are an explicit challenge to

BOX 4.1   THE DICHOTOMOUS NATURE OF SOCIAL RIGHTS

Do social rights:

accord people **emancipation** and freedom from Want	or	subject them to **control** and the regulation of need?
provide **entitlement** to social services	or	subject people to **discretion** and judgement?
offer **procedural guarantees** of equal life chances	or	ensure **substantive protection** across the life course?
ensure **proportional justice** as between individuals	or	promote **creative justice** amidst social diversity?

traditional paternalistic authority. There is a paradoxical resonance between this reservation about the consequences of a rights–based approach and that expressed by Richard Titmuss, as a representative of the, peculiarly British, 'Fabian' socialist tradition. Titmuss (1971) favoured 'creative' or 'individualised' social justice administered by compassionate experts, rather than formulaic 'proportional' justice bestowed by rights which are legally prescribed. There have, therefore, been those in both the conservative and the socialist camps who would question the need for social rights that might impair the exercise of benevolent authority in the interests of human welfare.

The history of the capitalist welfare state is in part a story of transition from relief based on charity and discretion to benefits based on legislation and entitlement. Though conservatives resisted the welfare state and Fabian socialists championed it, the common ground they shared was an attachment to the value of discretionary decision making. The compromise which both were prepared to strike with the liberal ideal of 'rights' can best be understood when it is realised that rights need not extinguish the scope for discretionary decision making. Dworkin (1977) makes the point that administrative institutions in advanced capitalist societies function in a discretionary 'void', surrounded like the hole in a doughnut by legal rules and principles. Rights created by legislation require the exercise of administrative discretion for the interpretation and application of those rules (see also Lipsky, 1980/2010). Rights come with strings attached. The creation of rights to welfare extended rather than diminished administrative power and retained a space for utilitarian moral authority through the refinement of conditionality (Garland, 1981). So it is that the expansion of the discourse of rights into the realm of social policy could be supported or at least tolerated across the board from within the broad swathe of the ideological centre ground.

Perhaps the most potent illustration of the ideological hybridity of capitalist welfare states is the extent to which they all, to a greater or lesser extent, adopt the social insurance principle as a mechanism for funding, regulating and delivering, whether wholly or partly, at least some elements of social provision. It is an internationally supported principle and remains a prominent feature in social policy reforms in several emerging economies and, for example, within the ILO's Social Protection Floor initiative (Batchelet, 2011; ILO, 2012b). The precedent for this was established not by a liberal administration, but at the end of the nineteenth century in Germany by Bismarck's conservative administration in its successful attempt to outmanoeuvre socialist opposition (Gilbert, 1966). And yet it was a precedent readily adopted by liberal and social democratic administrations across the capitalist world. The point about the social insurance principle is that it appeals both to individualistic and solidaristic ideals. It entails individual contribution and collective risk sharing. It is authoritarian insofar as membership and contributions are compulsory and insurance schemes are rule-bound. But it is also emancipating, since it can create indisputable rights to benefits, pensions or health treatment.

However, social rights, though born of an uneasy consensus, have generated new theoretical and practical concerns about the relationship between state authority and the individual citizen. And insofar as social rights are developing beyond the sphere of established capitalist welfare states, there are concerns as to how far this is feasible or appropriate.

Grand narrative critiques

Challenges to the nature and effects of social rights have come from the radical wings of both the political Right and the political Left, and from the 'grand narratives' (Lyotard, 1984) of both neo-liberalism and neo-Marxism. In each instance, the 'neo' prefix signals a revival or reapplication of an established ideological narrative or critique. Classical liberalism and Marxism provided an analysis and overarching explanation of political economy – contrasting stories about how, in the wake of the Western Enlightenment, the capitalist market economy functioned. The liberal narrative celebrated the achievements of capitalism; the Marxist narrative condemned them. Though each of these classical narratives had things to say about rights, neither provided an account of social rights or the welfare state. Modern thinkers, however, have remedied that (George & Page, 1995).

The neo-liberal challenge

In seeking to recapture and revitalise the classical doctrines of economic liberalism, neo-liberals would seek to restrict the rights of citizenship to civil and political rights, and primarily, to the negative liberties by which the free play of market forces may be guaranteed. Though the distributive outcomes of impersonal market forces may be unequal, this is neither intended nor foreseen and cannot therefore be unjust. According to Hayek (1976) the very idea of social justice, and of social rights that might compensate for such injustice, is no more than a mirage. If the rich and successful have moral obligations, how and to whom these may be discharged is a matter of choice: such obligations are not enforceable and give rise to no implication that those who fail to prosper have rights against those who succeed. Translating wants and needs into rights was once described by Enoch Powell as 'a dangerous modern heresy' (1972: 12).

Neo-liberal – or neo-liberal type – arguments are fundamentally sceptical towards the social rights created by capitalist welfare states and espoused within the UDHR. There are two kinds of objection: that welfare rights violate property rights, and that social rights do not meet the conditions necessary to qualify as basic human rights. Turning first to Nozick (1974), his argument is based on an interpretation of Kant's 'categorical imperative', namely that respect for other persons depends upon their being regarded as ends in themselves and not as means (see Chapter 3, this volume). This he uses to build a case against any form of social rights requiring redistribution. For Nozick, the inviolability of the individual is synonymous with the inviolability of the property in which her rights are vested. To redistribute any portion of that property to another is to treat that person as a means and not an end. We may not violate persons for the social good because, says Nozick – in words that prefigured British Prime Minister Margaret Thatcher's declaration that 'there is no such thing as society' (*Women's Own* magazine 31 October 1987) – 'there is no *social entity* with a good which undergoes some sacrifice for its own good. There are only individual people with their own individual lives' (1974: 32). Individuals may choose to undergo some sacrifice for their own or somebody else's benefit, but they should not be compelled to do so in the name of some other person's 'right'. Such compulsion does not create social rights, but rights of the state over the property of its own citizens – rights that violate the principle of respect for persons.

Second, there is, for example, Cranston's (1976) denial that social rights can be human rights. From a juristic rather than a political perspective, Cranston, as a legal positivist, draws the distinction we have previously discussed between legal rights (which are 'positively' defined) and human rights (which are 'morally' defined). According to Cranston, human rights have three tests of 'authenticity': practicability, paramount importance and universality. Civil and political rights by and large meet these criteria insofar as they are relatively easily secured by appropriate legislation, they are fundamentally necessary to the just functioning of capitalist society and they may be applied to everybody. Social and economic rights, however, are of a different order. The resources required for a social security system, for example, may be beyond the command of governments in the global South; social services and economic security may represent an ideal, but they are not essential; and the needs which social rights address are relative, not universal. Therefore,

> the effect of a Universal Declaration which is overloaded with affirmations of so-called human rights which are not human rights at all is to push *all* talk of human rights out of the clear realm of the morally compelling into the twilight world of utopian aspiration.
>
> (Cranston, 1976: 142)

Onora O'Neill (a distinguished neo-Kantian philosopher who, at the time of writing, chairs the Equality and Human Rights Commission in the UK) employs a similar logic. Addressing herself to 'The Dark Side of Human Rights' (2005), she observes that while it is clear that the duty to uphold negative rights may be assigned to the state, it isn't in all circumstances clear to whom the duty to uphold positive rights, such as the right to subsistence, can be practically assigned. The former entail claims to the forbearance of identifiable others, while the latter entail claims to performance by agents who cannot be conclusively identified.

Objections to these views are rehearsed elsewhere (Ashton, 2011; Plant *et al.,* 1980; Pogge, 2007; Watson, 1980: ch. 4). The two points which need to be drawn out are that what is here broadly characterised as the neo-liberal case against social rights rests first, on an assertion that social rights do not supplement but undermine the liberties necessary to the perpetuation of capitalism, and second, on concerns about the costs of achieving social rights and by whom they should be borne. Sen (1999: ch. 4) encompasses the first of these within what he refers to as the 'legitimacy' critique and the second in what he refers to as the 'coherence' critique.

The neo-Marxist challenge

From the opposite end of the ideological spectrum comes a contrasting set of arguments, but arguments that can be just as sceptical about the value of social rights. First, there is a group of academic writers who have sought to interpret Marxist principles in relation to the role which social rights play in regulating labour and sustaining, rather than undermining, capital. Second, there are theorists who have developed the Marxist critique of the form of individual legal rights in order to demonstrate the capacity of social rights for ideological mystification and control.

Turning to the first of these approaches, I want to be clear that there are different strands of thought within neo-Marxism. There is an *instrumentalist* strand which adopts from Marx's earlier writings the idea that the state under capitalism acts as no more than 'a committee for managing the common affairs of the whole bourgeoisie' (Marx & Engels, 1848: 69). There is also a *structuralist* strand that derives from Marx's later writing and which analyses state forms as an expression of the immanent logic of the capitalist system and its class antagonisms. When neo-Marxists came to analyse the twentieth-century welfare state and the significance of the development of social rights, both of these strands became to some extent intertwined.

The first kind of critique was developed by writers like Saville (1958), O'Connor (1973) and Gough (1979). They began to forge an account of how the welfare state had developed, claiming in essence that it was the product of three interacting influences. The first of these influences was the struggle by the working class for better living conditions. The social policy reforms obtained in this way had the effect of increasing levels of social consumption and general living standards, but they also benefited capital by furnishing an element of 'quantitative regulation' over labour power – partly by reducing the direct costs of labour, and partly by having the state look after people whose labour was not required. The second influence was capital's growing need for an efficient environment and a productive workforce. The reforms resulting from this influence amounted to the investment by the state in 'human capital' and the necessary 'modification' of labour power through the provision of health and education services so as to produce better workers. The third influence was a concern for political stability. The policies resulting from this influence involved the discharge of the 'social expenses' necessary for the 'qualitative regulation' of labour power, or, more crudely, for the production of contented workers through the provision of those benefits and services required to secure social order and a degree of ideological control.

The neo-Marxist writer to engage most directly with the idea of social rights was Claus Offe. One of his central arguments was that 'the owner of labour power first becomes a wage labourer as a citizen of a state' (1984: 99). Industrial capitalism required more than the passive compulsion of economic forces in order to get people to accept the burdens and risks associated with wage labour and a market economy. To make people actively participate it was necessary to have systems of political-administrative and normative control. Social policy is 'the state's manner of effecting the lasting transformation of non-wage labourers into wage labourers' (Offe, 1984: 92). This is the basis upon which Offe challenges T. H. Marshall's account of social rights. Social rights were not some optional extra or final refinement to citizenship under capitalism: they are, according to Offe, a necessary part of it. Without such rights citizens would not 'muster the *cultural motivation* to become wage labourers' (Offe, 1984: 94). Within Offe's account, social rights were necessary: first, as a precondition for the suppression of begging and modes of subsistence which might undermine the wage labour system; second, as the medium through which to justify the provision of facilities for improving the quality of labour power (in ways which individual self-seeking capitalists are incapable); and third, as a mechanism by which potentially or conditionally to exempt certain parts of the population from labour force participation (mothers, children, students, disabled people, older people). Social rights are as important as civil rights as a device for articulating labour power with the market.

Turning to the second kind of neo-Marxist critique, this is concerned less with the substance or effects of social rights as with their form. Marx had once argued that law and state apparatuses are no more than 'superstructural' phenomena, supported and indirectly shaped by the economic 'foundations' upon which they are constructed (1859). In *Capital* (1887, 1893, 1894), however, he went further and sought to demonstrate that the form of individual rights within bourgeois liberal ideology is a logically necessary consequence of capitalist production and market exchange. Because under market conditions goods must be exchanged as commodities, the producers and owners of such commodities must recognise in each other the rights of private proprietors and relate to each other on the basis of legal and contractual rules. Under capitalism it is not only materials, products and services that are traded but, following the destruction of feudal land tenure, real estate and even human labour are 'freed' to enter the market as commodities. Rights in ownership – of goods, land or labour power – become the universal foundation of human relationships. Unlike Hegel (whose account was similar – see Chapter 1, this volume), Marx dismissed rights in ownership as an illusion, a 'fetishised' form that obscures the fundamentally exploitative substance of the social relations of production under capitalism.

In the course of the twentieth century these ideas were taken up by other writers, foremost of whom was Pashukanis (1978). Writing in the 1920s, Pashukanis argued that, since it is the exchange of commodities that forms the very basis of social life, even such fundamental legal concepts as equity, restitution and entitlement are all derived from the commodity form. Just as 'value' is a concept that fundamentally defines our understanding of the nature and capacities of commodities, so 'right' is a concept that fundamentally defines our understanding of the nature and capacity of human beings. The individual juridical subject or citizen, as the bearer of rights, is the 'atom' – the simplest irreducible element – of legal and administrative theory. Pashukanis argued that this private form of possessive individual right has been rendered universal by being appropriated into the sphere of public and administrative law. This line of reasoning was developed by later theorists (e.g. Holloway & Picciotto, 1978) who have claimed that the form of the state – and the form of social rights – is 'derived' from capitalism's characteristic commodity form and from the nature of the wage relation as the most exploitative expression of that commodity form. The challenge here is that social rights are not all they seem. To cloak human welfare in an ideological discourse of 'rights' conceals the fundamental nature of relations of power under capitalism. It is nonsense to suggest that civil rights will guarantee that individual employees may bargain on equal terms with corporate employers, and it is nonsense to suggest that social rights will guarantee unemployed people, pensioners or disabled people power to negotiate their claims with departments or agents of the state. By proselytising the ideal of an abstract universal human individual, human rights discourse continues, it is claimed, to de-politicise the economic processes that give rise to social oppression; such an individual will never 'fully identify the kernel of their being with their particular social situation' (Žižek, 2005: 129). Social rights give expression to the ultimate dominance of capital over labour and serve to extend or permeate that dominance beyond the immediate sphere of the wage relation, into the sphere of state-citizen relations, and into everyday life.

Once again, objections to these views are rehearsed elsewhere (e.g. Campbell, 1983; Hall & Held, 1989). There are neo-Marxist or anti-capitalist theorists, such as Lukács (1971), de Sousa Santos (2001) and Hardt and Negri (2000), who clearly see an emancipatory role for law – and, by implication, for rights – in a future post-capitalist era (see Fine, 2002). However, in spite of differences between them, the essence of the neo-Marxists' case against social rights is first, that in ameliorating the exploitative impact of capitalism they help ensure its survival, and second, that under present circumstances, social rights provide a powerful mechanism for state/ideological control.

A post–grand narrative era?

We have touched in preceding chapters on the crisis that befell the capitalist welfare state towards the end of the twentieth century and the consequences of this for social rights. The era through which we are now living may be described as post-industrial (Bell, 1973), post-modern (Lyotard, 1984) or even post-social (Rose, 1996a). We live, arguably, in a different world than that in which T. H. Marshall expounded on social citizenship and the UN first proclaimed a Universal Declaration of Human Rights. However, contrary to the prophecies of some (e.g. Fukuyama, 1992), we have not seen the end of history. The grand narratives have not been superseded. The Marxist narrative appears to be in retreat and, although it is 'increasingly difficult to demarcate the boundaries of what Marxism is and is not' (Fine, 2002: 117), its influence is alive in all sorts of current thinking (Callinicos, 2007: ch. 13). The neo-liberal narrative on the other hand is ascendant and enduring (Amin, 1997; Taylor-Gooby, 1994, 2013). Its fundamental premises were reflected towards the end of the twentieth century in the global North, initially through the development of 'new right' approaches and the partial retrenchment of social rights (e.g. Levitas, 1986), and subsequently during the development of 'Third Way' thinking and the modification of social rights (e.g. Lewis & Surender, 2004). Its impact on the global South has been felt through the pro-market 'Washington consensus' (Williamson, 1990) that informed the development policies of the World Bank and the International Monetary Fund (IMF) – policies favouring free-market competition and minimal social safety nets. Though it is supposed by some (Stiglitz, 2003) that the implementation of the MDGs portended an end to such an approach, some would argue that its influence lives on (Deacon, 2007; Maxwell, 2005). Neo-liberal orthodoxies, it has been argued, have even survived the crisis of confidence that might have resulted from the global financial crisis that they precipitated in 2007–10 (Callinicos, 2010; Peck & Tickell, 2012). The implications of this for social rights will be pursued in future chapters. For now we shall consider other critiques bearing on social rights that have emerged during the transition to the current era.

The transition has fomented alternative insights, theories and critiques. I shall first discuss 'emancipatory' critiques associated with new social movements (specifically, the feminist, anti-racist and disability awareness movements). Second, I shall touch upon some of the 'defensive' critiques emanating from the new political pluralism. The distinction I make here between emancipatory and defensive approaches owes something to Habermas (1987: 393). Finally, I shall touch on theoretical post-structuralist critiques.

Challenges from emancipatory social movements

I refer here to critiques which attempted on behalf of particular constituencies to redeem the universal promises offered by the 'liberal' conception of rights (Hewitt, 1993), which questioned whether social rights did ensure equality and freedom from Want for women, for ethnocultural minorities and for disabled people. I referred fleetingly to a 'cultural turn' in critical thinking in the global North: a turn towards a politics of identity and recognition – a concern with dimensions of oppression and socially constructed differences other than those associated with socio-economic class.

Foremost, from the 1960s onwards, was the **second-wave feminist movement** (Fraser, 2010: ch. 6). Previous generations of liberal feminists had campaigned against limitations upon women's property rights and voting rights, and more latterly maternalist feminists began to campaign in favour of rights for citizen-mothers (Lister, 2003). Second-wave feminists, however, began to challenge the underlying form as well as the substance of their 'rights'. As in the sphere of civil and political rights, when it came to social rights women were 'second class citizens' (Lister, 1990: 56). There remained a liberal feminist strand whose concern was to promote equal opportunities legislation (Williams, 1989: 44–49), but the 1970s witnessed the birth of strands of feminism in which resistance to women's oppression was founded on the critical analysis of patriarchy, as a structural characteristic of human society. The central insight of the concept relates to the distinction between the socially constructed public and private spheres (see especially Pascall, 1986, 1997). The public sphere is where civil and political rights reside; it is the domain of the market and the state; it is the site of productive and administrative activity in which, by and large, men colonised the principal roles. The private sphere, in contrast, is not inhabited by rights; it is the domestic domain of hearth, home and family; it is the site for the reproduction of social life, a process in which women were assigned their principal roles. The public/productive sphere is separated from, yet dominates, the private/reproductive sphere. Social rights have been important to the articulation between the two. As Pascall puts it, the welfare state was originally forged 'in the void between the factory and the family' (1986: 26).

Social rights may have succeeded in redistributing resources from men to women (e.g. Falkingham & Hills, 1995), but women still face a higher risk of poverty than men, both globally (Chant, 2008), and even within capitalist welfare states (Pascall, 2012). Social rights have failed women on two counts: first, because they were instrumental in the supervision and enforcement of women's dependency in the private sphere, and second, because they did not compensate women for their disadvantage in the public sphere. The original architects and subsequent analysts of the capitalist welfare state were inured to the patriarchal norm of the male breadwinner household. They were criticised for failing properly to confront the reality that under capitalism 'men and women are "gendered commodities" with different experiences of the labour market resulting from their different relationship to family life' (Langan & Ostner, 1991: 131). As a consequence many capitalist welfare states incorporated social insurance schemes on the one hand, under which predominantly male heads of household claimed entitlements on behalf of predominantly female dependants, alongside social assistance systems on the other, under which predominantly female–headed households – including large numbers of lone parents and single female pensioners – claimed stigmatised means-tested benefits: the former have been characterised as 'masculine sub-systems', the latter as 'feminine sub-systems' (Fraser, 1989: 111–12). Recent policy reforms across the welfare states of the global North portend a shift away from assumptions based on the male breadwinner household model towards an 'adult worker model' (Lewis, 2000) in which men and women alike are expected to sustain themselves through participation in the labour market. This has resulted in the development of rights to childcare provision and to flexible working arrangements to facilitate work-family reconciliation. In practice, however, such policies may take little account of women's preferences or the opportunities available to them and would seem to be privileging paid employment at the expense of unpaid caring (Lewis, 2009). Women's socially constituted roles and identities remain systemically subordinate.

Like the feminist critique, the **anti-racist critique** of social rights claimed that ethno-cultural minorities living in capitalist welfare states were 'second class' citizens (see Lister, 1990: 52). Though there are important exceptions, ethnocultural minorities tend to experience a greater risk of poverty, unemployment, poor health and inadequate housing than ethnocultural majorities. (For a comprehensive account of evidence from the British case, see Craig *et al.*, 2012.) This can apply not only to diasporic migrant minorities but also to colonised indigenous minorities (Humpage, 2010; Salomon, 2005). What distinguished the anti-racist critique from liberal democratic concerns about racial discrimination was that it regarded racism not as an illiberal attitude, but as an ideology – an ideology that 'racialises' (Fanon, 1967) the relations of power by which social groups and the boundaries between them are defined. Racism first grew out of a mistrust of the 'otherness' of people deemed not to be civilised (Miles, 1989); it is even suggested that the very basis of modern law and rights of citizenship is grounded in a racist mythology (Fitzpatrick, 1992). Racism, therefore, is more than heterophobia or intolerance, but in the global capitalist context is historically situated in relation to processes of economic exploitation: slavery in the pre-capitalist era and class conflicts set in train as a result of conquests, colonialism, imperialism and global labour migration (Sivanandan, 1990). At the very least, the selective framing of social rights is implicated in the racialisation of the cultural differences through which ethnic identities are defined. Just as the sexual division of labour is rooted historically in the ideological construction of 'the family', so there is a racial division of labour that is rooted historically in the ideological construction of 'the Nation' (Williams, 1989: ch. 4).

The consequences pose peculiar dilemmas for the capitalist welfare state:

- Should migrants enjoy the same social rights as established citizens? There is a tension – the so-called liberal paradox (Hollifield, 1992) – between individual freedom of movement on the one hand and the principles of national sovereignty on the other. It is claimed that the welfare state 'requires boundaries because it establishes a principle of distributive justice that departs from the distributive principles of the free market' (Freeman, 1986: 52). Access to social security benefits, housing and other forms of welfare provision are generally conditional upon citizenship and immigration status or else social rights can be 'fine-tuned' to include or exclude different social groups (Lockwood, 1996; Morris, 2002). This is an issue to which we shall return.

- Should the members of settled ethnocultural minorities, contrary to liberal-individualist principles, be accorded group rights: for example, rights to the recognition of specific cultural or linguistic requirements? The trend in several capitalist welfare states towards the end of the twentieth century had been towards a variety of 'multiculturalism policies', intended to accommodate ethnocultural diversity rather than attempting to assimilate minorities and violate their right to cultural identity. The implications for social rights and the welfare state are widely debated (Banting & Kymlicka, 2006).

The **disability awareness movement**'s critique of social rights has direct parallels with those of the second-wave feminist and anti-racist movements. Born in the 1970s out of grassroots organisations *of* rather than *for* disabled people in several countries (Barnes & Mercer, 2010: ch. 1; Roulstone & Prideaux, 2012: ch. 1), the movement's primary claim was for self-determination through rights of citizenship (Townsend & Walker, 1981). Disability is something experienced when people are born with a genetic impairment, if they suffer illness or injury that limits their functioning, or if they suffer from degenerative conditions as they grow older. The impairments associated with disability may be physical or may entail mental health problems or learning difficulties. While the impairments or functional limitations to which human beings are subject generally relate to biological causes or the effects of physical injury, their impact on people's lives is in large part determined by social context: disability – like gender and ethnicity – is socially constructed. Prior to the development of capitalist welfare states, people adjudged to be physically, mentally or morally 'defective' were often confined in institutions or colonies or otherwise segregated from the 'normal' population. Post–Second World War welfare states developed policies and systems intended to ensure that disabled people should no longer be segregated from non-disabled society, but which succeeded nonetheless in excluding and continuing to 'disable' them. Provision was not necessarily framed as a social right but was shaped by an assumption that people with impairments are not fully competent citizens. The argument championed by the disability awareness movement was that disability should not be addressed as a personal tragedy that has befallen the individual or as an individual medical problem, susceptible to medical explanation and management. Rather, it should be understood in terms of the consequences of a hostile social environment that does not, or will not, accommodate the particular needs, or recognise the particular abilities, of people with impairments or functional limitations (Oliver, 1990).

The disability awareness movement has had some impact on the extension of social rights for disabled people (see Chapter 7, this volume), particularly with regard to the right to independent living. Nevertheless, there are enduring issues for the movement insofar as there remains a tension between the goal of enabling people with impairments and functional limitations to live independently, and the claim that as vulnerable citizens they also have a right to protective care and support (Shakespeare, 2006).

The emancipatory claims of feminism, anti-racism and the disability awareness movement have contested the basis of social rights. Rather than accommodate their demands to a one-size-fits-all universal or general conception of rights, emancipatory critics promote the particular needs claims of women, ethnocultural minorities and disabled people, albeit on the basis of universal principles. But should the objective of social rights be to ensure that everybody has effective opportunities and equal life chances regardless of gender, 'race' or disability (an equal opportunities approach), or practically to compensate individuals for the disadvantages that may result from socially constructed differences (a social welfare approach)? (See Dean, 2012a.)

The liberal *equal opportunities* approach is concerned with promoting tolerance and fairness. It has been implemented within capitalist welfare states primarily through various forms of anti-discrimination legislation (Bagilhole, 2009). However, equal opportunities approaches are preoccupied with observing formal rights. In so doing they ascribe fixed individualised identities on the basis of a person's membership of a particular social group. This may fail to address the fundamental causes of disadvantage and underlying relations of power between dominant and subordinate groups in society. The focus is on discriminatory attitudes and prejudices, not on social structural factors. Anti-discrimination legislation tends to reduce the problem of discrimination to the level of individual instances amenable to individual legal remedies. Second-wave feminists object to the equal opportunities approach when it effectively forces women to compete with men on men's terms. Anti-racists object to the equal opportunities approach if all it does is promote tactical compliance strategies on the part of employers and other bodies, leaving underlying institutional racism untouched. Elements within the disability awareness movement may object to the equal opportunities approach as currently conceived, since it does not positively or proactively intervene to ensure that disabled people have autonomy and proper control over their own lives.

The *social welfare* approach is concerned with protecting people and, arguably, with promoting solidarity amidst diversity. The danger is that such an approach may perpetuate and consolidate social differences, rather than confront their social implications. This is particularly the case if policy implicitly references difference in relation to some notion of a 'normality' that is, by default, male, white and able-bodied and which neglects the extent to which masculinity, majority ethnicity and 'ability' are themselves socially constructed. Compensatory approaches are preoccupied with identifying and meeting substantive human needs, but tend in so doing to prescribe the identity of the subject in a top-down fashion. Second-wave feminists may object that rights that support women in their role as mothers and carers or which make it easier for women to combine paid employment and unpaid caring responsibilities may lock women into dependency on men and perpetuate their status as second class citizens (Lister, 2003). Anti-racists object that rights intended to assist ethnocultural minorities more easily to celebrate their cultural identities while integrating with the majority communities in which they live may, in practice, trivialise ethnic differences or reify them, thus neglecting the structural root causes of disadvantage (Phillips, 1999, 2007). Activists within the disability awareness movement object that rights to special benefits and services for disabled people, though they alleviate personal suffering, do not necessarily confront the extent to which society is to blame for so many of the disadvantages that disabled people face (Morris, 1991, 2003).

We have focused on three particular social movements that have each sought to re-contextualise social rights in relation to social difference and diversity, but it is important to recognise that similar critiques can be developed in relation to other social groups, including young people, older people, gay people and people belonging to religious minorities.

Challenges from defensive political pluralism

The stirrings of a different kind of movement can also be traced back to the 1960s and '70s – movements concerned not so much with recognising social differences, as with defending humanity against military power (the peace movement), environmental exploitation and degradation (the green movement) and, in particular, excesses of administrative state power. The latter forms of defensive critique have been concerned with the defence of communities, the promotion of civil society organisations and fomentation of a different, more inclusive, participative and pluralistic form of politics (Scott, 1990). Social movements – broadly understood – have long had particular pertinence for social rights (Annetts *et al.,* 2009) and, in the context of current struggles for environmental and global social justice, they continue to do so, as we shall see in Chapter 10. It must additionally be borne in mind that movements favouring civil society alternatives to the state can be favoured from across the ideological spectrum, from the neo-liberal right to the social left (Kaldor, 2003; F. Powell, 2007). However, I am concerned here with a particular radical and nominally non-ideologically aligned shift of thinking that emerged, in part at least, as a backlash against the monolithic capitalist welfare state. The original impetus came from two quarters: the community development movement on the one hand, and radical communitarianism on the other – each of which sought to challenge the efficacy of social rights where these have been created through top-down, statist and undemocratic processes.

The 1960s and '70s witnessed largely unsuccessful attempts to establish poor people's movements, such as the National Welfare Rights Organization in the US (Piven & Cloward, 1977) and the Claimants Union movement in Britain (Jordan, 1973), movements that could not achieve formal sustainability in the way that organised labour and the trades unions had succeeded in doing, and which demonstrated the limits of informal resistance to the state administration of social rights. Lessons learned from such experiences informed, on the one hand, techniques of guerrilla-style community organisation (Alinsky, 1969) and, on the other, a variety of professionally organised urban community development and welfare rights projects, which we shall return to discuss in Chapter 8. In the same era, the acceleration of urbanisation in the global South was accompanied by the development of grass-roots urban social movements (Castells, 1983) and, for example, an explosion of illegal squatting, a phenomenon to which policy makers were, increasingly, obliged to accede (Hardoy & Satterthwaite, 1989). Contemporaneously, radical new critiques of the oppressive or disempowering nature of modern state-organised education and healthcare systems from intellectuals such as Paulo Friere (1972) and Ivan Illich (1971; Illich *et al.,* 1977) began to percolate debate in the global South and the global North alike.

The resulting pluralist critique of the capitalist welfare state achieved a certain level of orthodoxy within parts of the voluntary or NGO sector. This was distilled and exemplified in Hadley and Hatch's (1981) attack on the centralised nature of the welfare state and the character this afforded to the administration of social rights. Unitary government, they claimed, is an inheritance that had suited parties of both Left and Right and was now entrenched by virtue of its own internal momentum. The result was bureaucratic, unaccountable and inefficient. It gave to professionals and officialdom unwarranted power to control the behaviour of clients and service users. The supposedly non-ideological solution was in part a shift to welfare pluralism with a greater role for the voluntary and informal sectors (see discussion in Chapter 1, this volume), but partly also the development of bottom-up 'participatory alternatives' to centralised social services. The nature of such participatory alternatives would have been to give clients or service users a more active role in negotiating the nature of the services they received. The performance of such services, it was argued, should be judged with reference to outputs, rather than inputs.

This emphasis on results or outcomes, rather than resources or 'rights' represents a theme espoused in common with some radical communitarians, such as Walzer (1983). Walzer has contended that *justice* is more important than 'rights', since distributive justice or equality represents outcomes (which can be assessed) rather than objectives (which cannot). Justice itself, however, 'is a human construction, and it is doubtful whether it can be made in only one way' (Walzer, 1983: 5). Equality, Walzer argues, does not require the elimination of difference and what justice must entail is egalitarianism 'without the Procrustean bed of the state'. The bed in the Procrustean legend was one to which victims were fitted by being forcibly stretched or butchered, and Walzer's case is that human beings need not be so abused; it is social goods, not citizens, that should be controlled or made to fit. What is required is not universalism, but a form of 'complex equality'. (This is, incidentally, a rather different sort of communitarianism than that of either traditional conservatives or 'new' communitarians such as Etzioni (1995) or Putnam (1993) and more in tune with elements of the work of Sandel (1982), Taylor (1992) and MacIntyre (2007), who challenge a reductive rights-based understanding of equality.)

The common theme of these 'defensive' critiques is a rejection of the generality of the *dirigiste* state and social rights based on prescription. The emphasis on participation, especially political participation, has had particular resonance amongst social movements in the global South in which there has been resistance to ideas premised on the old-style state corporatism of the global North (Foweraker & Landman, 1997) and to social rights as the mere 'politics of demand' (Waterman, 2001).

Post-structuralist critiques

Coinciding with the 'crisis' of the capitalist welfare state, the 'cultural turn' in ideological thinking and the birth of a 'post-modern' era, there have been important developments in social theory and a plethora of new insights into the functioning and limitations of social rights. Foremost among these has been the contribution of post-structuralist thinking. Theorists of post-modernity have called into question whether the Western Enlightenment that gave birth to 'modernity' was ever a dispassionate quest for truth and reason. On the contrary, according to Bauman (1987: 80), it was an exercise in two parts:

> First, in extending the powers and ambitions of the state, in transferring to the state the pastoral functions previously exercised by the church, in reorganising the state around the function of planning, designing and managing the reproduction of social order . . . secondly, in the creation of an entirely new and consciously designed mechanism of disciplinary action, aimed at regulating and regularising the socially relevant life of the subjects of the teaching and managing state.

What was obscure under modernity is more transparent within the post-modern world of information technology and new managerialism in which, for example, scientists are hired 'not to find truth, but to augment powers' (Lyotard, 1984: 46). Bauman and Lyotard are echoing here the arguments of Michel Foucault, whose claim had been that modernity was based not on scientific reason and rationality but the 'will to power'; that the legitimacy of modern governance was an effect of power and not truth or justice; and that the reality behind the veil of democratic-welfare-capitalism was that of an inherently 'disciplinary society' (see especially Foucault, 1977).

Foucault's general arguments have also influenced some particular critiques of the disciplinary aspects of social policy (e.g. Dean, 1991). The basis for such approaches has been a re-examination of the history of the welfare state and of the increasingly sophisticated surveillance and disciplinary processes associated with the administration of social rights. These approaches invoke a relational theory of power, which holds first, that the shift from feudalism to capitalism was associated with a shift from coercive to administrative (welfare) state power. Administrative state power has had as much to do with the regulation of human behaviour as the 'dull compulsion' of economic forces. The development of state welfare and social rights has involved new technologies of power and pervasive new disciplinary techniques. The characteristic of these technologies and techniques is that, unlike class power, they bear upon *individual difference*. In place of unbiddable mass movements is the controllable individual subject.

In place of the indiscriminate giving of alms to the anonymous poor there has been erected the complex panoply of the capitalist welfare state, which scrutinises and documents each individual 'client' or 'case'. In place of careless humanitarianism there has been inserted meticulous paternalistic control. In place of such practices as the public whipping and branding of vagrants there have emerged more discreet and gentle forms of coercion based on benefit penalties and disqualifications. In place of an explicit Malthusian desire to punish the poor there have developed more subtle forms of containment. In place of crude processes of classification and surveillance associated with the workhouse and the Poor Laws there have been constructed administrative systems based on legal definitions and regulations to which citizens must submit in order to exercise their 'rights'. In place of the prying concern and moralistic edicts of philanthropists and overseers of the poor has emerged a voluntaristic discourse based on the idea that citizens of the welfare state are juridical subjects with the freedom to exercise their rights and a responsibility to abide by the rules. The history of the welfare state is therefore seen, not as a story of progress towards the development of universal social rights, but as a story of developing state power and increasingly sophisticated methods of social control. It is additionally argued that, far from dismantling state power, recent policies of welfare retrenchment have often involved subtle refinements to the disciplinary mechanisms which underpin social rights, and have ushered in a new disciplinary logic of 'governmentality' (Foucault, 1991), through which new forms of conditionality and behavioural management may be brought to bear, especially in relation to labour market activation (Henman & Fenger, 2006).

Summary/conclusion

This chapter has considered several critiques of social rights and their practical consequences. These critiques are diverse. The element they seem to have in common is a recognition that social rights of citizenship must inevitably involve some propensity for social control. Where the critiques differ is in the reasons for which they consider such a propensity to be problematic.

The neo-liberal objection is that rights involving the redistribution of income or property are corrupting. They are not rights at all; on the contrary, they are an infringement of real (i.e. property) rights or a distraction from properly enforceable (i.e. civil and political) human rights. The neo-Marxist objection is that social rights, in spite of the advantages they have brought the working class, are exploitative. They are a necessary component in the process by which labour power is reproduced and articulated with the capitalist market system, and they are a source of ideological mystification.

Feminists, anti-racists and disability activists complain that women, members of ethnocultural minorities and disabled people can be systematically excluded from effective social rights or that social rights are so framed as merely to accommodate them in a world that is largely shaped by and for 'white', able-bodied men. There are also related defensive critiques whose concern is with the undemocratic nature of social rights and their capacity to impose conditions of social uniformity. The post-structuralist objection is that the extension of social rights is constituted as an extension of administrative state power, based on an increasingly sophisticated array of disciplinary techniques for the definition and control of individual subjects.

Inevitably, this complex spectrum of arguments has been somewhat simplified, but the purpose of this chapter has been to demonstrate that social rights are controversial. Throughout the rest of the book we shall return to some of these controversies and will consider whether, for all their potentially adverse and controlling propensities, social rights are important and can be strategically deployed or developed. We shall also (particularly in the next chapter) consider further questions about whether the social rights framed for the capitalist welfare states of the global North can, under the auspices of the human rights framework, be meaningfully transposed to countries of the global South.

PART TWO
Social rights in practice

5

SOCIAL RIGHTS IN GLOBAL CONTEXT

We have seen that social rights were initially framed as rights of citizenship through substantive social legislation by capitalist welfare states, but also formulated as general principles within the UDHR. This chapter will consider to what extent social rights can and may yet be extended globally. I shall start by discussing in general terms the contested role of social rights in human development, before providing a brief overview of the various ways in which social rights have in practice been developing in different parts of the world. I shall then turn to consider whether it is appropriate to introduce social rights into all societies and cultures and whether it is possible to protect and promote human wellbeing without recourse to concepts and discourses of rights. Finally, I shall say something about globalisation: the ways in which social rights are being promoted on the global stage and the implications of global trends for social rights, including trends in migration.

Social rights and human development

Human development, we might suppose, is the process by which the human species organises to meet its needs. However, it is an ambiguous term of relatively recent provenance. Insofar as I am asserting that social rights may be understood as articulations of human need, we might by extension assume that social rights are essential to human development. However, we saw in Chapter 2 that social policy making and rights declarations have not succeeded in ensuring that all human need is met: manifestations of social inequality and poverty remain evident globally, and even within established welfare states. The UNDP attempts to measure human progress around the world by means of a composite index, the Human Development Index (HDI), which combines within a single integer measures of standard of living (gross national income (GNI) per capita), health (life expectancy) and education (mean and expected years of schooling). Countries can then be ranked in terms of their 'performance'. The results imply a correlation between national wealth and development, but a more complex picture emerges when account is taken of the extent of inequality, poverty and, for example, public social security expenditure within each country (see Table 5.1). There are important debates about

TABLE 5.1 Human development data: Selected countries[1]

	HDI Classification[2] 2011	HDI ranking[2] (out of 187 countries) 2011	GNI per capita[2] ($US at PPP) 2011	Inequality by income quintile[2] (80/20) ratio 2000–2011	Inequality adjusted ranking[2] 2011	% population 'in poverty' (by differing criteria)	Public social security expenditure as % of GDP 2001–2006[5]
USA	very high	4	43,017	8.5	23 (–19)	17[3]	8.9
Germany	very high	9	34,853	4.3	9	8[3]	19.0
UK	very high	28	33,296	7.2	24 (+4)	12[3]	14.3
Russia	high	66	14,561	8.2	59 (+7)	1.3[4]	8.3
Brazil	high	84	10,162	18.0	97 (–13)	2.7[4]	9.6
China	medium	101	7,476	8.4	102 (–1)	13[4]	4.1
India	medium	134	3,468	5.6	133 (+1)	54[4]	3.1
Nigeria	low	156	2,069	9.5	162 (–6)	54[4]	?
Ethiopia	low	174	971	4.2	173 (+1)	89[4]	6.5
Congo (DR)	low	187	280	9.2	187	73[4]	0.9

PPP = purchasing power parity; GDP = gross domestic product.

[1] All having populations in excess of 60 million (NOTE: the three highest HDI ranking countries – Norway, Australia and the Netherlands – have relatively small populations of 5, 23 and 17 million respectively).

[2] Source: UNDP, 2011.

[3] % below 50% median household income (2000–05) – source: UNDP, 2009.

[4] % poor under Multidimensional Poverty Index (2000–09) – source: UNDP, 2011.

[5] Excluding health expenditure – latest available year – source: ILO, 2010.

the meaning of 'development' and in particular the relative importance of, and interaction between, economic and social development as components of human development.

A contested concept

In times past, explanations of relative wealth and poverty at the international level were framed in terms of development and underdevelopment (George, 1988). Development was considered to be synonymous with industrialisation, and the world was divided into the Western 'First World' of industrialised capitalist nations, an Eastern 'Second World' of partly industrialised communist nations, and the 'Third World' of supposedly underdeveloped nations. Such terminology has been rendered obsolete by a variety of global factors: the acceleration of economic globalisation and the international mobility of capital; the eclipse of industrial manufacturing, the rise of the service sector (so-called tertiarisation) and the proliferation of new information-based technologies; and the collapse of Eastern Bloc communism and rapid economic growth in parts of East Asia and Latin America. However, we have yet to develop entirely satisfactory alternatives. In this book I have on occasion adopted the shorthand convention of referring to the world of capitalist welfare states as the global North (whether or not they are situated in the Northern Hemisphere) and the rest of the world as the global South. This I acknowledge to be far from satisfactory, not least because there appears to be little agreement or consistency about the criteria by which countries are deemed to achieve global North status. The club of capitalist nation states has been joined, on the one hand, by post-communist countries in which social rights had developed very differently than in Western welfare states, and, on the other, by countries which – though they have moderately or even *very* high HDI rankings (e.g. South Korea) and have attained membership of the Organisation of Economic Co-operation and Development (OECD) and the G20 group of nations – have welfare states that are recently instituted and as yet comparatively immature. The anomalies are legion, but the difficulties entailed in defining and measuring 'development' speak to a deeper problem.

The dominant conception of development imported a hegemonically Western theory of 'modernisation', which assumes there is an optimum, even unilinear, path to democratic-welfare-capitalism (e.g. Lipset, 1963; Rostow, 1971). Insofar as some countries remain chronically poorer than others, it is supposed that this reflects a failure to 'modernise', occasioned by technological, political or cultural deficiencies. Poor countries must be encouraged or assisted to 'catch up' with their richer capitalist neighbours. Structuralist critics of this view (e.g. Frank, 1971; Hayter, 1971) began to suggest that the continued disadvantage of the world's poorer countries should be attributed not to internal failings, but to external factors – in particular, the historical and structural economic dependency of poor and economically weak nations upon rich and powerful ones. Recent commentators have observed the ways in which poor nations are more vulnerable than rich ones to the power of mighty transnational corporations; and they can, in practice, be impeded rather than assisted by the regulatory interventions of supranational bodies, such as the IMF and the World Bank (Deacon *et al.,* 1997). Pressure, largely from countries of the global South, led in 1986 to the UN's adoption of a Declaration on the Right to Development (DRtD), expressing demands from poorer countries for self-determination and the right to develop on their own terms. Nevertheless, it may be argued that there are limits to economic growth, both social (Hirsch, 1977) and ecological (Jackson, 2009; Meadows *et al.,* 1972). And so-called post-development critics (e.g. Escobar, 2012; Sachs, 2010) now claim that the global race for capitalist economic development, in which there must be winners and losers, can be inherently damaging to human wellbeing. It results, according to James Midgley, in 'distorted development' (1995, 2013b).

Economic development vs. social development

What, therefore, is the goal of development? Is it the creation of wealth, or is it the provision through social rights of food security, clean water, sanitation, shelter, healthcare and education? Amartya Sen's contention is that the goal is the wider realisation of human capabilities or freedom, but this still leaves open the question of the relationship between economic development and social development. Are social rights a prize to be earned through economic growth or a precondition for economic success? What has been referred to as the Washington consensus, which has informed the thinking of key international agencies (see Chapters 2 and 4, this volume), was premised on the neo-liberal 'trickle-down' thesis: in a free world market, it was believed, wealth would eventually trickle down from rich to poor nations, just as it should trickle down from rich to poor people within each nation. What matters from this perspective, is that the engine of economic growth and development should be fired up and kept running: most certainly, that wealth creation must precede the development and funding of social rights. It was a thesis supported by economists such as Kuznets (1955), who proposed the 'Kuznets curve', suggesting that as per capita income in a country grows, inequality will initially increase before plateauing and then fall as general living standards rise and as the economy can support the costs of redistributive social rights. Just as influentially, the US sociologist Harold Wilensky (1975) specifically demonstrated a direct correlation between economic development and social security spending, from which he inferred a causal relationship: the former, he claimed, facilitates the latter.

However, contrary evidence was provided by Newman and Thompson (1989), who assembled data from the 1960s and '70s from some 46 developing countries and observed that provision for basic needs (measured by indices of basic literacy, perinatal mortality and life expectancy) tended to precede, rather than result from, economic development. Since then, the data assembled for early versions of the UNDP's annual Human Development Reports demonstrated that there is no automatic link between economic growth and social development (UNDP, 1993). More recently, it was observed that the association between income and non-income dimensions of human development has weakened over time (UNDP, 2010): in other words, rising per capita income does not necessarily translate into better social outcomes. Even in the European context, the evidence can be interpreted as suggesting that measures to enhance 'social quality' through social rights may assist rather than impair economic competitiveness (Gough, 1997). But regardless of whether social rights help or hinder economic development, opponents of Wilensky's contention – that social rights are a spin-off from economic prosperity – have long argued that it takes insufficient account of the part that political processes play in determining the level of spending on things like social security provision (Castles, 1982). Social rights clearly can arise as political achievements in their own right and not as an incidental outcome of the capitalist development process. The historical and political context matters.

Regions and regimes

In Chapter 1 we considered Esping-Andersen's influential taxonomy of capitalist welfare state regimes which had been based, in part, on an empirical evaluation of the extent to

TABLE 5.2 Three main paths to social rights development in the global North

Paths to 'modern' citizenship[1]	Welfare 'regime'[2]	Role of social rights[3]	Form of social rights[4]
Constitutionalist settlement - Anglophone	Liberal (low level of de-commodification)	Residual safety net for the needy	Selective rights to meet particular needs
Post-absolutist power brokerage - Continental European	Conservative/ Corporatist (medium level of de-commodification)	Paternalistic protection for workers	Protective rights to meet common needs
Reformist compromise - Nordic	Social Democratic (high level of de-commodification)	Emancipatory guarantee for all	Citizen rights to meet universal needs

[1] Loosely derived from Mann's (1987) overview of the different strategies by which in the eighteenth and nineteenth centuries the often chaotic transition from despotic monarchy to democratic citizenship was negotiated and finally resolved.

[2] The ideal-type categories established by Esping-Andersen (1990). It is important to note that they are heuristic categories, which elide the complexities of history and the extent to which all welfare regimes are more or less hybrid in nature. In the 1950s and '60s, for example, the Anglophone UK and the Continental European Netherlands might each have been regarded as more or less Social Democratic regimes and it is only more recently that the former has generally been regarded as a Liberal and the latter as a Conservative/Corporatist regime.

[3] See Chapter 1.

[4] Based on Dean's (2010) taxonomy of needs and rights and the analysis summarised in Figure 3.1. It should be borne in mind that in all regimes the legacy of pre-modern poor-relief systems (perspective β in Figure 3.1) may to a greater or lesser extent live on.

which different welfare states had sought to moderate or regulate the commodification of labour under capitalism. We can reconsider that taxonomy in the context of an analysis of different paths to social rights development. The analysis is illustrated in Table 5.2, which demonstrates how different historical paths have led to different social constructions of social rights. Critics of this kind of model point out that it doesn't adequately account, for example, for the different histories and cultures of the southern European or the Antipodean welfare states (Castles & Mitchell, 1993; Leibfried, 1993). Esping-Andersen contends, nonetheless, that it is generally possible from within his taxonomy to characterise the dominant influences and assumptions at work in established capitalist welfare states (1999). Whether or not this is so, the primary purpose of this chapter is to consider the evolution of social rights and the wide variety of potential paths to social development to be found *beyond* the predominantly Western capitalist welfare states, where conventional regime theory may have limited, if any, relevance (Midgley, 2013a).

Alternative legacies

To that end, let us go back to the negotiations that took place between the states parties represented on the Commission on Human Rights during the drafting of the UDHR in the 1940s (see Chapter 2, this volume, and U. Davy, 2013). The dominant, essentially liberal, conception of social rights proposed by the US and broadly supported by European representatives was confronted by two alternatives: the developmental view expressed by Latin American countries and the statist view from the Soviet Eastern Bloc.

What is here described as the developmental view stemmed from a belief in development as a process that was both economic and social and which represented an explicit policy goal: a goal already expressed in the national constitutions of several Latin American countries. Development and social rights were regarded as all of a piece. At that time, the region sought to transcend the corporatist-conservative traditions of its colonial past and was infused by a heady if conflictual blend of both liberal and socialist influences. The Latin Americans pushed for the specification of collectively guaranteed individual social rights in greater detail than the US and Western European nations wished to countenance.

In the end, Latin American ambitions were thwarted, not so much with regard to the drafting of the UDHR's final text – on which they had some influence – as with regard to the substantive development of social rights within their own region. Latin American economies were destined to grow spectacularly, if erratically, on the back of unregulated inward investment, but the extension of social rights provision lagged behind. Characteristically, Latin American countries already had partially developed welfare states, dating from earlier in the twentieth century, based on highly stratified and fragmented social insurance arrangements, quite extensive employment protection measures, and reasonably well-developed public health and education provision. Provision, however, was largely restricted to the formalised employment sector and urban areas, whereas substantial swathes of Latin America remained, and still are, economically informal and rural. Uneven economic growth was accompanied by substantial increases in poverty and inequality. In the 1980s the region was gripped by economic recession and was dependent for recovery on assistance from international financial institutions, conditional on neo-liberal 'structural adjustment' policies. These led to extensive privatisation of social insurance arrangements, the de-regulation of labour markets and the decentralisation of health and education provision. The end result, according to Barrientos (2001, 2004), was a transition to what had once been a conservative-informal welfare regime to a kind of liberal-informal welfare regime. From the 1990s onwards, the attitudes of the international financial institutions began to change, favouring support for social safety nets, based on conditional cash transfers (Bastagli, 2009; Leisering & Barrientos, 2013). At the same time, several Latin American countries elected left-leaning political leaders, committed to poverty reduction, within the constraints to which the region remains subject. Poverty has been somewhat reduced, but social inequality remains stubbornly high. Nevertheless, Latin American countries may be defined as welfare state regimes, in which social rights are recognised, albeit that they are incompletely or unevenly implemented.

The statist view, expressed by the Eastern European countries (led by the USSR), stressed a different interpretation of social rights. Initially they had abstained from participation in debates about social rights and did not join the discussions until the third session of the commission. For them, the issue was not that of achieving a balance between state powers and individual freedoms, but of ensuring state guarantees of work and social security. They sought to strengthen the obligations of other states parties to prevent unemployment and to fund social insurance, not through individual contribution by workers, but directly. Their influence on the final text of the UDHR, and later in the framing of the ICESCR, turned out to be negligible (U. Davy, 2013).

Prior to 1989, Soviet-style communism in Central and Eastern Europe represented a distinctive welfare regime that provided extensive social rights through guaranteed employment, subsidised prices and extensive state-enterprise-based social benefits. The demands that led to the eventual fall of that system were for the political and civil rights that such a regime had withheld. For their part, the architects of such regimes had believed they were forging a new form of civilisation, premised on transformative social rights and services by which, according to the slogan of the Moscow sports clubs, they were 'mending the human race on scientific principles' (cited in Webb & Webb, 1935: 805).

Towards the end of the Soviet era, however, state guaranteed jobs were often highly unproductive and the guaranteed minimum wage had fallen below the poverty line: workers joked 'they pretend to pay us, we pretend to work' (cited in Standing, 2009: 43). The real value of insurance benefits and pensions had dwindled, and the quality of health services and state housing had declined, with access to the best provision reserved for party *apparatchiks* (George, 1993). After 1989, the countries of Central and Eastern Europe, under the guidance of Western 'shock therapists', withdrew price subsidies and exposed state enterprises to market competition, but without first ensuring that alternative forms of social protection were in place (Standing, 1996). The immediate result was staggering increases in poverty and social inequality and a decline in health and life expectancy. The process of recovery entailed a contest between economic liberalism and the legacy of state paternalism (Deacon, 1993; Deacon *et al.*, 1997), in the context of fragmentary social provision by burgeoning numbers of NGOs (Stephenson, 2000). As in Latin America, living standards for many were sustained only through a resilient and extensive informal economy (Jordan, 1998: 165). What has since emerged within the Soviet Bloc is a variety of post-communist welfare states with different kinds of social rights, with a divide between the more Easterly states, most notably Russia, and the Central European and Baltic states. The former had tended towards post-communist corporatism (albeit that Russia's recent oligarch-led economic recovery has been accompanied by selective marketization of social provision) (Davidova & Manning, 2009). The latter are now mostly members of the European Union (EU), albeit that these countries have tended to varying degrees towards liberal welfare regime characteristics (Cerami & Vanhuysse, 2009; Fenger, 2007).

Outwith the rights agenda?

Asian and Arab states, though they contributed, did not exercise a concerted influence during the original deliberations over social rights by the Commission on Human Rights (U. Davy, 2013). They remained by and large marginal to the central debate. The explanation for this might in part be cultural and this we shall consider in a moment. But there are other explanations. The fundamental conditions for the development of social rights in the Marshallian mould were, on the one hand, a formalised economy and labour market and, on the other, an effective and legitimate state apparatus. Where these conditions do not apply, conventional welfare regime theory loses relevance (Gough *et al.*, 2004), and the conventional concept of social rights has little foundation. Even in the case of Latin America and Eastern Europe we have seen that the existence of a substantial informal sector could displace or inhibit social rights development. In the Latin American context especially, the term 'social exclusion' has been applied to refer not as in Western societies to the marginalisation of aberrant minorities, but to the wholesale exclusion of entire populations – in rural areas or 'slum' settlements – from social rights of development and the 'social project' (Munck, 2005; Rodgers *et al.*, 1995). However, for regions of the world that had little semblance of a formal economy or a modern state apparatus, the social rights debate was a secondary or remote concern of limited or no immediate relevance. Within some regions, this still applies.

The South Asian sub-continent consists largely of countries defined by Gough *et al.* (2004) as 'informal security regimes', denoting that practical provision for human need stems not so much from state-administered rights as from family, kinship and community. India, the largest country in the region, does have a pervasive but often dysfunctional state bureaucracy, bequeathed from its British colonial past (Townsend, 1993: ch. 8), and the country has formally incorporated directive social rights principles into its written constitution (Muralidhar, 2008). Despite this, 42 percent of children under age five in India are malnourished (Naandi Foundation, 2011). Across the South Asian region as a whole, social protection programmes, education and healthcare provision are at best uneven or fragmentary and, in rural areas, they may be non-existent. There have been initiatives, such as locally co-ordinated food-for-work schemes, national work guarantee schemes and micro-credit schemes which, even with NGO involvement can sometimes be subverted by patronage and clientalism at the community level (Davis, 2004).

As a region, sub-Saharan Africa is the poorest in the world. It may be noted that all three low HDI ranking countries in Table 5.1 are in sub-Saharan Africa. The region consists largely of countries defined by Gough *et al.* (2004; and see Bevan, 2004) as 'insecurity regimes', denoting that practical provision for human need depends not necessarily on state administered social rights, but in many instances on local leaders, war lords, mafia bosses, corrupt officials or benign aid workers. In much of the region colonial domination was succeeded not so much by Western inspired models of governance as by a form of modernity without development, in which, outside urban areas, the populations are not so much citizens as subjects (Mamdani, 1996). Despite some progress in relation, for example, to education and healthcare, there has been a tendency for temporary measures to become institutionalised, creating what Cerami (2013) has characterised as 'permanent emergency welfare regimes'.

In contrast, the Arab countries of the Middle East/North Africa include several spectacularly rich oil producers, as well as some poorer nations. Though based in lands hailed as the ancient cradle of civilisation, these countries are all as nation states relatively modern creations. They have tended until lately to encompass relations of power that remain in some respects pre-modern, if not semi-feudal. Destremau (2000) had characterised some such countries as 'rentier states': lacking productive economies, they are heavily dependent on external revenues from oil exports, financial revenues and tourism. The wealth so created has enabled their rulers to develop public services, including healthcare and educational provision, but shares in the nation's 'rent' may be unevenly distributed and are not rights-based. The characteristically patrimonial form of capitalism observed across the region has tended towards a kind of welfare regime that has been 'neither democratic nor socially inclusive and [whose] developmental role has been limited' (Karshenas & Moghadam, 2006: 18). In recent years, parts of the region – which is more complex and diverse than can be conveyed in any thumbnail sketch – have been variously subjected to external military intervention, internal civil strife, and inter-factional tensions based on sect, religion and ethnicity. The 'Arab Spring' of 2011 witnessed insurgent demands for democracy, but this has been followed by counter-revolution, chronic instability and, in some instances, violent extremism. At the time of writing it is difficult to predict whether and in what form social rights may now develop.

Emerging economies

Finally in this section, we discuss places around the world where economic development has been, or is currently, especially evident and where the conditions for the evolution of Marshallian-type social rights might more recently have come into being.

Foremost, have been countries in East Asia. It should of course be noted that Japan, as an established industrialised power had already developed a welfare state, albeit one difficult to categorise using Esping-Andersen's typology. In the 1960s a group of smaller East Asian countries (South Korea, Hong Kong, Taiwan and Singapore), the 'Tiger Economies', began to take off. Their approach to social provision and social rights was pragmatic, involving selective copying of policies from Japan or other industrialised countries, but with comparatively low levels of social spending and with particular emphasis on human capital development (i.e. education and healthcare). More recently, the rapid growth of the original East Asian Tigers, where economic growth slowed in the 1990s, has been replicated by 'Tiger Cubs', like the Philippines and Indonesia, with a similarly modest approach to the extension of social rights (e.g. Comola & de Mello, 2010). Goodman and Peng (1996) have argued that the emerging model should be characterised as 'Japanese-style welfare-systems', but other commentators prefer to define these new capitalist nations as 'productivist' regimes (Gough *et al.,* 2004; Holliday, 2000), reflecting the extent to which they prioritise economic production over social rights.

Also within East Asia is the world's most populous country, China: a country which in many ways defies categorisation. China is the last major communist nation, albeit that, following market liberalisation, it is best regarded as 'state capitalist' (The Economist, 2012). The People's Republic of China in the 1950s had nationalised most land and industry, giving it over to collectives and co-operatives, creating an 'iron rice bowl' by which to ensure life-long employment and 'five guarantees': enough food, clothes and fuel, education for children and an honourable funeral. Market liberalisation began in 1978, leading, according to some critics, to a dismantling of the iron rice bowl (Leung, 1994). A revised constitution in 1982 identified certain social rights: to work, education, rest, retirement and 'material assistance' in the event of illness or disability. As economic growth accelerated, new forms of state social provision have been introduced, often based on Western-style state welfare models but on a limited scale (Chan *et al.,* 2008) and with extensive variations around the country (Shi, 2012), including disparities between affluent urban coastal regions and largely impoverished rural western China.

It should always be borne in mind that there can be significant diversity and differences between countries within the same region, and the above account is crude. If indeed it is economic growth that drives social rights development, we should perhaps review the prospects of the largest and most rapidly developing economies. At the turn of the twenty-first century, economist Jim O'Neill (2001) first coined the acronym BRIC for a group of leading emerging economies and G20 members: Brazil, Russia, India and China. The countries thereafter formally established themselves as a co-operative grouping and were joined in 2010 by South Africa. More recently, the acronym MINT (Fraser, 2011) was coined for a further group of nations with large populations and rapid economic development: Mexico, Indonesia, Nigeria and Turkey. At the time of writing, economic performance of the BRICS and MINT countries, though fluctuating, is generally outstripping that in North American and Western European countries, and the diversity of their trajectories challenges orthodox analyses of how social rights development might occur.

Russia is an oligarchic capitalist/post-communist welfare regime. Brazil and Mexico are Latin American liberal-informal welfare regimes (Mexico is an OECD member). China and Indonesia are radically contrasting East Asian countries – the former being set potentially to become the mightiest economy in the world, and the latter being one of the vibrant young capitalist Tiger Cubs – but each has uneven social rights provision. South Africa and Nigeria are radically contrasting African countries: the former – an exceptional case in the African context – which despite its legacy of Western-style industrial development during its apartheid era suffers entrenched poverty and inequality; the latter (Nigeria) has very high levels of poverty and simmering social divisions, despite its expanding, largely oil-based economy. Turkey might until recently have been characterised as a Middle Eastern regime, subject to authoritarian paternalist rule, but with an incipient welfare state it had been moving towards democratic-welfare-capitalism and EU accession, albeit subject in recent times to strong neo-liberal policy tendencies (Boratav & Özuğurlu, 2006; Manning, 2007). These may be the countries to watch, but there is no discernible pattern as to the prospects or the most likely manner in which social rights might develop.

The cultural critique

The third of the three broad critiques of the human rights agenda identified by Sen was the 'cultural' critique (the other two being the 'legitimacy' and the 'coherence' critiques – see Chapter 4, this volume), the essence of which is that concepts of 'rights' forged during the Western Enlightenment and developed within democratic-capitalist-welfare states are inimical, for example, to Asian cultures. Attempts to impose them in the name of development amount to ethnocentrism (e.g. Polis & Schwab, 1979) if not cultural imperialism. There are two questions we might ask: is this true; and just why does it matter?

Cultural values and practices

We have explored how the ethical foundations of rights discourse lie in Western philosophy and value systems, but there are Eastern philosophies and value systems – Confucian, Hindu, Buddhist, Muslim – through which other cultures and traditions have been shaped and which may, for example, prize loyalty, self-reliance and obedience above individual rights. Early attempts to characterise welfare state regimes emerging in East Asia sought to characterise them as Confucian welfare regimes constructed on principles of hierarchical community building and in the manner of a traditional extended Confucian family (Jones, 1993). This characterisation has since been questioned, not only because it oversimplifies complex influences, but because it can be 'a convenient excuse, with a persuasive historical and cultural camouflage, to filter responses to social welfare needs' (Walker & Wong, 2005: 215). It is a characterisation that also sidesteps the fact that, as we have seen, even China has written certain social rights into its constitution, as do for example a number of Islamic states (Jung et al., 2013). The Organisation of the Islamic Conference in 1990 adopted the Cairo Declaration on Human Rights in Islam. The declaration insists that the roots of such rights lie in Sharia, not Western law, but it includes, for example, the following statement: 'The State shall ensure the right of the individual to a decent living which will enable him to meet all his requirements and those of his dependents, including food, clothing, housing, education, medical care and all other basic needs' (Article 17 [c]). And though the Association of Southeast Asian Nations' (ASEAN) Declaration of Human Rights, which was adopted in 2012, has been held by Amnesty International, Human Rights Watch and the UN High Commissioner for Human Rights on several grounds to be flawed, it does contain an explicit array of social rights.

Sen (1999: 231–8) suggests that allusions to non-Western values may not be used to explain or justify authoritarian policies or systemic inequalities. He claims that values associated with tolerance and equality have deep-rooted counterparts within several Asian philosophies, pointing by way of example to parallels between the ancient teachings of Kautilya, the Indian philosopher and royal adviser, and Aristotle, with whom he happened to have been a chronological contemporary. Kautilya was a strong advocate of personal liberty for the privileged elite in Indian caste society – as was Aristotle for the Athenian city elite – but like Aristotle, he advocated no such thing for slaves or the members of lower castes, for whom nevertheless he advocated paternalistic governmental assistance to relieve their misery. Historical trajectories vary, but cultural constructions may at times concur.

A case can be made for the existence within a variety of non-Western philosophies of ethical or moral principles that, I would argue, are implicitly or even explicitly consistent with the ideal of shared responsibility for meeting individual needs and therefore with some sort of basis for social rights as articulation of shared human needs (though not necessarily framed in the language of rights):

- The Confucian idea of *Rén,* which translates as human-ness and is the ultimate state to which all should aspire through the observance of such values as filial piety and loyalty (Chan, 1999). There is, to my mind at least, a resonance between *Rén* and the Aristotelian notion of *eudaimonia,* as a state of fulfilment as a *social* being, concerned not with personal pains and pleasures, but with one's harmony of existence with other beings.
- The ancient pan-African belief system, *Ubuntu,* whose essence is captured in the aphorism, 'a person is only a person through other persons'. It implies an inherently solidaristic, albeit potentially conservative philosophy, which can nonetheless inform caring and sharing practices between and within human generations (Ramose, 2003; Whitworth & Wilkinson, 2013).
- The Islamic principle of *Zakat:* one of the pillars of the Muslim faith based on a religious obligation to share a portion of one's individual wealth with needy members of the *Ummah* (the worldwide community of the faithful). At the heart of Islam lies a quite particular conception of social justice (Dean & Khan, 1997).

I do not suggest that we should romanticise the manner in which these ideas have over the centuries been interpreted and reinterpreted. My point is that 'non-Western' value systems are by no means incommensurate with social rights. They entail theories of personhood with implications for the way in which human needs are to be understood and provided for, whether or not the framing of needs-based claims involves an explicit discourse of rights. However elusively, the examples I give contain prefigurative elements of the γ or even the δ perspectives outlined in Figure 3.1 in Chapter 3 in this volume.

The cultural critique, however, has relevance not only for the real or imagined tensions between Western and Eastern philosophical traditions, but also for the very practical tension between the social standards that are promoted in the global North and the social customs that apply in the global South. A well-intentioned attempt in 2000 to establish a set of 'Global Social Policy Principles' distilled from the raft of relevant UN conventions and declarations (see Ferguson, 1999) foundered at the UN's Copenhagen plus 5 Social Summit, amidst charges of hypocrisy against its proponents by representatives from the global South (Deacon, 2007: 139–140). The proposals were resented as an unacceptable interference with the sovereignty of nations in the global South and, without a transfer of resources from North to South, they would amount to an unachievable imposition. The imposition of ILO labour standards, has long been and remains a thorny issue for many countries (Felice, 1999). It is claimed that the protection of highly exploited women workers and the abolition of child labour in certain parts of the world cannot necessarily be achieved without endangering the limited sources of income available to women (Kabeer, 2004) and without imposing Western cultural conceptions of childhood and of children's legitimate role in social and economic life (Edmonds & Pavcnik, 2005).

Conflicting epistemologies

There is a problem about transposing notions of rights constructed largely within the capitalist North to other parts of the world, but is this a cultural problem or an epistemological issue? Culture, undeniably, is dynamic, syncretic and evolving (Phillips, 2007). In a riposte to the cultural critique, Donnelly hones in on precisely this argument, asserting that 'culture is not destiny' (2003: 88). At the same time, however, he also dismisses the possibility that there can be, or ever were, non-Western conceptions of human rights. He suggests that just as cardinal principles of mathematics have universal validity even though they were invented in the Arabic world, so the principles of human rights have universal validity even though their origins are 'Western'. His argument is redolent of Meyer's 'World Society' idea: the idea that systems of management and governance around the world conform to increasingly similar assumptions (Meyer, 2007; Meyer et al., 1997). Human rights, Donnelly implies, are a modern epistemological triumph and just because older philosophies defined that which was 'right' did not mean that they satisfactorily conceptualised the 'rights' that inhere to the individual human being. Though certain margins of appreciation may apply when it comes to differing interpretations of human rights, cultural relativism, according to Donnelly, should be confined within proper limits. Donnelly is right about culture, but mistaken, I believe, about the epistemological status of human rights.

So far as social rights are concerned, these may have been incorporated into the UDHR and subsequent international covenants, but we have already seen first, that social rights in the Marshallian sense had already been substantively formulated as legislative entitlements within various types of welfare state, and second, that the terms on which they were incorporated as human rights were not discovered or deduced, but *negotiated* by representatives from many nations. They are not eternal verities. They might yet be renegotiated. So far as human rights more generally are concerned, the issue is not a conflict of cultures so much as an epistemological or ideological conflict between what was referred to in Chapter 2 as a hegemonic liberal-individualist conception on the one hand and the critical minority conception on the other: the former is premised on what Arendt described as the 'arrogant myth' (1951: 439) of inborn individual dignity; the latter is premised on an understanding of the shared vulnerability that is the human condition (e.g. Turner, 2006). In an increasingly 'multi-polar world' (Held, 2010: 2), it isn't so much that Western and Eastern assumptions and beliefs converge or that the global South must adapt its understanding of rights to that of the global North, but that East and West, South and North can and will, it is hoped, negotiate and evolve broader understandings.

Reflecting on the significance of the global justice or anti-globalisation movement in general and the deliberations of the World Social Forum in particular, Boaventura de Sousa Santos suggests that their potential role is to supersede the hegemonic mono-cultural and technocratic epistemology of the global North with an insurgent epistemology of the South. The former entails an axiology of progress through capitalist development; the latter entails an 'axiology of care' (2006: 31). In the process of framing future alternatives for the articulation of human needs-claims, such an axiology (or theory of value) might draw on insights or precepts from the past and present. We shall return to both these issues in Chapter 10.

Globalisation

The existence of an *anti*-globalisation movement is testimony to the extent to which globalisation, like development, is a contested concept (Held & McGrew, 2007). The concepts and the processes they purport to define are interconnected. Supporters of globalisation regard the process as coterminous with that of human development. Its opponents fear that the hegemonic neo-liberal form of the globalisation process promotes a socially and environmentally damaging form of economic development, at the expense of effective and inclusive social development: that the age of neo-liberal globalisation 'has now superseded the age of development' (Sachs, 2010: vii). The direction and pace of global change and human development are affected by global events: acts of terrorism, military interventions, financial crises and climatic disasters. But the extent of the interdependence and interconnectedness of countries, regions and transnational corporations is ever more intense as they interact within a social space that is increasingly de-territorialised: 'Globalization is synonymous with a process of time-space compression – literally a shrinking world – in which the sources of even very local developments, from unemployment to ethnic conflict, may be traced to distant conditions or action' (Held & McGrew, 2007: 3).

Global institutional framework

One of the consequences in the course of the past half-century has been that the context and the relevance of social rights have been changing. Bob Deacon has argued that we have been witnessing 'the globalisation of social policy and the socialisation of global politics' (2007: 3). The spirit of optimism that followed the end of the Cold War led some commentators to envision a global community and a form of global citizenship based on shared objectives of peace, social justice and ecological sustainability (Falk, 1994). The reality has been less harmonious, not least because of a drive towards the 'securitisation' of citizenship and concerns with risk containment, rather than socially inclusive development processes (Nyers, 2009). Nevertheless, there is an increased awareness that social policy in one country or region cannot be made without reference to the global context, and that global poverty and social inequalities have potential implications for every country and region. Neo-liberal globalisation (as a process entailed by the ascendancy and contradictions of the Washington consensus) obliges its supporters and opponents alike to think systematically about what Deacon calls the three 'Rs': global Redistribution, global Regulation and global social Rights (2007: 1).

TABLE 5.3 Social rights at the United Nations

	Specialist agencies/programmes	concerned with rights to:
Principal organ with responsibility:		
• **ECOSOC**	• **ILO** ➤	Livelihood/standard of living
(Economic and Social Council)	(International Labour Organisation)	('work' and social security)
Relevant Departments/Offices:	• **WHO** ➤	Health
• **UNDESA**	(World Health Organisation)	
(United Nations Department of Economic and Social Affairs)	• **UNESCO** ➤	Education
• **OHCHR**	(United Nations Educational, Scientific and Cultural	
(Office of the High Commissioner for Human Rights)	Organisation)	
	• **UNDP** ➤	(Social) development
Relevant finance and trade-related agencies/organisations:	(United Nations Development Programme)	
• **IMF**	• **WFP** ➤	Food/standard of living
(International Monetary Fund)	(World Food Programme)	
• **World Bank**	• **UN-HABITAT** ➤	Housing
• **WTO**	(United Nations Human	
(World Trade Organisation)	Settlements Programme)	

The Byzantine panoply of UN agencies and organisations includes several of direct relevance to social rights. Table 5.3 identifies the key agencies, though there are many others. Under the overarching authority of ECOSOC, these agencies are between them responsible for providing or overseeing financial aid to countries in need of assistance; for developing regulatory frameworks or codes of conduct in relation to social protection and international trade for states parties and, for example, multinational corporations; and for promoting and monitoring the observance of social rights. Within the UN Secretariat there is a department dedicated to social rights matters (the UNDESA), and the promotion of human rights in general is overseen by a high commissioner, through her/his office (the OHCHR). A group of agencies, originally proposed in 1944 by the Bretton Woods Monetary and Financial Conference, provide a contextual framework by attempting to ensure global monetary stability (the IMF), to finance social and economic development projects (the World Bank) and to regulate world trading systems (the WTO – which prior to 1995 had been known as the General Agreement on Tariffs and Trade). Three specialist agencies that had existed in some form since 1919 under the auspices of the erstwhile League of Nations have responsibility for labour standards and social security (the ILO), for public health and healthcare standards (the WHO) and for educational, scientific and cultural development (UNESCO, previously the International Committee for Intellectual Co-operation). Finally, there are several more recently created specialist agencies, including the UNDP (founded in 1966 and which has previously been mentioned), the WFP (founded in 1961 and responsible for food security) and UN-HABITAT (founded in 1996 and the only UN agency with a brief explicitly focused on housing standards).

The world over which the UN system presides is very different from that for which it was created in the aftermath of the second of the world wars to have occurred in the twentieth century. However the relevance of a supranational perspective on the promotion and implementation of social rights is, arguably, greater now than ever before.

Global consumers and regulatory standards

Nicola Yeates (2001) has suggested that a distinction may be drawn between a 'strong' and a 'weak' globalisation thesis. Clearly, there is a spectrum of interpretations as to whether globalisation is an inevitable process and as to what its implications are for the future of social rights. At the 'strongest' end of the spectrum of beliefs it is supposed that globalisation has ushered in a wholly new era (Fukuyama, 1992), in which markets will rule supreme, and in which our rights to income security and pensions, to health and social care, education and housing will all be met on the basis of our rights as consumers of financial products and human services offered competitively by private and/or transnational providers in a global market place. Insofar as there may be aberrant minorities or communities who cannot access such provision, there should be publicly provided safety nets, but these should be selective, conditional and temporary. Though this is something of a caricature of the neo-liberal perspective, it is arguably consistent with the free-trade agenda of the WTO, which has developed mechanisms by which to open the provision of public social services to competition – a process which could unfold globally if established welfare states start to relinquish overall public control over key services (Holden, 2008). At the 'weaker' end of the spectrum, it is contended that the significance of globalisation is overstated (Hirst & Thompson, 1996). The process of internationalisation in trade, technology and ideas is a long-term secular trend, and welfare state development is pretty much an irreversible phenomenon: mature welfare states are durable and can survive even in the context of a more pluralistic welfare mix (Mishra, 1990; Rieger & Leibfried, 2003). Such a perspective is broadly consistent with, for example, the ILO's promotion of an international social protection floor (ILO, 2012b) and commitment to social insurance-based rights and corporatist principles of social partnership.

If indeed these were the models imposed by globalisation on existing and emerging welfare states alike, the trend to a neo-liberal American-style solution would entail a 'race to the bottom' as existing welfare states compete to establish the lowest levels of publicly funded social protection. The trend to European-style social protection, on the other hand, would entail a hard climb to the top for countries with limited or incipient welfare states: a fear, as we have seen, often voiced by such countries. Globalisation does not necessarily entail a straightforward transfer of social policies and the rights they supposedly impart from global North to global South (Hulme & Hulme, 2008). Social policies are not necessarily popularly equated with rights. And the framing of social rights as concessions to an international human rights agenda can have the effect, especially for vulnerable and marginalised people, of making rights seem abstract and distant from immediate needs and concerns (e.g. Soysal, 1994). Mishra (1999) has suggested that international regulation of social development would establish, not rights, but social standards.

Measures taken by the UN to promote social development have fallen short of regulation, but have included the introduction of the MDGs (UN General Assembly, 2000; and see Box 5.1) – a set of extremely important, if relatively modest, targets against which some progress has been made (UN Secretary General, 2013), but which by 2015 will not have been fully met throughout the world. In 2015 the MDGs will be succeeded by a set of 'Sustainable

BOX 5.1 THE MILLENNIUM DEVELOPMENT GOALS

Goal 1: Eradicate extreme poverty and hunger

- *Target 1A: Halve, between 1990 and 2015, the proportion of people living on less than $1.25 a day*
- *Target 1B: Achieve decent employment for women, men and young people*
- *Target 1C: Halve, between 1990 and 2015, the proportion of people who suffer from hunger*

Goal 2: Achieve universal primary education

- *Target 2A: By 2015, all children can complete a full course of primary schooling, girls and boys*

Goal 3: Promote gender equality and empower women

- *Target 3A: Eliminate gender disparity in primary and secondary education preferably by 2005, and at all levels by 2015*

Goal 4: Reduce child mortality rates

- *Target 4A: Reduce by two-thirds, between 1990 and 2015, the under-five mortality rate*

Goal 5: Improve maternal health

- *Target 5A: Reduce by three-quarters, between 1990 and 2015, the maternal mortality ratio*
- *Target 5B: Achieve, by 2015, universal access to reproductive health*

Goal 6: Combat HIV/AIDS, malaria and other diseases

- *Target 6A: Have halted, by 2015, and begun to reverse the spread of HIV/AIDS*
- *Target 6B: Achieve, by 2010, universal access to treatment for HIV/AIDS for all those who need it*
- *Target 6C: Have halted, by 2015, and begun to reverse the incidence of malaria and other major diseases*

Goal 7: Ensure environmental sustainability

- *Target 7A: Integrate the principles of sustainable development into country policies and programs; reverse loss of environmental resources*
- *Target 7B: Reduce biodiversity loss, achieving, by 2010, a significant reduction in the rate of loss*
- *Target 7C: Halve, by 2015, the proportion of the population without sustainable access to safe drinking water and basic sanitation*
- *Target 7D: By 2020, to have achieved a significant improvement in the lives of at least 100 million slum-dwellers*

Goal 8: Develop a global partnership for development

- *Target 8A: Develop further an open, rule-based, predictable, non-discriminatory trading and financial system*
- *Target 8B: Address the special needs of the least developed countries (LDCs)*
- *Target 8C: Address the special needs of landlocked developing countries and small island developing states*
- *Target 8D: Deal comprehensively with the debt problems of developing countries through national and international measures in order to make debt sustainable in the long term*
- *Target 8E: In co-operation with pharmaceutical companies, provide access to affordable, essential drugs in developing countries*
- *Target 8F: In co-operation with the private sector, make available the benefits of new technologies, especially information and communications*

Development Goals' (SDGs) to be achieved by 2030 and, at the time of writing, these are still under discussion (see Köhler & Pogge, 2014). The MDGs – and, it would seem, the proposed SDGs – are equivocal phenomena, resonating distantly with earlier social development approaches premised on the BNA, yet influenced by the capabilities-oriented human development approach (see Chapter 2, this volume), and bearing the stamp of a neo-liberally inspired form of mangerialism. By setting measurable performance targets the MDGs reflect the application of an essentially managerialist technique and exhibit elements of new public management thinking extended to the global level (see Chapter 1, this volume). It amounts to a technocratic colonisation or de-politicisation of the social development agenda and, it may be argued, the marginalisation of social rights (e.g. Porter & Craig, 2004; and see Chapter 9, this volume). The goals and targets set have implications for social rights, but are framed in terms of technical benchmarks, not social rights.

Rights of migrants

However, one of the effects of globalisation that does explicitly engage with the social rights agenda is that of migration and the rights of migrants in relation to employment, social security, healthcare, education or housing. Migration has been integral to the history of humanity, but it has particular significance in the context of current trends. It affects more countries and regions than ever before and there is more urgency, diversity and complexity to migration flows as people move around a rapidly changing and sometimes volatile world in pursuit of employment opportunities or better living standards – or as they flee from poverty, danger or persecution (Castles & Miller, 2009). We observed in Chapter 4 that one of the dilemmas facing capitalist welfare states is whether recent migrants – whether they be economic migrants or refugees – should enjoy the same social rights as settled citizens. There is a fundamental tension between rights of citizenship based on nationality and 'postnational' citizenship or human rights (Soysal, 1994).

The issue has particular pertinence when it comes to rights that require access to limited public funds and/or when migrants are subject to xenophobic or racist hostility (Craig, 2008). These two aspects – civic status and entitlement on the one hand and cultural inclusion or exclusion on the other – are critical. When Lockwood (1996) observed the way in which social rights could be 'fine-tuned' to exclude or include different social groups he referred to the process as 'civic stratification': stratification based not on class, but civic status constituted through differential entitlement. Lydia Morris has extended this analysis to consider how the granting and withholding of social rights becomes 'a valuable tool in the management of population and society' (2006: 54). The civic (by which we here mean 'public') dimension to economic and social rights may be taken as referring to the terms on which an individual is enabled to engage with the market and the state.

We have been using the term social rights to encompass what are referred to in the UDHR as economic, social and *cultural* rights, yet we have not so far discussed cultural rights. Cultural identity and expression might be thought of as being a 'private' rather than a public or civic issue. As individual human rights they appear to have been included, according to Eide (2001: 289), 'almost as a remnant category'. Specifically, the ICESCR (Article 15) provides for the right to take part in cultural life and the right to enjoy the benefits of scientific progress and its applications. The intention is ambiguous. Insofar as we are concerned with social rights as articulations of human need, the socio-cultural component of social rights is concerned with participation, identity and knowledge. Migrants may be inferred to have a right to participate in the life of the society to which they have migrated; to have access to educational opportunities; to take part in creative and leisure activities; and to share equally in the benefits of technological progress enjoyed by that society, whether this relates, for example, to having access to the latest advances in medical treatment, or more generally to prevailing living and housing standards. Migrants might also claim the right to preserve their own language, religion and customs, and it is on this basis that cultural rights may be regarded as an element of collective or group rights to self-determination (e.g. Kymlicka, 1995). But that is conceptually distinct from the contention that a migrant has a right to cultural inclusion in the life of a 'host' society and, by implication, to be protected from discriminatory treatment.

A full discussion of immigration policies and debates surrounding multiculturalism lies beyond the scope of this book, but it behoves us nevertheless to consider how the different perspectives on social rights, human needs and responsibilities – as outlined in Figure 3.1 in Chapter 3, this volume – play out in terms of competing approaches to migrants (this analysis is developed from Dean, 2011):

- The α perspective will be accepting of the right of free movement by migrants, who can expect to experience some degree of civic inclusion and cultural tolerance. Their social rights may well be conditional in nature. But the migrant is socially constructed as a potential settler.
- The β perspective is likely to be actively hostile to the admission of migrants, who can expect to experience civic exclusion and cultural rejection. Their social rights are likely to be minimal in nature. The migrant is socially constructed as an unwelcome alien.
- The γ perspective will be accommodating to migrants, who can, however, expect to experience restricted civic status and cultural isolation. Their social rights are likely to be sufficient, but not necessarily equivalent to those of a citizen. The migrant is socially constructed as a transient guest.
- The δ perspective will ostensibly be openly welcoming of migrants, who can expect to experience the benefits of full civic status and cultural inclusion. Their social rights are likely to be universalistic in character. The migrant is socially constructed as a new citizen.

This model is clearly no more than a heuristic device with some value for the interpretation of approaches to the social rights of migrants moving from low-income to high-income countries. Liberal welfare regimes such as the UK and the US have in the past actively encouraged inward migration at times when cheap labour was required but, in the case of the UK, this was restricted to migration from former colonies and since the 1960s has been radically curtailed. Practices in social conservative regimes vary: Germany, where citizenship is restricted to the indigenous ethnic group and migrant labour is accorded 'guest worker' status (with separately defined rights), is quite different from France, which – in theory at least – is more open to new citizens. Social democratic Nordic countries, which had been welcoming towards migrants, have lately come under pressure to restrict the social rights of migrants. Reactionary moral authoritarian tendencies can come into play within any substantive welfare regime.

Summary/conclusion

In this chapter we have considered the relevance of social rights to human welfare in a wider global context.

Social rights are by no means the automatic outcome of capitalist development. We have attempted to deconstruct the concept of 'development' and the nature of human progress. Human development can be defined and evaluated in terms of economic growth and material productivity on the one hand, and in terms of social progress and the satisfaction of human needs on the other. Clearly, these two dimensions of human progress are related, but there is controversy as to how. That controversy is fundamental to the subject of this book and to any understanding of social rights. As articulations of human need, social rights will develop in different ways and it is possible to trace the different pathways along which they have developed. In the modern Western world social rights developed differently depending on just how the transition from feudal relations of power to democratic-welfare-capitalism had been achieved. The emergence of liberal, conservative and social democratic welfare regimes reflected differently inflected social or ideological constructions of social rights. In the communist world of the Soviet Union, and its Central and Eastern European satellites, an alternative form of state-driven social rights had developed, but these were undermined by the collapse of Soviet communism and have been or are being re-established in different ways. In Latin America, the enthusiastic pursuit of social rights development was constrained by uneven economic development, while in East Asia social rights development took second place to economic development. In other parts of the world, it is forms of governance as much as the nature and extent of economic development that have constrained the emergence of social rights. In different regions of the world there are now several strongly emerging capitalist (or essentially capitalist) economies, albeit that there is at present no clear pattern to the way in which social rights are being or are likely to be established.

We have discussed the obstacles to the realisation of social rights, whether in the form envisaged by T. H. Marshall or that prescribed by the UDHR. There are real or imagined cultural obstacles. The Western concept, or at least the language, of rights are alien to some cultures, albeit that at the root of non-Western philosophies it is usually possible to detect ideals that are consistent with respect for individual human need and, by implication, for an understanding of what might be meant by 'social rights'. The fundamental issues, it may be argued, are as much epistemological as cultural or linguistic: they may relate to the inherent conflict between liberal-individualistic and social-solidaristic understandings of the human condition. Just as much as the economic consequences, the ideological and cultural impacts of neoliberal globalisation raise vital issues so far as any evolution or constructive reframing of social rights is concerned. Globalisation has entailed the growth of an extensive supranational machinery of governance, and we have examined those elements of that machinery that have bearing on social development and the realisation of social rights. It is suggested that the processes entailed have taken on a managerial character concerned not so much with the promotion of social rights, as the regulation of social standards. However, the effects of supranational governance in ameliorating the adverse consequences of economic globalisation and the unevenness of social development have been limited. One of the associated phenomena has been accelerating levels of global migration, and we have discussed the various ways in which the resulting conflicts between citizenship-based and human rights-based social rights claims may be played out. It is an issue that brings into focus the constitutive tension between, on the one hand, rights founded on global doctrines or universal principles and, on the other, rights claimed on the basis of local realities and everyday needs.

We may conclude that social rights have essential significance in the global context, but we have uncovered a trail of questions as to how to interpret and realise their meaning.

6
RIGHTS TO LIVELIHOOD

If one considers the fundamental human needs that may be translated into rights one might start from the idea of a right not merely to life, but to livelihood – to the *means* of achieving human personhood. Human beings interact symbiotically with Nature in order to satisfy their needs. The basis of humanity's 'species-being' has been conceptualised as a process of social-ecological metabolism – a consciously organised 'exchange of matter between Man and Nature' [*stoffwechsel*] (Marx, 1887; and see Dean, 2014b). Human beings lay claim to natural resources in order to survive and to flourish. In the earliest forms of human society, what we might now identify, in effect, as social rights would have been constituted through the customary expectations and practices by which human communities engaged with Nature and, in so doing, with one another.

In a bid to theorise the causes of famine, Sen (1981: 2) has suggested that there are four categories of 'entitlement' to food (and here he is talking not about rights, but effective command over resources): production-based entitlement, own-labour entitlement, transfer entitlement or trade-based entitlement. In other words, we can *work* in order to feed ourselves from Nature, by growing food or earning it in kind; and/or we can *subsist* by receiving gifts of food in kind (from family, community, charity or the state) or by buying food (if we have the means, which may be obtained through paid labour or through transfers). Development theorists have since introduced the concept of 'sustainable livelihoods' to define the processes by which people mobilise resources – natural, human, financial, physical and social – in order to sustain themselves from generation to generation (Chambers & Conway, 1992). There has been a proliferation of alternative approaches to analysing 'livelihood frameworks', encompassing the diverse ways in which such frameworks may be culturally as well as materially constituted (see Gough *et al.*, 2004). But for the purposes of reflecting on *rights* to livelihood I want for the moment to focus on those rights that are premised on needs-based claims in relation to work on the one hand and subsistence on the other. Human personhood is achieved through a person's practical doings and material wellbeing – her 'work' (broadly understood) and her level of subsistence, accepting, of course, that the latter may depend on the former.

The right to work

If we are to regard work as purposeful and constructive human activity – as socially engaged metabolism with Nature – it amounts to more than just paid labour. It includes unpaid care work, domestic labour and voluntary work; community, political and religious activism; studying; and all kinds of artistic and creative pursuits. Even recreational activities or 'amateur' pursuits, necessary to human wellbeing, may entail effort, training and the application of skill. Work is what people *do* and, insofar as we *need* to work in order to be fully human, we may argue for a right to work. In practice, however, the rights we shall now discuss relate narrowly to rights to, or in, paid labour. I shall first discuss such rights as are defined under the human rights framework, before turning to the ways in which rights relating to work tend to be constituted within nation states when defined as rights of citizenship.

International labour rights

We observed in Chapter 5 that the ILO, which sets international labour standards through conventions and recommendations, was originally founded after the end of the First World War as an agency of the League of Nations. Its constitution (1919: Preface) did not speak of rights, but of the extent to which world peace could be imperilled by social injustice and, specifically, by unjust conditions of labour. Towards the end of the Second World War the ILO's Declaration of Philadelphia (1944) explicitly situated the aims of the organisation within a human rights context, while also declaring, controversially that 'labour is not a commodity' (Article I [a]).

   The context for the post–Second World War human rights agenda had been set not so much with the aim of de-commodifying labour, as by principles fostered in the course of the preceding century by the international campaign for the abolition of slavery and the prohibition of *forced* labour (Drescher, 2009) – a campaign that had culminated in the League of Nations' Slavery Convention of 1926. The primary emphasis within much of the subsequent international human rights agenda has been on the principle that 'work' should be freely chosen and remunerated.

- The UDHR of 1948 declares that 'everyone has the right to work, to free choice of employment, to just and favourable conditions of work and to protection against unemployment' (Article 23[1]).
- The ICESCR of 1966 'acknowledges' the right of everyone to the opportunity to gain her living by work which she freely chooses or accepts (Article 6), but also (under Article 7) to 'fair wages' (including equal pay for equal work as between men and women) and a 'decent living', safe working conditions, equal opportunities for promotion at work and (reiterating UDHR Article 24) reasonable working hours and paid holidays.
- The Council of Europe's Social Charter of 1961 (revised in 1996) provides for a person's right to earn her living in an occupation freely entered upon, but more generally to the benefits of economic and social policies designed, *inter alia*, to ensure full employment (but also, for example, vocational training and free employment services). Additionally, in the European context, the European Union's Charter of Fundamental Rights of 2007 provides more cautiously for 'the right to engage in work and to pursue a freely chosen or accepted occupation' and 'the freedom to seek employment [and] to work'.
- The American Convention on Human Rights of 1969 (to which most Latin American nations are a party, but which the US never fully ratified) includes provision for freedom

from slavery (Article 6) and a provision (Article 26) for the progressive development of economic, social, educational and cultural standards set out in the Charter of the Organization of American States of 1948 (as amended in 1967), which refers in general terms to 'fair wages, employment opportunities and acceptable working conditions for all' (Article 34 [g]). The Additional Protocol of San Salvador to the American convention (not signed by the US) includes ambitious and detailed provision (under Article 7) for 'Just, Equitable and Satisfactory Conditions of Work', including the abolition of night work and the right of every worker to follow her vocation.

- The African Charter on Human and People's Rights of 1981 states simply that 'every individual shall have the right to work under equitable and satisfactory conditions and shall receive equal pay for equal work' (Article 15).

Of course the implementation of human rights may not be fully realised at the domestic level. But in any event it appears there is no unequivocal obligation on states parties under any of the above instruments actually to provide a citizen with a job. While the right to work is established as a human right, its availability as a right of citizenship may not necessarily or unequivocally be guaranteed. And even in developed welfare states some have been more willing than others to protect citizens from the adverse consequences of wage labour through, for example, intervention to regulate wages and the terms and conditions of employment.

Domestic labour rights

In Chapter 4 I mentioned Claus Offe's argument that in industrial capitalist societies people became wage labourers as citizens of a state. The terms on which they sell their labour power and the conditions under which they are supposedly free to do so can be shaped in part by social legislation. But ultimately they will be governed by market forces. Though citizens are supposedly free to sell their labour, Polanyi (1944: ch. 6) has suggested that because labour cannot be separated from the person who labours, labour should be regarded as a 'fictitious' commodity. By the same token we might regard the right to labour (as opposed to a right to work in its broader sense) as a fictitious right. We saw in Chapter 5 that jobs were, after a fashion, guaranteed under Soviet communism, but the availability of employment in the context of a capitalist market economy is subject ultimately to market forces.

Macroeconomic and local development policies may aim to create jobs, but employment for all cannot necessarily be guaranteed, unless governments themselves are prepared to act as employers of last resort (Sawyer, 2003). Relatively high levels of public sector employment have in the past assisted social democratic welfare states to maintain near full employment, but insofar as such states had also relied on fiscal, active labour market and wages policy to maintain full employment, this would have been an incidental effect (Kananen, 2014). Counter-recessionary public works programmes, such as those in the US following the financial crisis of 2008–11 under the so-called Obama Jobs Act (see *The Guardian,* 9 September 2011), have never guaranteed jobs for all. There has been a recent attempt in India to introduce a National Rural Employment Guarantee Scheme: a programme that offers up to 100 days of unskilled manual labour per year on public works projects for any rural household member who wants such work at a stipulated minimum wage rate. However, implementation of the scheme has been partial and selective and there remains considerable unmet employment demand in all parts of the country (Dutta *et al.,* 2012).

If work equates with paid employment, a right to work under capitalism will remain elusive. Welfare states provide rights to social security protection for workers and these we shall consider in the next section of this chapter. However, welfare states have developed a significant array of rights *at* work for citizens who are in employment. It is to these that we shall now briefly turn. Though it may be difficult or impossible to ensure a right to work, it is arguably reasonable to demand a right to 'decent' work, as is the aim of a campaign currently mounted by the ILO (1999).

The first thing to be said about the rights of citizens who are in employment, is that their employment is governed in law by a contract with their employers, whether that be written or implied. The employees' rights are primarily civil rights, not social rights. Workers have the freedom and a right – in theory – to negotiate the terms of their contracts of employment, though the disparity of power between workers and employers may make this practically impossible. Through social legislation, however, policy makers can impose certain terms and conditions on such contractual arrangements. And in a democracy, workers can – in theory, once again – exercise their political rights in an attempt to influence policy makers, though bringing influence to bear on the policy-making process can be difficult.

There is a variety of possible employment protection or social regulation measures, some of which are expressly required of those states parties that have ratified human rights treaties or the conventions of the ILO, though some of these measures evolved over time in advance, or independently, of international human rights frameworks. These are some of the more important forms of regulatory intervention that give rise to rights at work:

- *Minimum wage* regulation may be applied on a nationwide basis or selectively in different regions and/or in different employment sectors within a country. Over 190 countries worldwide claim to fix minimum wages (ILO, 2012a). The rates set and methods of enforcement are highly variable. In some countries, such as Brazil, the level of the national minimum wage is used as a benchmark for fixing a range of other social entitlements. Countries that don't have minimum wages, including the Nordic countries, consider that to do so would undermine the principle of free wage bargaining. Britain abandoned a fragmentary system of wage regulation in the 1980s, only to reinstate a national minimum wage in 1999. Neo-liberal opponents of minimum wages assert that they increase unemployment, a claim that remains largely unproven (Coates, 2007). In London and other parts of Britain, there are currently voluntary schemes under which employers agree to pay a 'living wage' at a rate higher than the prevailing national minimum wage, and there is a campaign for the replacement of the minimum wage by a living wage scheme (Bennett & Lister, 2010).

- The regulation of *working hours* became a concern of policy makers in the first industrialised countries during the first half of the nineteenth century, as factory-based production systems began to develop (e.g. Fraser, 2003), culminating in Britain in 1844 with a restriction in the working hours of women and children to 10 hours a day. The very first ILO convention in 1919 established the principle of 8 hours a day and 48 hours a week, and the UDHR in 1948 specifically demands the 'reasonable limitation of working hours' (Article 24). Currently, working hours legislation can be identified in over 100 countries worldwide, with a trend towards a dominant, but by no means universal, standard of 40 hours per week (Lee *et al.*, 2007), albeit that actual working hours vary considerably. The European Union Working Time Directive provides for a maximum

48-hour week, from which certain professions may be excluded and individual employees may opt out, though France, for example, has legislated for a 35-hour week. Working hours regulations may include provision for rest periods, holiday entitlements and night work restrictions.

- Occupational *health and safety* standards similarly developed because of concerns about the hazards associated with industrial production methods, which resulted, for example, during the second half of the nineteenth century in Britain in a series of factories acts and legislation relating to safety measures and compensation for workplace injury. The right to safe and healthy working conditions was included in the ICESCR (Article 7 [b]) and, as with the regulation of working hours, ILO conventions and EU directives have evolved. Legislation and systems of enforcement are identifiable in more than 120 countries worldwide (ILO, 2009). Such systems generally provide for inspection regimes with penalties against employers for non-compliance, rather than specifically defined rights for workers, other than regulated rights to civil compensation after the event for industrial injuries or diseases.
- Protection against arbitrary or *unfair dismissal* is something that developed more recently. Relevant legislation was first introduced in Britain in 1971, and the ILO later agreed on a convention in 1982 (developed from prior recommendation in 1974). Some form of regulation relating to the termination of employment can be identified in more than 100 countries (ILO, 1995). The right not to be unfairly or unjustifiably dismissed is to be distinguished from the civil right not to be wrongfully dismissed insofar as it is a right established by legislation which specifies the grounds on which a dismissal can be fair or justifiable. These characteristically include grounds associated with the worker's capability or conduct or because of redundancy (where the worker's job has ceased to exist), in which case there is provision in some countries for statutory redundancy compensation.
- Rights to equal opportunity or *non-discrimination* have their origins in the UDHR, which declared that everyone has the right 'without any discrimination, to equal pay for equal work' (Article 23 [2]), explicitly interpreted in the ICESCR as discrimination on the grounds of sex, albeit that the right was extended by the International Convention on the Elimination of All Forms of Racial Discrimination of 1965, and subsequently, the Convention on the Rights of Persons with Disabilities of 2006 (Article 27). The ILO's Discrimination (Employment and Occupation) Convention of 1958 had defined discrimination as including 'any distinction, exclusion or preference made on the basis of race, colour, sex, religion, political opinion, national extraction or social origin, which has the effect of nullifying or impairing equality of opportunity or treatment' (Article 1 [a]). The convention has been ratified by an unusually high proportion of ILO member states (169 out of 183) and there is evidence that legislative and institutional initiatives continue to develop worldwide (ILO, 2011). By way of example, the history of such legislation in Britain dates back to the 1970s with legislation that now encompasses provision of individual rights against discrimination on a multiplicity of grounds, including age and sexual orientation, buttressed by an Equality and Human Rights Commission with powers of investigation and enforcement.
- Initiatives to promote *work-life balance* or work-family reconciliation are ostensibly of more recent provenance. Capitalist welfare states had been initially constructed with the male breadwinner model in mind (see Chapter 4, this volume), but since the 1990s, policy makers in the global North have been driven to facilitate the mutual accommodation

of labour markets and household living and earning strategies, by introducing extended parental leave schemes, the enhancement of childcare and the promotion of 'family friendly' employment practices (Lewis, 2006). However, the foundations for some such initiatives had in part been laid in the form of maternity leave provision (introduced in several countries in the mid-twentieth century, and specifically required by Article 10 of the ICESCR), and, for example, the extension of non-discrimination principles in the European Social Charter (Article 27) and ILO Convention 156 – Workers with Family Responsibilities.

Of critical relevance to the right to work is the role of trades unions. The right to form and join a trade union stems from the right to freedom of association and might therefore be considered to be as much a political right as a social right. Nevertheless it is explicitly present both in the UDHR (Article 23 [4]) and the ICESCR (Article 8 [1] – which includes the right to strike) as a component of the right to work. Trades unions have been and are important for their role in negotiating the framing of workers' substantive rights, whether formally (as in corporatist and social democratic welfare regimes) or through lobbying and campaigning activity (as in liberal regimes) – and in defending their members' rights, whether collectively or through support provided to individual workers. However, though trades unions remain resilient in some countries, the effects of neo-liberal economic globalisation are reflected in a decline in union power and recruitment (Visser, 2006). What is more, despite their importance, trades unions have been subject to criticism for their 'labourist' approach (e.g. Standing, 2009): their adherence to an institutional model of industrial capitalism, favouring protection for labour market insiders, often at the expense of marginalised, precariously employed and informal sector workers. What were once called 'atypical' workers – part-time, temporary, casual or agency workers – who in many instances tended to be legally excluded from the protections outlined above, have seldom been represented by trades unions. However, the polarisation and flexibilisation of labour markets around the world (Doogan, 2009) have meant that what was once 'atypical' has become the norm for large numbers of workers, even within the formal economy. Increasingly those workers with limited skills and qualifications are consigned to low-paid, insecure work with little or no prospect of advancement. As mentioned in Chapter 2, Guy Standing has referred to this emerging class of workers as the 'precariat'. Though legislators in established welfare states have sought to extend protection to 'atypical' workers, employers have found new devices – zero hours contracts, bogus self-employment arrangements, etc. – to circumvent protection. And as we saw in Chapter 5, in many parts of the world, much if not most work is not formalised and enjoys no protection.

The right to subsistence

In discussing rights to livelihood it is difficult to disentangle work and subsistence. A subsistence farmer may achieve subsistence through her own work, but cannot satisfactorily do so in the absence of transactions with other human beings: she is likely to barter or sell some part of her own produce or labour in order to obtain food stuffs, tools or materials she cannot herself produce. As suggested above, in the absence of any formal legal framework this might require the implicit development and exercise of what would amount to customary rights. But when it comes to formal rights in the context of a market economy, the relationship between work and subsistence becomes more problematic. If a right to work for wages cannot be guaranteed, to what extent can a right to subsistence be ensured? Once again, I shall first discuss such rights as are defined under the human rights framework, before turning to the ways in which rights relating to subsistence tend to be constituted within nation states when defined as rights of citizenship.

Human rights framework

A general right to subsistence or to an adequate standard of living was established in the following terms by the UDHR of 1948:

> Everyone has the right to a standard of living adequate for the health and well-being of himself and of his family, including food, clothing, housing and medical care and necessary social services, and the right to security in the event of unemployment, sickness, disability, widowhood, old age or other lack of livelihood in circumstances beyond his control.
>
> (Article 25 [1])

This wide-reaching statement begs a variety of questions, of which the most obvious is whether the right is to be established through the provision of goods in kind, or cash? In the case of the right to food, is this a right to a food parcel or to a cash transfer? Insofar as the world faces enduring challenges from hunger and malnutrition, the UN's World Food Programme, established in 1961, has continuing responsibility for international food aid in order to protect livelihoods in emergencies (World Food Programme, 2013). At the national level there are past examples of a right to food being provided through food stamps in the US (a scheme dating from the 1930s – see Elsinger, 1998) or through various experiments with food parcels or food tickets under Brazil's Zero Hunger Programme during the 1990s (da Silva *et al.,* 2005). Supporters of a right to food in kind would argue that it is more redistributive than cash transfers; it can be used to support local agricultural production and to promote adequate nutrition. Opponents complain that it is paternalistic and potentially stigmatising: people should be allowed to choose what they eat, and by and large – with the exception of emergency provision – a right to food for citizens without the means of subsistence is usually met by way of cash transfers.

A right to food may be underwritten by states parties not directly through provision to individual citizens, but more generally. The San Salvador Protocol to the American Convention on Human Rights of 1988 sets a high standard for the right to adequate nutrition, insisting it should guarantee 'the possibility of enjoying the highest level of physical, emotional and intellectual development' (Article 12 [1]). But the protocol also suggests that states parties must 'undertake to improve methods of production, supply and distribution of food, and to this end, agree to promote greater international cooperation in support of the relevant national policies' (Article 12 [2]). We see here an example of rhetoric that links social rights to a wider international social development agenda (cf. Chapter 5, this volume).

Article 25 [1] of the UDHR also provides for rights to clothing, housing, medical care and necessary social services. The right to clothing appears to be largely a 'forgotten right' (James, 2008), except insofar as it is indirectly provided for through cash transfers. Housing, medical care and social services will be discussed in Chapter 7, since these may be considered as human services as opposed to subsistence goods. These too may be provided in kind – through public sector provision – or their cost to the individual may be met though cash transfer schemes specifically intended to cover rents, fees and charges.

Social security systems

We move therefore to consider the complex realm of cash transfers or – the term we shall now be using – social security. The term social security is mired in a certain amount of misunderstanding, since it can refer to different things in different parts of the world. However, by social security we are alluding to the UDHR's reference in Article 25 to 'security in the event of unemployment, sickness, disability, widowhood, old age or other lack of livelihood'. Curiously, the provision relating to social security in the ICESCR of 1966 is startlingly brief. It says only that the states parties 'recognise the rights of everyone to social security, including social insurance' (Article 9): a clumsy compromise reflecting unresolved disagreement as to the meaning of social security (U. Davy, 2013).

Michael Hill (2006: 67) has provided what is perhaps the simplest definition of social security: 'Collective action to protect individuals against income deficiencies'. Collective action may take a variety of forms: social assistance funded through general taxation; social insurance funded through specific contributions; universal social allowance schemes; tax allowances; or the public regulation of private provision. We shall be considering each in turn. The complexity of social security and the different mechanisms or systems it can entail stem partly from the different contingencies or circumstances in which a right to social security might arise – but partly also from the proviso that the right does not arise other than in circumstances where individuals' lack of livelihood is 'beyond their control'. Rights to social security are, to a greater or lesser extent, conditional.

Social assistance is the term applied to forms of relief that are conditional on proof of need, usually a test of means. 'Traditional' forms of social assistance have their roots directly in the Poor Laws: forms of poor relief characteristically to be found in Western countries prior to the development of welfare state regimes. The receipt of relief under such schemes had been based not on rights, but upon the exercise of administrative discretion. The Poor Laws superseded charitable forms of relief with organised relief – funded from local rates or taxes. Relief was at best judgemental – being reserved only for those deemed to be sufficiently deserving – and at worst punitive, requiring supplicants to submit to incarceration in workhouses, where they were subject to conditions that were deliberately contrived to be worse than those endured by even the poorest independent labourer (e.g. Fraser, 2003). Social assistance schemes under capitalist welfare regimes can vary in terms of the degree of discretion vested in those who administer them, but they are usually framed as a right for the poorest in society and as a social safety net. Subject to conditions, social assistance may be dispensed for the maintenance of persons and the households of such persons where the household has no or insufficient income from any other source. It is a characteristic feature of 'liberal' welfare regimes (see Table 5.2 in Chapter 5, this volume), though usually not as the only form of social security provision (the exceptions here being Australia and New Zealand). The advantage of social assistance is that it can target assistance where it appears to be most needed. Its disadvantages are that it can stigmatise those who receive it (because they are identified by their poverty); it is inevitably complex to administer (because the household circumstances of every recipient must be assessed); and it can create perverse incentives (since relief is withdrawn should recipients receive other income from earnings or savings). In the

US, social assistance is not thought of as a form of social security, but as 'welfare' – a term that has acquired distinctly pejorative associations, wholly distinct from social insurance. But in Australia and New Zealand, where means-tested benefits are the mainstay of social security, they attract less stigma.

Social assistance programmes have been emerging in the global South: the *dibao* system in China (Yan, 2014), and the Child Support Grant in South Africa (Lund, 2008). But most prominent have been 'new' forms of social assistance, known as conditional cash transfers (Bastagli, 2009). These were first developed in Latin America – e.g. *Opportunidades* in Mexico and the *Bolsa Familia* in Brazil – but schemes have proliferated elsewhere. Characterised as a form of 'social citizenship for the global poor' (Leisering & Barrientos, 2013), these locally based schemes provide cash incomes to poorer households on the condition that mothers report with their younger children to health clinics, while older children attend school. The explicit aim was not merely to relieve current poverty, but to underwrite investment in human capital so as to ensure higher levels of productivity among future generations. The schemes have generally been popular with recipients, though there have been practical issues relating in some instances to the inaccessibility of health clinics and the poor quality of education available in schools. There is also, potentially, a matter of principle at stake because of the way such schemes make the household's right to subsistence interdependent with their children's rights to healthcare and education. Whereas 'traditional' social assistance, with its roots in the Poor Laws, reflects elements of the β perspective on social rights (see Figure 3.1 in Chapter 3, this volume), the 'new' form of social assistance, which is strongly supported by the World Bank, reflects elements of the α perspective.

Social insurance may be remembered as one of the big ideas of the twentieth century. I made the point in Chapter 4 that social insurance entails a principle that can be embraced from either an individualistic or a solidaristic perspective: the term may encompass a fully funded scheme where individual entitlements are strictly dependent on individual contributions, and which is 'social' only in the sense that it is state administered (or administered as a provident fund on behalf of the government as, for example, in Hong Kong); or it may be a scheme where the state itself maintains a fund on behalf of workers from which benefits and pensions are paid, and which is insurance-based only in the sense that everyone has 'assured' protection (though it was only under Soviet communism that any such scheme existed). In practice, contemporary social insurance schemes can represent compromises that sit somewhere between these extremes: they are 'pay-as-you-go' (PAYG) schemes into which workers and employers pay contributions, while the state underwrites the ability of the scheme to meet current liabilities for benefits and pensions. But globally, some fear that the social insurance principle is being marginalised in favour of social assistance safety nets on the one hand, and regulated private insurance schemes on the other (e.g. Rys, 2010).

Nevertheless, social insurance against life's risks – including and especially the risks of unemployment; sickness, injury or disability; and old age – continues as a substantial and resilient component of most established social security systems and is being incrementally adopted by some newer ones, including China (Chan *et al.,* 2008). The essence of social insurance is that membership and therefore contributions are compulsory, but that risks are shared. Statutory social insurance arrangements sometimes subsumed voluntary schemes, begun by civil society organisations in the nineteenth century. However, the range of risks or contingencies and the populations or employment sectors covered by such insurance varies from country to country. Contributions and benefits rates also vary and the redistributive effects of such schemes will depend on just how such rates are set. The advantage of social insurance schemes is that they provide benefit recipients with a clear sense of entitlement and they are usually, therefore, popular. Their disadvantage is that they may tend primarily to benefit only certain workers: labour market 'outsiders', especially women, can be excluded. Social insurance schemes characteristically reflect elements of the γ perspective on social rights (see Figure 3.1 in Chapter 3, this volume). However, fully funded forms of social insurance reflect elements of the α perspective, while generous and universally inclusive forms reflect elements of the δ perspective.

Universal social security schemes, sometimes called 'social allowances', are universal in the sense that they are non-means-tested and non-contributory. In practice, schemes are not so much universal as 'categorical'; they are benefits payable in some welfare states to persons in particular demographic groups or categories, including the following:

- Children or families with children. The right to social security for children (specifically restated in the UN's Convention on the Rights of the Child of 1989) can be realised through social assistance provision to the low-income households in which children reside, or through child additions to social insurance benefits payable to parents. Alternatively or additionally, however, provision can be made through universal family allowances or child benefits payable to all households with children. (Britain's Child Benefit scheme had been an example of this, although entitlement has now been directly withdrawn from certain high-income households, making it effectively means-tested.)
- Disabled people and carers. People who become disabled in the course of their working lives may have previously 'earned' an entitlement to benefits under social insurance schemes, and those who have been disabled from birth or since childhood may be entitled to relief under social assistance schemes. Additionally, however, social security provision may be made by way of universal benefits, intended to compensate not for lack of earnings, but for the additional living costs experienced by a disabled person. Entitlement, however, is subject to medical assessment criteria. Universal social security may also be instituted for people who provide full-time unpaid care for a disabled relative. (Britain's Personal Independence Payment and Carer's Allowance schemes, respectively, are examples, though entitlement criteria for the former have recently been tightened, and the level of support provided by the latter is very modest indeed.)
- Older people. For people above a specified retirement age, social assistance schemes may provide a safety net or else social insurance schemes may pay retirement pensions. However, it is also possible for governments to provide a universal state funded retirement pension to all older citizens. (New Zealand currently provides an example, and such a possibility has been mooted from time to time in Britain.)

There has been long-standing debate around the idea of a fully universal basic income, social dividend or citizen's income (Fitzpatrick, 1999; Torry, 2013), and limited experiments with such ideas have been attempted in Namibia (Haartmann et al., 2009) and India (Standing, 2013). The advantages of universal benefits schemes is that they are simple to administer (since they involve no means-testing or contributions) and they are symbolically highly solidaristic. The perceived disadvantages are that unless benefits are set at a low level, the levels of progressive taxation required to pay them would be high – and that people with high incomes would pay high taxes while receiving a benefit they do not need. Depending on *exactly* how they are designed and implemented, universal benefits schemes can appeal either to a **δ** or an **α** perspective on social rights (see Figure 3.1 in Chapter 3, this volume): in theory, at least, they can help to underpin either a substantively or a formally egalitarian society.

Richard Titmuss (1958) coined the terms **'fiscal welfare'** and **'occupational welfare'** to refer to systems that run in parallel with the kind of social security systems outlined above. By fiscal welfare he was referring to systems of tax allowances or tax credits that can be of benefit to people who already have taxable incomes. And by occupational welfare he was referring to the panoply of perks and benefits that can be made available by employers to their employees. Titmuss's particular concern was that such systems were more likely to be of benefit to individuals and households with higher incomes and better opportunities, and it was important that state administered social security should not be reserved primarily for the poorest or least advantaged in society. Nevertheless, fiscal and occupational welfare have played a part in providing social security. Of particular importance in many countries has been the development not only of occupational pension schemes operated by employers, but also the range of private savings schemes and financial products that governments can both actively promote and regulate with a view to ensuring optimal security for older citizens. The World Bank (1994; and see Holzmann & Hinz, 2005) has recommended that all countries should establish pension systems based on three 'pillars':

- First pillar: a guaranteed publicly funded minimum safety net − whether means-tested, flat-rate social insurance-based or universal. (Possibly, an earnings-related social insurance scheme might provide for an intermediate 'pillar' above the first pillar and the next one.)
- Second pillar: a mandatory savings scheme, either an occupational or a personal pension plan, subject to government regulation.
- Third pillar: voluntary additional private insurance or savings. (Arguably, informal intra-family or inter-generational transfers represent a final 'pillar'.)

The right to social security may be interpreted as a right to secure subsistence across the life course, but its most problematic aspect relates to its intersection with the right to work.

The subsistence rights of workers

We have seen that the UDHR provides a right to social security for individuals and their families in the event of unemployment. It additionally provides that 'everyone who works has the right to just and favourable remuneration ensuring for himself and his family an existence worthy of human dignity, and supplemented, if necessary, by other means of social protection' (Article 23 [3]). The prevailing assumption is that human beings will normally sustain themselves within families and through paid employment, but if they cannot, they should have a claim upon the state for protection. It is not said, but perhaps implied, that it is a person's reciprocal responsibility to sustain herself in such a manner. The bearer of rights is primarily constituted as a potential wage labourer who during her adulthood should work to sustain herself, her children and, as need be, her spouse or adult partner. In the two preceding sentences I have deliberately used the feminine possessive pronoun, though the instruments by which rights are declared or instituted have classically been framed using the male possessive pronoun: in the minds of those who framed such instruments, the bearer of rights would have been envisaged primarily as male (e.g. Lister, 2003). The foundational assumptions upon which such rights had been framed have long since been challenged by such trends as the increase in women's labour market participation and, in the global North, the changing dynamics of family life. These trends have cast new light on how the rights of men and women, as workers and carers, breadwinners and home-makers, may be interpreted.

The normative ambiguity of the social rights agenda was exposed in other ways by the critical backlash that began in the 1970s (see Chapter 4, this volume): in particular, a hardening neo-liberal consensus among the capitalist welfare states of the global North that the responsibilities of citizens-as-workers should be more explicit. The mantra that achieved a virtual consensus by the turn of the millennium was that there should be 'no rights without responsibilities' (Giddens, 1998: 65). In the global South, meanwhile, the fragmentary nature of formal labour markets and state administration meant that the nexus of rights and responsibilities within families and in relation to work were differently understood (Gough & McGregor, 2007; and see Chapter 5, this volume). Nevertheless, welfare programmes developing in some emerging economies – for example South Korea's Self Sufficiency Programme (Jo & Walker, 2014; Kim, 2011) – demonstrate clear similarities with trends in the global North.

This section of the chapter will focus on transitions that have been occurring in the welfare states of the global North: transitions variously described in terms of a transition from passive to 'active' welfare states (Esping-Andersen, 2002), from welfare states to 'workfare' states (Jessop, 2002), and from protective to 'enabling' state models (Gilbert, 2004). It is important, however, to note first, that such transitions often entailed changes of emphasis, rather than substance; second, some of the principles informing such transitions can already be seen to be informing developments in emerging economies. The fundamental issues for welfare states, whether established or incipient, are how to make workers work; how to make work pay; and how to make workers' families self-sustaining.

Labour market activation

There has undoubtedly been an increase in the degree of conditionality attaching to the receipt of benefits or cash transfers for welfare state citizens of working age (Dwyer, 2004). Conditionality, however, is nothing new. Since unemployment benefits were first introduced in industrialised countries around or even before the early part of the twentieth century, the right to benefits was invariably conditional. In the British case, benefits could be withheld if the claimant had become unemployed voluntarily or through misconduct, and entitlement was in any event conditional on the claimant's continued availability for work (Gilbert, 1966). The subsequent evolution of social security for unemployed people – or 'job-seekers' as they came to be known in the 1990s – entailed a relentless tightening of rules, procedures and sanctions intended to encourage, assist or compel people to engage or re-engage with the labour market (Lødemel & Trickey, 2000). The trend was consistent with a shift from Keynesian macro-economic orthodoxies to supply-side economic measures, whereby governments sought to attract private investment by maximising labour market participation and 'driving up' the skills and motivation of their domestic labour force.

The initial impetus towards 'welfare-to-work' schemes has been associated with developments in the US (Mead, 1997) but such provision rapidly spread to Britain and other welfare states (Peck, 2001). However, there were significant variations in the approach taken (see Dean, 2007; and Box 6.1).

BOX 6.1   VARIETIES OF WORKFARE

Work-first. Policies that seek to move unemployed people rapidly into available employment, however low paid or insecure, on the premise that any job is better than no job and may provide a stepping stone to a better job. Characteristically, claimants will have benefits immediately withdrawn if they refuse a job offer. The approach is consistent with a β perspective on social rights (see Figure 3.1, this volume).

Human capital. Policies focused directly on the labour market supply side that emphasise the need for skills training and making people job ready. Characteristically, claimants will be allowed time to engage with the labour market, though claimants may have benefits withdrawn if they refuse appropriate training or work experience or if they fail to co-operate with employment services staff. The approach is consistent with an α perspective on social rights.

Insertion. Policies that seek to 'insert' marginalised or hard-to-place workers into the labour market, often in temporary jobs, with minimum coercion on the one hand, and taking care not to disrupt existing labour relations on the other. The approach is consistent with a γ perspective on social rights.

Flexicurity. Policies that seek to adapt social security provision to a flexible labour market by coupling relatively generous short-term social protection measures for unemployed people with strenuous labour market activation measures on the one hand and policies to promote life-long learning and work-family reconciliation measures on the other. The approach is consistent with a δ perspective on social rights.

NOTE: This is a heuristic taxonomy. The models can overlap and actual workfare regimes generally combine elements of more than one model. For these reasons the terms used above may be used in slightly different ways in different contexts.

Part and parcel with labour market activation measures have been policies to 'make work pay'. Such measures are not wholly new. In England towards the end of the eighteenth century at a time when the Poor Laws were less draconian than they would later become, a system of relief, known as the Speenhamland system (after the name of the parish in which it was first instituted), was introduced in parts of the country where agricultural wages had fallen beneath subsistence level. Under the Speenhamland system, local justices supplemented workers' wages from the Poor Rates (de Schweinitz, 1961). The system was later abolished, but since the 1970s, a number of countries have introduced a variety of means-tested wage top-up or tax credit schemes in order to sustain the functioning of low wage economies (Dean, 2012c), sometimes as an alternative, but often in addition, to minimum wage regulation. Though framed as a right of low-paid workers, such schemes function in effect as an indirect subsidy to their employers. The rationale, however, is that supplementing low wages in this way provides an incentive for citizens to engage with the labour market, while enabling employers to employ them on wages beneath subsistence level.

Labour market activation has not only been intensifying, it has been extending to new groups of citizens, including lone parents and disabled people. Each group in its way has been problematic for the capitalist welfare state. Lone parent households, which tend to be female-headed, are hardly a new phenomenon: in any era and community in which average male life expectancy is relatively low, the numbers of widowed mothers are likely to be relatively high. Such circumstances applied prior to and during the early part of the Industrial Revolution (and still applies in some parts of the world today). But despite increased longevity associated with rising living standards, greater diversity and fluidity in patterns of family formation were associated in the last part of the twentieth century with an unexpected growth in the incidence of different kinds of lone parenthood throughout the global North (Duncan & Edwards, 1997; Lewis, 2001). As divorced, separated and never partnered lone parents with the care of dependent children became a major component of social assistance case loads, attempts were made to encourage, assist or coerce them into the labour market by incorporating them into the various kinds of scheme outlined in Box 6.1, while simultaneously seeking ways to provide or to subsidise childcare provision to enable them to do so (Knijn *et al.*, 2007). Practice between countries varies as to how soon after the birth of her youngest child a lone parent (or, for that matter, any non-working parent in a household supported by social assistance) should be expected or required to substitute the unpaid work of full-time parental childcare for paid employment.

Disabled people, similarly, would once have been a more or less accepted part of any human community, though in the early part of the modern industrial era there had been a trend towards the development of institutional care for disabled people, on the premise that they were a burden if not a threat to the productivity of the labour force (Oliver, 1990). But following the formation of modern capitalist welfare states there had been a new trend – driven in part by the disability awareness movement (see Chapter 4, this volume) – towards greater integration of disabled people in society. However, growing concern in recent decades about the numbers of long-term sick and disabled people in receipt of social security benefits has driven some capitalist welfare states to tighten eligibility tests for such benefits and/or to evaluate disabled people's capacity for work with a view to incorporating them into the kinds of schemes outlined in Box 6.1 (e.g. Roulstone & Barnes, 2005).

Enforcing family responsibilities

The other prevailing assumption implied in the way that rights to social security are framed is that workers are responsible for maintaining their families. In most jurisdictions there is legal liability established by statute whereby parents may be held *financially* responsible for dependent children, spouses are held responsible for each other and, in some instances, adult children may be held responsible for their aged parents. Whether statutorily defined intra-familial liabilities give rise to intra-familial rights is a moot point. The evidence suggests that attempts by legislators to interfere with the complex ways in which responsibilities within families are negotiated can be ineffectual at best and counterproductive at worst (Finch, 1989). The moral rationality of, for example, those parents who see virtue in caring for their children rather than working for wages is at odds with the utilitarian logic of prevailing policy environments. Welfare state societies have been experiencing changes in cultural expectations with regard to what people seek in familial and intimate relationships (Beck & Beck-Gernsheim, 1995). Nevertheless, there are certain instances in which it is through conditions imposed on a working-age citizen's right to social assistance that the state may seek to impose its interpretation of where material responsibilities lie.

The first of these arises in the administration of household means-tests conducted for the purposes of assessing social assistance entitlement. These characteristically assume that all members of a cohabiting household unit will maintain one another. In calculating a household's entitlement, account is taken of every household member's resources (including savings and income from part-time employment, child maintenance, pensions and other social security benefits). The assumption applies not only to adults' responsibilities to child dependents within a household but to mutual responsibility between adults, where they are married, in a civil partnership or cohabiting *as if* they were in such a relationship. The implication, when this arises, is that adults in a conjugal relationship are required to be financially interdependent, whether or not they are so in reality, or would choose to be (McLaughlin, 1999; Tranter *et al.,* 2008). The consequence of this constraint on citizens' rights to social assistance is that they might lose their right to benefits upon entering a cohabiting relationship. In Britain, when concern about the rising numbers of lone parents in receipt of social assistance began to surface in the 1960s and '70s considerable administrative effort was invested into the intrusive investigation of lone parent claimants suspected of cohabiting relationships (Dean, 1991; Fairbairns, 1985).

The second instance relates to provision by absent parents for the financial support of their children. In Britain this was a matter of perennial concern to parish authorities during the Poor Law era, but in more recent times such matters had been regarded as private matters and had been left by and large to the civil courts to administer (Wikeley, 2006). However, where a lone parent with care of a child is in receipt of social assistance, the state has a direct interest in the enforcement of such liabilities so as to limit claims upon the state. Arrangements vary between countries, but in recent decades there have been attempts in several Anglophone countries (including Britain, the US and Australia) to introduce specialised child support schemes specifically intended to enforce the liabilities of what in the US were called 'deadbeat dads': feckless fathers who had walked out on their children (Garfinkel *et al.,* 1998). Though a parent with the care of children could file for support from an absent biological parent, the state itself could also institute action directly against such a parent to recover child support. In Britain at one stage, lone parents in receipt of social assistance could be penalised with a reduction in benefits if they failed to co-operate with the authorities in tracking down an absent parent (Garnham & Knights, 1994). The British scheme has since been modified, but fundamental issues remain with all such schemes: should parents with care (predominantly women) be *forced* to depend on absent parents (predominantly men) for the means to sustain the children, or should they and their children have a right to subsistence regardless of such relationships as they may have had in the past? Related to such questions is should a lone parent's right to assistance be conditional on her not having any more children? The US applies 'family cap' policies, which restrict a lone parent's social assistance entitlement so as to exclude additional help for the support of children conceived while she remains in receipt of state assistance (Walker, 2005).

Summary/conclusion

In addressing the notion of a right to livelihood, this chapter has considered the right to work, the right to subsistence, and some of the complex intersections between them.

Insofar as 'work' may be understood as something more than wage labour – as activity constitutive of human personhood – rights to work inscribed in international human rights instruments and in domestic social legislation are narrowly framed. They reflect a construction of work that is essentially fettered to capitalist relations of production. The international human rights framework constructs the right to work in the first instance as a right to free-dom from slavery – an undeniably essential claim on behalf of all humanity. By implication, however, it then constructs the right to work as a right to freely chosen and justly remuner-ated paid labour. Meanwhile, at a national level, the wage labourer has been constituted as a citizen of a welfare state. Citizen-workers have indeed been able – to a greater or lesser extent – to enjoy rights *at* work, including rights to minimum wages, restricted work-ing hours, health and safety protection, protection against unfair dismissal, rights to equal opportunities and, most recently, rights to 'work-life balance' (thus explicitly acknowledging a certain disjuncture between work as wage labour and the other aspects of human life). It should be noted, however, that nowhere is there to be found an unequivocal right to paid work, that is to say, a specific right to a job.

The right to subsistence is ineluctably entangled with the right to work. It is framed within the international human rights framework in terms of a right to an adequate standard of living, to be underwritten by provision for the social security of those who are otherwise unable to obtain a livelihood – by implication, if they are unable to 'work'. At a national level, welfare states have demonstrated different understandings of 'social security'. In prac-tice, however, it is possible to identify a number of mechanisms or systems through which social security can be provided: social assistance safety nets; preventative social insurance measures; and universal benefits for people in particular demographic categories. Addition-ally, governments can act to maintain citizens' incomes through tax allowances and regula-tory intervention in order to promote and safeguard provision through privately managed schemes. Each approach has its advantages and disadvantages, and the different ways in which countries develop and combine different approaches in relation to the rights of different social groups – including children, disabled people and older people – can be complex and messy.

Most complex and messy of all is provision for people of 'working age', whether they are unemployed, sick or partially disabled, or full-time carers. The question of when within the human life course a person is expected to engage in paid labour and when they might be allowed to desist is socially determined, but such determinations are written into the rules and conditions that govern the subsistence rights of workers. Similarly, the explicit socially determined assumption within the human rights framework and within national social legislation is that workers should sustain not only themselves, but their families – an assumption that translates itself into the rules and conditions that attach to the subsistence rights of working-age adults, as parents and partners within families. In this chapter we have considered recent developments in the field of labour market activation or 'welfare-to-work' policy, and the paradox that though welfare states may not guarantee a right to work, they may enforce a duty to work. And we have considered how welfare states, in the process of administering rights to subsistence within families, may seek to enforce the financial respon-sibilities of parents and partners in ways that can, in some instances, conflict with prevailing understandings of care and responsibility.

Rights to livelihood are in one sense about how people can put food on their tables. But they are about more than that. This is a point to which I shall return in Chapter 10. But in the next chapter, we shall consider rights to some of the human services that are also essential to an adequate standard of living.

7

RIGHTS TO HUMAN SERVICES

The term 'social services' can and has been used (see Titmuss, 1958) to apply to the entire spectrum of governmental interventions intended to meet human needs. However, a distinction may be drawn between, on the one hand, rights to livelihood involving payments of cash transfers intended to enable people to *buy* essential commodities and, on the other, the right to *receive* goods and services that have been to some extent de-commodified or which, having the status of 'merit' goods (Musgrave, 1959), are supplied subject to governmental regulation or oversight. The line between these kinds of social service can be a fine one, but for practical purposes we shall refer to the latter as 'human services'.

Human services, in this sense, are of various kinds. If we consider the right to shelter, we have seen that the right to housing is included in the UDHR as part of the right to an adequate standard of living (Article 25 [1]): housing represents a merit good in relation to which governments may provide services for the planning of the habitable environment and control over the supply of dwellings. The provision of healthcare and education might be regarded as 'bedrock' services: these are the services through which our universal life course needs for health and autonomy (Doyal & Gough, 1991) are met, and which provide the foundation of a civilised human existence. Finally, there are what may be called 'personal' social services which are not universal, but are reserved for the care and protection of the most vulnerable members of society: services for children, disabled people or older people who are at risk or in need of specialised social support.

We have already seen that rights in paid employment, though they may be regulated by social legislation, are fundamentally contractual or civil rights, and this also applies in relation, as we saw in Chapter 6, to rights to occupational or private pensions. The same can be said in relation to rights to the human services identified above, if and when these are provided privately and on a contractual basis. We saw in Chapter 2 that the ICESCR allows for the 'progressive realisation' of social rights, by which it is required that state parties should (see CESCR General Comment 12; and e.g. Shue, 1980):

- in the first instance, *respect* such rights – for example, by refraining from forcibly evicting citizens from their homes, and from disrupting or preventing private or NGO sector educational or health and social care provision;

- second, *protect* such rights – for example, by regulating private or NGO sector housing, educational or health and social care provision; and
- third, *fulfil* such rights – for example, by subsidising and/or directly providing housing, educational or health and social care provision.

Social rights can be promoted or fulfilled through intervention short of direct public sector provision, in which case, where human services are not free at the point of delivery, contractual arrangements between service providers and service users are entailed. The social rights and the contractual/civil rights agendas interact at the point where policy makers intervene in such arrangements. Where governments are concerned to protect or promote human services, they may be concerned to ensure fair and equal access – by providing selective subsidies for those least able to afford the use of services – or to ensure equality of opportunity for women and girls and/or for ethnic or religious minorities. Governments may seek to regulate markets in human services or the terms of contractual relationships so as to guard against the consequences of power imbalances between providers and users, and the risk that users may be exploited. But, where governments seek to provide directly for human need through public sector institutions, social and civil rights may interact in a quite different way: for example, to safeguard the freedom of the service user lest it be jeopardised through the exercise of over-weaning or paternalistic state power. In the realm of human service provision, social and civil rights cannot easily be disentangled.

I shall, in barest outline, discuss generic issues and principles relating to rights to housing, education, healthcare and social care.

Rights to shelter

Like nourishment and raiment, shelter is one of the most elemental of human needs. As with food and clothing, 'housing' is a need that will be met in different ways depending on climatic and cultural conditions. Before human beings ever built 'houses', they established customs or rights as to how spaces and structures for human habitation should be allocated. The idea of what constitutes a 'home' and a 'household' is entirely socially constructed: but so too is the concept of property. We saw in Chapter 1 how the invention of property and the commodity form shaped modern understandings of rights. While the commodification of labour has been fundamental to the framing of the right to work, the commodification of land has been fundamental to the framing of the right to housing. But like labour, land cannot be an ordinary commodity. Land, whether initially occupied by settlement or conquest, or arbitrarily bestowed as the gift of a ruler or despot, is not only an essential livelihood resource, but also, potentially, a source of power and profit. To establish land as private property required a doctrine not of tenure, but title: inalienable and exclusive ownership, with protection against expropriation, the foundations for which were laid in the Fifth Amendment to the US Constitution of 1791 and the French Declaration of the Rights of Man of 1789, the substance of which would be encapsulated in 1948 in the UDHR, which provides for the permissive right to own property and not to be arbitrarily deprived thereof (Article 17; and see Jacobs, 2013). This does not confer a right to housing, but it does furnish the terms on which people may or may not establish the tenure of their homes: as owners, as lessees or tenants, as licensees, or as bare occupants or trespassers. The rights that flow from this – where they exist – are civil not social rights.

At the same time as land – and thereby the housing on which it stands – was turned into a commodity, so the way in which human beings house themselves began to change. Industrialisation depended on the mobility of labour, and this was facilitated as freedom of movement was afforded to agricultural workers, who had in previous eras been tied to the land. In 1800 barely 2 per cent of the world's population lived in cities. By 2000 three-quarters of the 'developed' world's population and nearly a half of all humanity were urban dwellers (UN-HABITAT, 2003). The rapid urbanisation associated with economic development necessitates local governmental intervention to secure the supply of housing and urban infrastructure and to prevent or control the emergence of the 'slums', 'shanty towns' or *favelas* in which the poorest urban inhabitants are likely to find housing. This is the context in which rights to or in relation to housing, as substantive social rights, have emerged. Broadly speaking, such rights fall into four categories:

Consumption subsidies

As intimated in Chapter 6, social security or income maintenance provision can be extended to enable citizens to pay for housing. This may take a variety of forms: as supplements to means-tested social assistance or as separate social assistance–based housing benefit schemes. Such provision, axiomatically, is specifically targeted to low-income households: to provide public sector tenants with rent rebates; to support private or voluntary sector tenants with the payment of rent; and to assist home owners with mortgage interest payments. Such assistance is likely to be conditional not only on a test of means (with all the implications discussed in Chapter 6), but on a variety of other factors. Assistance may be withheld or reduced depending on the age and status of applicants; whether there are members of applicants' households (such as adult sons and daughters) who can be called upon to contribute to housing costs; or whether applicants' housing costs are deemed to be excessive, or their accommodation is deemed to be larger than they require. In Britain, attempts in 2013 to limit the eligibility of low-income households for assistance in high housing cost areas and of public sector housing tenants with 'spare bedrooms' resulted in the displacement of tenants and a condemnatory report by the UN's Special Rapporteur on Housing (Rolnik, 2013). Alternatively, fiscal benefits may be made available to home owners in the form of tax relief, though this is likely indiscriminately to benefit higher income groups – a practice that in Britain, for example, was discontinued in 2000.

Controls over landlords

The history of measures against forcible eviction can in England be traced back to the fourteenth century, when the concern was to prevent summary dispossession. In more recent times landlord and tenant law has developed – both through common law and statute – to maintain principles that protect legitimate tenants and home owners from eviction without due process, though protection for illegal occupants or 'squatters' may be limited. There is insufficient space in this chapter to address the Byzantine complexities of landlord and tenant law in jurisdictions around the world, but it is possible for governments by way of legislation:

- to impose certain minimum obligations upon landlords as implied covenants – for quiet enjoyment and the conduct of repairs – in any or every tenancy agreement;
- to define categories of residential tenancy with specific terms as to security of tenure;

- to supplement remedies available in civil law by the creation of criminal sanctions for illegal eviction or harassment; and
- to regulate the rents that landlords may charge (e.g. McQueen, 2013).

By and large, however, such legislation does not create social rights, so much as support or supplement them through modifications to civil rights.

Environmental protection

The process of urbanisation has provoked governmental concerns with a wide range of spatial governance activities (UN-HABITAT, 2009), including public health controls on the one hand, and strategic and regulatory planning on the other. Public health intervention evolved in industrialised countries when in the nineteenth century overcrowded and insanitary conditions in growing metropolises and conurbations threatened the health of rich and poor alike. Formal processes of urban planning emerged when the unsustainable consequences of unregulated development and land use became self-evident. The resulting interventions, including slum clearance schemes past and present, may indeed promote social rights by raising general living standards, but they do not directly bestow social rights. And, for example, where slum clearances lead to enforced evictions, they may even violate rights (as in the celebrated case of Irene Grootboom before the Constitutional Court of South Africa in the 1990s) (see Liebenberg, 2008). However, public or environmental health legislation may directly benefit people living in substandard conditions when it includes, for example, the imposition of fitness for habitation and overcrowding standards on landlords – especially when rights of complaint are extended to tenants – or provision for home improvement grants for home owners on low incomes (e.g. Stewart, 2001).

Social or public sector housing

Governments can fulfil the right to housing through direct provision. Practices among established welfare states, and over time, have varied enormously. There are some fundamental issues: whether social housing is to be provided to meet general needs or whether it is a form of residual and potentially stigmatised housing tenure reserved for poor and vulnerable people; whether rents chargeable for social housing should be market rents or whether they should be subsidised; whether and how access to social housing should be rationed; and whether people should 'qualify' for social housing on the basis of how long they have been waiting to be housed, the nature and strength of their connections to the locality in which they are seeking to be housed, or simply the urgency of their need. Some welfare states have legislated for a right of homeless persons to be housed (Fitzpatrick & Stephens, 2007), though definitions of 'homelessness' differ and there are no instances in which citizens enjoy an unconditional right to housing. In the British case, for example, the right is restricted to households with children or who are vulnerable and who can establish that their homelessness is genuine and unintentional (Burrows *et al.,* 1997; Liddiard, 2001). A country's decision or self-imposed duty to provide housing may be met by funding voluntary housing bodies to provide suitable accommodation, but it is to be expected that social sector housing – whether provided by a public or a voluntary sector body – will be let subject to a tenancy that affords similar rights and protections to those afforded to private sector tenants.

Rights to education

The right to education articulates a number of needs. On the one hand it gives expression to the basic human need for personal autonomy, though it is necessary here to distinguish between 'thin' and 'thick' understandings of autonomy. Doyal and Gough (1991: 67) contend that though 'basic' autonomy of agency may be minimally necessary for human existence, optimal needs satisfaction requires 'critical autonomy' – a level of autonomy that enables a person actively to participate as a fully fledged social and political actor. On the other hand, the right to education articulates the need of human society to reproduce itself: to perpetuate skills, knowledge and values. This raises questions as to whether education is more of a social requirement of the individual than a right. With whom should responsibility for that requirement rest? The UDHR requires that 'education shall be directed to the full development of the human personality and to the strengthening of respect for human rights and fundamental freedoms' (Article 26 [2]). This envisages that the right is concerned in part with the need for autonomy, and in part with the need to perpetuate a particular set of values.

Insofar as the right to education is concerned with the human individual's need for autonomy, it has been argued that it is not so much a social right as a foundational right – a precondition for the exercise of civil and political rights (e.g. Nowak, 2001). The capacity to function as a citizen in a democratic-welfare-capitalist society requires a minimum level of literacy and basic knowledge. And to function optimally, it needs a great deal more. A citizen's right to 'decent work' may very well depend on the education they have received. There is also a sense in which the realisation of cultural rights, which afford a person the right to share in the benefits of scientific and artistic endeavour (see Chapter 2, this volume), are linked with or depend on educational provision. The ICESCR stresses that 'education shall enable all persons to participate effectively in a free society' (Article 13 [1]). It is significant that in 1966 the right to education was incorporated by the Council of Europe, not in the European Social Charter, but in the European Convention on Human Rights, which is primarily concerned with civil and political rights and states that 'no person shall be denied the right to education' (First Protocol, Article 2). This right is cast not as a positive right, but in terms of freedom of access to provision that is assumed already to exist – as a declaration of the autonomy that is supposed to define the human subject in the first place: a 'freedom right' (Mehedi, 1999).

Insofar as the right to education is concerned with human society's need to reproduce itself, this will inevitably depend on the form of the society it aims to reproduce. When provision for compulsory elementary schooling was first introduced in England, the declared aim was to underwrite the nation's industrial prosperity and the 'safe working of [its] constitutional system' (Forster, 1870). Education has always had an instrumental function as an investment in what has lately been termed 'human capital' (e.g. Giddens, 1998: 47–48) and the means by which children are made ready for the labour market. The development of public educational provision in the global North was regarded as a means to promote national efficiency during the late nineteenth and early twentieth centuries. It was an aim that acquired added momentum following the crisis of the capitalist welfare state in the late twentieth century when there was a renewed utilitarian emphasis on 'vocationalism' (Chitty, 2009). The UDHR, as we have seen, refers to the socially reproductive function of education in rather different terms; it speaks of promoting respect for the noble values expressed in the declaration itself. There is, inevitably, a fine line to be drawn between promoting respect for particular values and indoctrination. The inter-American 'Protocol of San Salvador' of 1988 (sponsored and adopted primarily by Latin America and not the US) elaborates on the values which education should promote by including 'respect for . . . ideological pluralism', which hints, perhaps, at a challenge to hegemonic liberal-individualist assumptions. However, a very different and morally authoritarian interpretation of the reproductive role of education may be seen in the African Charter on Human and People's Rights which in Article 17, having asserted that 'every individual shall have the right to education', then declares: 'The promotion and protection of morals and traditional values recognized by the community shall be the duty of the State', which hints quite strongly at the possibility that education might serve as a means for behavioural control. The development of state education in the global North – certainly during the early part of the twentieth century – quite explicitly entailed mechanisms for the surveillance of children and the supervision of their physical and moral welfare (Donzelot, 1979; Ellis, 2000).

What emerge are four different perspectives on the right to education:

The right to equality of access

Education as a social or 'inter-psychological' process (Vygotsky, 1978) is integral to the human life course, including and especially the processes of informal learning that occur within families during childhood. However, the origins of *formal* education outside the family may be traced to antiquity and the beginnings of human civilisation (Pointer, 1896). Education was implicated in the social divisions and relations of power that were so created, such that formal learning was synonymous with privilege and secular authority, on the one hand, or with religious teaching on the other. Though the Western Enlightenment fomented a spread of learning, education of any substance remained by and large the preserve of the elite. Education for the children of the poor, if it existed, generally amounted to basic instruction provided out of charity or by the church. This remained the case until it became 'almost a self-evident axiom that the State should require and compel the education, up to a certain standard, of every human being who is born its citizen' (Mill, 1859: 175). This realisation, however, did not lead to equality of access.

Expensive private institutions have continued to provide for children of the elite, while the effectiveness of provision in state schools varies – in relation, generally, to the socio-economic circumstances of the households from which their students come (Ball, 2008). The current evidence clearly suggests that across OECD countries the socio-economic background of students and schools appears to have a powerful influence on performance (OECD, 2010). Beyond socio-economic inequalities there are also issues concerning equality of access for women and girls; for ethnic, religious or linguistic minorities; and for disabled people. Segregated or exclusionary education systems provide conspicuous instances of discrimination, and were an early focus for the criticisms of new social movements (see Chapter 4, this volume). They prompted UNESCO in 1960 to adopt the Convention against Discrimination in Education. Later UN conventions against discrimination (see Box 2.3 in Chapter 2, this volume) were to follow. But inequalities endure. Not only are there still parts of the world where girls are effectively excluded from education (UNESCO, 2013), but even well-developed education systems may, for example, offer an essentially gendered 'hidden curriculum' (Pascall, 1997: ch. 4). Though systemic racial segregation in schools (for example, in the US and South Africa) has been ended, effective segregation and educational disadvantage may persist as a result of social exclusionary processes, and the aims and objectives of 'multicultural' education remain controversial (Modood, 2007). Despite demands that children with special educational needs should so far as possible be integrated within mainstream educational provision rather than consigned to suboptimal segregated schooling (UNESCO, 1994; Warnock, 1978), progress towards this aim has been uneven. In England, it seems, such progress may have recently been reversed, despite clear evidence of the consequent educational disadvantages for disabled children (CRAE, 2013: para. 79; Roulstone & Prideaux, 2012: ch. 4).

The right to education that is free, but compulsory

There is a certain paradox that the right to education is now framed as an enforceable requirement. The moral duty of parents to teach their children or to have them in some manner schooled may once have been policed or supplemented by religious authority, but the encroachment of the state meant that, for it to be compulsory, education had to be free. For households in which subsistence might depend on the labour of children, compulsory schooling imposes a burden to which it is unreasonable or impractical to add by charging school fees. The systematic extension of compulsory education for all children – not only elementary or primary education but in due course secondary education – had already begun in industrialised countries even before the UDHR of 1948 declared that elementary education, at least, should be both free and compulsory (Article 26 [1]). Giving effect to the declaration, the ICESCR of 1966 (Article 13) clarified that secondary education should also be made 'generally available'; that higher education should be available on the basis of merit or 'capacity'; and that both secondary and higher education should be accessible to all and 'progressively' (i.e. eventually) free.

Internationally, therefore, it is only primary education that is unequivocally a right, though domestic legislation within established welfare states and many emerging economies has extended that right to secondary education, characteristically by imposing an enforceable duty on parents to make arrangements for the education of their children up to a specified age (for overview, see UNESCO, 2011). Arrangements for higher education are highly variable and in England, for example, free tuition at the higher education level has recently been withdrawn (Callender, 2010). But, though tuition at primary and (in some countries) secondary levels may be free, education does not necessarily come free of all costs. There are wider issues for all education systems as to whether parents should have to pay for their children to travel to school; for school meals and uniforms; for books, materials and extra-curricular activities; or whether there may be undue pressure in some schools upon parents to make 'voluntary' financial contributions: such costs may represent a barrier to educational access (e.g. Smith & Noble, 1995).

The rights of parents

There is some ambiguity as to whom the right to education belongs. In one sense it is the right of parents to have their children educated. In practice, however, parents' rights are for the most part restricted to 'a prior right to choose the kind of education that shall be given to their children' (UDHR, Article 26 [3]), though the ICESCR makes clear that parents must be at liberty 'to choose for their children schools, other than those established by the public authorities, which conform to such minimum educational standards as may be laid down or approved by the State' (Article 13 [3]). Additionally, both the ICCPR (Article 18 [4]) and the ICECSR accord parents the right to ensure that the religious and moral education of their children is 'in conformity with their own convictions'. Parental rights of choice may, therefore, enable parents to educate their children independently or privately (subject to regulatory oversight); to send their children to religious schools conforming to minimum educational standards; to choose between single sex and co-educational schools; to withdraw their children, for example, from any religious or sex education lessons of which they disapprove; and to choose between state schools.

The consequence of this is that it is possible for social segregation or differentiation between schools to occur not by design, but through the effects of parental choice, and for inequalities between schools to multiply. What is more, parents lacking the resources to pay for private alternatives to state education, or the ability to move between neighbourhoods, may in practice have limited or no choice as to which school to send their children. Nevertheless, the right of choice between state schools may in some countries be linked to the idea that parents should be encouraged to behave as consumers in a market, and that they should have the right to receive published information regarding the performance of the schools between which they must choose. This has been the case, for example, in England, where the introduction of new public management principles has been used to drive competition between schools through the production and publication of performance-based league tables, enabling parents to discriminate between schools (Chitty, 2009).

However, though parents may in theory have a right of choice between schools, they generally have no choice but to send their children to school, and they may be liable to prosecution and penalties should they fail to do so and have not made satisfactory alternative arrangements. We have already noted (in Chapter 6) that in some parts of the world a right to conditional cash transfers may be provided as an incentive for parents to send their children to school, albeit that this may be withdrawn as a sanction should they fail to comply.

The rights of children

We might suppose that the right to be educated belongs to the child, but we have seen that education up to a certain level is supposedly compulsory and that it is parents, not children, who have the right of choice over the manner of their children's education. As Daniel and Ivatts put it, although education policy is, in effect, social policy for children, 'rather than children's needs being placed at the forefront of education policy consideration, a variety of adult concerns and perspectives determine the policy outcomes' (1998: 168). Critics of the National Curriculum, first introduced to English schools in the 1980s, complained that it conformed to a 'factory-farm model of education, in which each child, like a battery hen, is to assimilate as much as possible of the food offered to it' (Kelly, 1994: 94). Similar critiques have been advanced in relation to educational systems throughout the world (Freire, 1972). Nevertheless, the UN Convention on the Rights of the Child (UNCRC) of 1989 explicitly recognises the right of the child to education (Article 28) and elaborates this broadly in accordance with the principles of the UDHR and ICESCR.

While the notion that children might be regarded as having inalienable rights as autonomous persons is in several respects contentious (for a discussion, see Freeman, 2000), the UNCRC establishes two general principles of particular significance in the context of children's relationships with parents, teachers and educational establishments (not to mention other welfare professionals and institutions):

- that 'In all actions concerning children, whether undertaken by public or private social welfare institutions . . . the best interests of the child shall be a primary consideration' (Article 3); and
- that a child who is 'capable of forming his or her own views' should be assured 'the right to express those views freely in all matters affecting the child, the views of the child being given due weight in accordance with the age and maturity of the child' (Article 12).

In theory, this might give children the rights to some say in their education, though in practice the provisions conflict so long as it is adults who are the arbiters of the child's best interests.

Rights to health

Health is one of the two basic needs specified by Doyal and Gough's (1991) theory of human need. The preamble to the 1946 Constitution of the World Health Organisation (WHO) declared that the 'the enjoyment of the highest attainable standard of health is one of the fundamental rights of every human being', a principle echoed in the ICESCR (Article 12 [1]) which commits states parties to recognising the right both to physical and mental health. Other than in its constitution, however, the WHO has for the most part avoided the language of rights. Nevertheless, the UN's Special Rapporteur on Health has lately argued that the right to health is to be understood as the right to 'an effective and integrated health system, encompassing both healthcare and the underlying determinants of health' (Hunt, 2006: para. 4). He further stressed that 'an effective health system is a core social institution, no less than a court system or a political system' (para. 20). With this in mind, the principal issues are as follows.

The determinants of health

In the preamble to its constitution, the WHO defined health as 'a state of complete physical, mental and social well-being and not merely the absence of disease or infirmity'. This sets an ostensibly *un*attainable standard: nobody can be completely healthy for the whole of her life! The significance of the definition, however, lies in the emphasis on social context of health, not just the treatment of individual illness (Marks, 2013). Here, the right to health intersects with the right to housing (see above) and to a healthy environment. The ICESCR of 1966 committed states parties to 'the improvement of all aspects of environmental and industrial hygiene' (Article 12 [2]). Two decades later environmental issues had moved up the global political agenda, and the right to a healthy environment was regarded as a component of a 'third' generation of human rights (Boyle, 2007; and see Chapter 9, this volume). For example, the Protocol of San Salvador explicitly declared that 'everyone shall have the right to live in a healthy environment' (Article 11). It is speculated that, had he been alive, T. H. Marshall might have added environmental rights as a category of citizenship rights (Newby, 1996; Van Steenbergen, 1994).

But before this, as we have seen, public health had already become a predominant concern informing the development of urban infrastructure in the global North. Indeed, the history of public health technologies – of water supply and sanitation – can be traced back further, to ancient Egyptian, Greek, Roman and Inca civilisations. And such concerns are now a major preoccupation in many parts of the global South (UNDP, 2006; UN-HABITAT, 2009). Good health is dependent on a variety of preconditions: most fundamentally, a safe water supply and adequate sanitation. In the current era it also requires protection against risks from environmental pollution, occupational hazards and overcrowded or substandard housing. And beyond the infrastructural determinants of health, as medical science and knowledge advances, it has become possible to protect human populations from infectious diseases through immunisation programmes, health promotion initiatives and health education (Cahill, 2002; Toebs, 2001; WHO, 2008). Public or environmental health policies may not directly fulfil the right to health, but vitally, they promote it.

The accessibility of healthcare to all

The ICESCR commits states parties to 'the creation of conditions which would assure to all medical service and medical attention in the event of sickness' (Article 12). As with education, the history of medical practice and the provision of healthcare date from antiquity (Bynum, 2008). In the pre-industrial era in the West it had assumed the form of fee-paying services for those who could afford to pay and informal or charitable provision for those who could not. Industrialisation, however, gave employers a potential interest in healthcare provision (at least, for their more highly skilled workers), while the people for whom sickness coincided with destitution placed growing demands on the Poor Laws (Doyal, 1979). What would emerge was a mixture of private and voluntary health insurance arrangements, which in some countries were subsumed into national health insurance schemes – and alongside, a variety of public and municipal healthcare institutions, which in some countries were subsumed into a national health service.

The accessibility of healthcare and the precise content of the right to health is largely dependent on the model of funding that applies within any particular country, of which there are, broadly speaking, three: the private market–based model with a medical assistance safety net; the social insurance model with state co-ordinated medical provision; and the tax-funded national health service model. (There is a direct conceptual parallel with the distinction between social assistance, social insurance and universal/contingent models of social security provision, discussed in Chapter 6.) In practice, health service provision around the world may comprise elements from more than one model and tends currently to be in a process of flux or reform (Watson, 2013). Inevitably, systems that are more heavily dependent on private provision provide less equal access than national health services that are free to all at the point of use. Nevertheless, even services that are free at the point of use may systemically fail to provide adequately for patients whose health needs are the greatest (Marmot, 2010; Tudor-Hart, 1971). And, where rights of access are conditional on citizenship, the rights of migrants may be denied (Toebs, 2001; Weaite, 2013; and see Chapter 5, this volume).

Rights of patients

An individual person's right to health implies a correlative duty on others. The duties of private healthcare providers will be defined by contracts and service-level agreements. The duties of healthcare professionals will be governed by professional doctrines or codes of conduct (of which the most famous is the Hippocratic Oath). The duties of states are defined in human rights instruments and/or are self-imposed through social legislation. For example, the British National Health Service (NHS), founded in 1948, was established on the basis of legislation that placed a clear duty on the minister of health to establish a comprehensive health service for the prevention, diagnosis and treatment of illness – a duty modified in 2012 as the government of the day sought to devolve the administration of a largely state funded, but increasingly fragmentary and marketised, service to local commissioning bodies (Pollock & Price, 2013). Critics contend that this dilutes the right to health, but even prior to this the courts had ruled that though NHS patients had rights of access to and a choice of providers, they had never had a direct right to NHS resources (Lenaghan, 1997; Weaite, 2013). We shall see below and again in Chapter 8 that disputes over access to expensive medicines and treatments have been a salient issue throughout the world.

But for now we are concerned with just what a right to health guaranteed by the state can in practice amount to. Returning to the example of the British NHS, Box 7.1 sets out the charter of patients' rights provided in the NHS constitution for England. It may be seen that this does not embody an unequivocal right to health, which arguably would be impracticable for any state. It falls short of a right to demand a specific treatment, but one of the important substantive rights afforded in charters of this nature is the patient's right of informed choice and her right to refuse such treatment as is offered. However, in the case of patients with mental health problems there is legislation in place in many countries to allow treatment, subject to procedural safeguards, to be administered compulsorily (WHO, 2005). The issue of choice, however, is problematic not only for people whose ability to exercise choice may be impaired through mental health problems, but for all human beings when they may be suffering illness, because of fundamental disparities of power between patients and healthcare professionals. The fiercest critics of such disparities complain of the risks of iatrogenic medicine: practices that may worsen rather than improve health (e.g. Illich et al., 1977). Critically important to the individual right to health is just who is entrusted with the duty to meet that right and on what terms.

Rationing healthcare

I have already indicated that there can seldom in practice be a right of unqualified access to particular drugs or medical treatments. The resources necessary for healthcare are likely to be rationed because, on the one hand, resources may be scarce, while on the other, demand for healthcare can accelerate as a result of population ageing (Grover, 2011) and the multiplication of 'technical needs' generated by scientific discovery and new medical treatments (Forder, 1974). The right to medical intervention may therefore be made conditional, for example, on a prediction of a person's 'quality adjusted life years' (QALYs – a system controversially developed in Oregon, USA) or on generic guidance issued on the basis of an official cost-benefit analysis of different drugs and medical procedures (such as that provided in England by the National Institute for Health and Care Excellence (NICE) – see Box 7.1). More generally, there are questions about whether public funds should be allocated to treat potentially avoidable illnesses – such as obesity or diseases attributable to tobacco or excessive alcohol consumption – or to provide fertility treatment, cosmetic surgery or other arguably non-essential procedures that may nevertheless have great significance for those who seek them (Bochel, 2005).

BOX 7.1 COMMENTARY ON PATIENTS' RIGHTS CONTAINED IN THE NHS CONSTITUTION FOR ENGLAND, 2013

Access to health services:

*   to receive NHS services free of charge, apart from certain limited exceptions sanctioned by Parliament.[1]
*   to access NHS services. You will not be refused access on unreasonable grounds.[1]
*   to expect your NHS to assess the health requirements of your community and to commission and put in place the services to meet those needs as considered necessary, and in the case of public health services commissioned by local authorities, to take steps to improve the health of the local community.[2]
*   in certain circumstances, to go to other European Economic Area countries or Switzerland for treatment which would be available to you through your NHS commissioner.[1 & 3]
*   not to be unlawfully discriminated against in the provision of NHS services including on grounds of gender, race, disability, age, sexual orientation, religion, belief, gender reassignment, pregnancy and maternity or marital or civil partnership status.[3]
*   to access certain services commissioned by NHS bodies within maximum waiting times, or for the NHS to take all reasonable steps to offer you a range of suitable alternative providers if this is not possible. The waiting times are described in the *Handbook to the NHS Constitution.*[1]

Quality of care and environment:

*   to be treated with a professional standard of care, by appropriately qualified and experienced staff, in a properly approved or registered organisation that meets required levels of safety and quality.[3]
*   to expect NHS bodies to monitor, and make efforts to improve continuously, the quality of healthcare they commission or provide. This includes improvements to the safety, effectiveness and experience of services.[2]

Nationally approved treatments, drugs and programmes:

*   to drugs and treatments that have been recommended by NICE for use in the NHS, if your doctor says they are clinically appropriate for you.[1]
*   to expect local decisions on funding of other drugs and treatments to be made rationally following a proper consideration of the evidence. If the local NHS decides not to fund a drug or treatment you and your doctor feel would be right for you, they will explain that decision to you.[2]
*   to receive the vaccinations that the Joint Committee on Vaccination and Immunisation recommends that you should receive under an NHS-provided national immunisation programme.[1]

Respect, consent and confidentiality:

*   to be treated with dignity and respect, in accordance with your human rights.[3]
*   to accept or refuse treatment that is offered to you, and not to be given any physical examination or treatment unless you have given valid consent. If you do not have the capacity to do so, consent must be obtained from a person legally able to act on your behalf, or the treatment must be in your best interests.[3]
*   to be given information about the test and treatment options available to you, what they involve and their risks and benefits.[3]
*   of access to your own health records and to have any factual inaccuracies corrected.[3]

- to privacy and confidentiality and to expect the NHS to keep your confidential information safe and secure.[3]
- to be informed about how your information is used.[3]
- to request that your confidential information is not used beyond your own care and treatment and to have your objections considered, and where your wishes cannot be followed, to be told the reasons including the legal basis.[3]

Informed choice:

- to choose your GP practice, and to be accepted by that practice unless there are reasonable grounds to refuse, in which case you will be informed of those reasons.[4]
- to express a preference for using a particular doctor within your GP practice, and for the practice to try to comply.[4]
- to make choices about the services commissioned by NHS bodies and to information to support these choices. The options available to you will develop over time and depend on your individual needs. Details are set out in the *Handbook to the NHS Constitution*.[1 & 4]

Involvement in your healthcare and in the NHS:

- to be involved in discussions and decisions about your health and care, including your end of life care, and to be given information to enable you to do this. Where appropriate this right includes your family and carers.[4]
- to be involved, directly or through representatives, in the planning of healthcare services commissioned by NHS bodies, the development and consideration of proposals for changes in the way those services are provided, and in decisions to be made affecting the operation of those services.[4]

Complaint and redress:

- to have any complaint you make about NHS services acknowledged within three working days and to have it properly investigated.[5]
- to discuss the manner in which the complaint is to be handled, and to know the period within which the investigation is likely to be completed and the response sent.[5]
- to be kept informed of progress and to know the outcome of any investigation into your complaint, including an explanation of the conclusions and confirmation that any action needed in consequence of the complaint has been taken or is proposed to be taken.[5]
- to take your complaint to the independent Parliamentary and Health Service Ombudsman or Local Government Ombudsman, if you are not satisfied with the way your complaint has been dealt with by the NHS.[5]
- to make a claim for judicial review if you think you have been directly affected by an unlawful act or decision of an NHS body or local authority.[3]
- to compensation where you have been harmed by negligent treatment.[3]

Notes/commentary:

1. A right subject to qualification or dependent on judgements by some higher authority.
2. A right to *expect* something: not a substantive right.
3. A right already established in international or domestic law (e.g. equalities or data protection legislation) or, for example, implied by professional codes of practice.
4. A right to choose a service provider, express a preference or to be involved in decisions: not the same as a definitive right to receive a specific treatment.
5. A right of complaint: not a substantive right of appeal against a disputed decision or clinical judgement.

Rights to social care

Finally, in this chapter I turn to social rights that pertain to particularly vulnerable groups in society. Whereas everybody needs the means of subsistence, housing, education and healthcare in the course of their lives, they do not *necessarily* require social intervention to protect them from abuse when they are children; to assist them with physical, mental or intellectual impairments during their life course; or with frailty during old age. Any of us might very well experience such needs at some stage (especially as we grow older), but they call for forms of care or support that may be specialised and that we might group together using the collective term 'social care'. They are forms of care and support that have been characteristically provided or organised by professional social workers (Glasby, 2012). Insofar as we may speak of rights to social care, such rights were not clearly bestowed either by the legislative frameworks of capitalist welfare states or by the international human rights framework. Though there had been provision for the 'protection' of children, the 'rehabilitation' of disabled persons and the 'welfare' of older people, it is comparatively recently that the specific rights of children, disabled persons and older people have achieved discreet and specific international recognition. And it was only the European Social Charter of 1961 that committed contracting parties 'to promote or provide services which, by using methods of social work, would contribute to the welfare and development of both individuals and groups in the community, and to their adjustment to the social environment' (Article 14 [1]). By and large, therefore, rights to social care had been implicitly inferred from the statutory duties and professional codes of social workers. These are rights that in a sense do not fit with the liberal ideal of the autonomous rights-bearing individual because they are rights asserted by or on behalf of persons whose autonomy is (or is assumed to be) compromised by immaturity, impairment or age – and whose claims are rooted in potential or manifest vulnerability. And yet they are social rights precisely because vulnerability and lack of autonomy are in some measure socially constructed. They are artefacts of the ways in which society determines the following: the character and effective duration of childhood dependency and when and how responsible adulthood is assumed to begin (Gittens, 1993); the social significance and practical implications of physical, mental or intellectual impairment (Oliver, 1990); and the substantive meaning and lived realities of chronological ageing, and the point at which active social engagement is assumed to diminish (Townsend, 1991). Though they have important issues in common, I shall consider the rights of each vulnerable social group in turn.

Children's rights

I have already touched on the rights of children in relation to education and the significance of the UNCRC's emphasis on the paramountcy of the best interests of the child (Article 3). It is a principle that sits awkwardly with the idea that children should also be allowed a right to identity (Article 8) and respect for their views (Article 12), but critically it expresses a right to care and to be cared for. The UNCRC clarifies the extent to which the social rights proclaimed in the UDHR should apply to children, but it goes further in addressing issues largely glossed over in other major human rights instruments by specifying an explicit duty on the part of states parties to take legislative measures 'to protect the child from all forms of physical or mental violence, injury or abuse, neglect or negligent treatment, maltreatment or exploitation, including sexual abuse, while in the care of parent(s), legal guardian(s) or any other person who has the care of the child' (Article 19 [1]). The significance of this is that it places into a rights-based framework social work practices that had been developing for at least a century. The earliest forms of social work practices in the late nineteenth century in England, for example, had entailed interventions by philanthropic and state bodies who were concerned with rescuing the children of the perishing classes, while controlling the children of the dangerous classes (Younghusband, 1964). Children and young people at risk were both a worry and a threat – a target not only for care, but also discipline. The subsequent development and ethos of professional child protection or 'safeguarding' work has been strongly influenced by contemporary behavioural and social scientific theory and psycho-therapeutic methods (Halmos, 1973; Howe, 2009). But its practical functions are the support and supervision of families in which children are in need or at risk and of children engaged in dangerous or illegal activities; in addition, child protection services provide alternative care for children deprived of, or who have been removed from, their families.

Children's rights to social care arise when their families may be judged to be dysfunctional. In recent years the scope of this right has been extended to embrace a particular concern with early childhood care and education programmes, which are believed to enhance children's cognitive development and improve their subsequent educational attainment, economic productivity and prospects for social mobility (Allen, 2011; UNESCO, 2007). This raises complex issues. In much of the global North, there has been pressure to extend early years' childcare so as to facilitate greater labour force participation by mothers, but there remains some controversy regarding the boundary between care and education and just how to define the best interests of the child (Moss, 2005). Also implicit in the linking of early childhood care and education with the aim of enhancing social mobility is a suggestion that it is parental neglect or incompetence rather than the material disadvantage experienced by poorer families that accounts for enduring social inequalities: the best interests of children might better be served through rights to higher living standards (Morabito *et al.*, 2013). Social care, in its literal sense, must be understood in its broadest context.

Disabled persons' rights

Every human being is subject to some degree of vulnerability during childhood, but any human being may also experience vulnerability – sometimes from childhood, sometimes later in life – as a result of disability. I have already discussed disability and its meaning in Chapter 4, in the context of the critiques of social rights emanating from the disability awareness movement. Disability may be evaluated and understood not as a direct effect of biological impairment or dysfunction, but of society's response: as a consequence of the substance, character and adequacy of social care. For so long as disability is regarded as a medical problem, disabled people may be accorded rights to social security – though subject, as we have seen, to whether they might be adjudged capable of paid employment; to housing – though this may depend on the extent of structural adaptations and personal supervision this might entail; to education – though subject, as we have seen, to how their 'special needs' might be accommodated; and to healthcare – though this is likely to focus on measures to rehabilitate or 'normalise' the patient (Wolfensberger, 1972). The UN's adoption in 2006 of the Convention on the Rights of Persons with Disabilities is comparatively recent. It addresses the extent to which the impairments experienced by disabled people 'in interaction with various barriers may hinder their full and effective participation in society on an equal basis with others' (Article 1).

This emphasis accommodates the 'social model' of disability, but the emphasis throughout the document is very much on individual autonomy and choice – independent living and the principle that disabled people should so far as possible enjoy equal access to the built environment, the labour market, and to commercial and public services. This rather elides the right to respectful care and a reasonable quality of life for those disabled people with limited agency and extensive needs (Shakespeare, 2006). Article 19 of the convention expressly endorses the existing drive towards social inclusion and care in the community: the right to 'have access to a range of in-home, residential and other community support services, including personal assistance necessary to support living and inclusion in the community, and to prevent isolation or segregation from the community'. Social workers and other care workers engage increasingly in the organisation and/or delivery of residential or domiciliary care for disabled people within or as near as possible to the community. But critics have questioned whether care *in* the community can be the same as care *by* the community (Bornat *et al.,* 1993). It is difficult to legislate for 'community' or social care in this last sense. Legislation in Britain, for example, has for some years entitled disabled people (including children with special educational needs) to an assessment and statement of their needs, and albeit that the resulting statement does not statutorily oblige social care, health or educational agencies provide for the needs identified (Balloch & Hill, 2007). The problem, in part, is that social care in its widest sense necessitates a holistic understanding of needs. If public resources are scarce and responsibility is fragmented between separate, often relatively specialised, social service agencies, planning and co-ordination is difficult.

Older people's rights

Human beings generally hope or at least expect to grow old. The process has implications for their autonomy and for their health. As with childhood and disability, the experience is shaped by social context, specifically, by customs and expectations relating to 'retirement' – to which Townsend once referred as a 'kind of mass redundancy' (1981: 6); and with regard to housing and living arrangements. Rising living standards and medical advances mean it is possible for people not only to live longer, but also to remain healthy and to live independently for longer than ever before. Nevertheless, the extent to which this occurs is highly unequal around the world (WHO, 2008), and it remains the case that the need for healthcare resulting from degenerative disorders is likely to be at its greatest during the final years of life. However, frailty during old age entails needs for care that are broadly similar to those of disabled people that we have discussed above. The UN has not adopted a convention on the rights of older people, but as part of an International Plan of Action on Ageing, it did adopt certain 'Principles for Older Persons'. These might be inferred as a statement of rights and they include a specific set of 'principles' under the heading of 'care' (see Box 7.2). While acknowledging that family and community care may accord with a society's cultural values, pronouncements as to the freedoms, autonomy and respect that should be accorded to older people set certain standards of care, and there is clear reference to 'appropriate levels' of institutional care. The ability of families in advanced or post-industrial societies to provide sustained and intensive care for frail elderly relatives is much diminished as a result of

BOX 7.2   THE RIGHTS OF OLDER PERSONS TO CARE

According to the United Nations Principles for Older Persons, adopted by the General Assembly on 16 December 1991, older persons should:

- benefit from family and community care and protection in accordance with each society's system of cultural values;
- have access to health care to help them to maintain or regain the optimum level of physical, mental and emotional well-being and to prevent or delay the onset of illness;
- have access to social and legal services to enhance their autonomy, protection and care;
- be able to utilize appropriate levels of institutional care providing protection, rehabilitation and social and mental stimulation in a humane and secure environment; and
- be able to enjoy human rights and fundamental freedoms when residing in any shelter, care or treatment facility, including full respect for their dignity, beliefs, needs and privacy and for the right to make decisions about their care and the quality of their lives.

demographic, economic and cultural factors, and some countries are already establishing social insurance arrangements to assist with the costs of long-term social care for older people (Barr, 2010; Peng, 2002). More broadly, however, it is particularly in the sphere of social care for frail older people that the right to care as a social good (Daly, 2002), and the distribution and management of that good, becomes contentious. In what circumstances can social care be care that is – as of right – supervised, assisted or even provided by the state?

Summary/conclusion

This chapter has considered social rights to human services, that is to say, to such essential goods as housing, education, health provision and social care. They are rights that nation states have been enjoined to respect and, so far as possible, promote and/or fulfil. Rights to such services may be understood as *social* rights insofar as they are articulations of human needs, but where needs are met by the market or by market mechanisms social rights necessarily intersect with *civil* rights.

The right to housing intersects with the realm of land-related private property rights. Social rights may come into play in the form of rights to assistance with the costs of housing; rights that flow directly from statutory controls over rent levels and the conduct of landlords; rights that flow indirectly from government attempts to regulate and plan the built environment; and rights that result from the promotion, subsidy or provision of dwellings, including in some instances, a right to be housed in the event of homelessness.

The right to education appears to articulate ambiguous needs or purposes: it may serve fully to develop the human personality or specifically to shape the values and skills of the individual. Social rights may come into play in the form of rights to equality of access to educational opportunities; rights to education that is free, but which is nevertheless compulsory; rights on the part of parents to choose how their children shall be educated; and rights of children to be educated, albeit that it is a right they cannot refuse.

The right to health, to be optimally effective, depends on processes that must be systemic, integrated and sustainable. This is inherently difficult to achieve. Social rights come into play in the form of rights that flow indirectly from government attempts to maintain a healthy environment; rights of access to personal healthcare services, whether provided in the private or the public sector; rights in some instances to choose from whom to seek, and whether to accept, medical treatment; and rights which, under conditions of escalating demand and scarce resources, are likely to be subject to constraint and fall short of an unconditional right to treatment.

The right to social care articulates the needs of vulnerable members of society. Though it is a right that might apply to anybody, it can too easily be marginalised: it requires specialised provision, yet a holistic understanding of human need. Social rights come into play in the form of the right of children to be safeguarded from the effects of abusive or negligent care; the right of disabled people to be socially included, which requires that in addition to their right to optimise their health and autonomy, they have the right to respectful care; and the rights of older people, who may need safeguarding from the consequences of socially inflicted disempowerment, but whose rights to care in the event of significant frailty in old age are the same and just as important as the rights of other 'disabled' people.

We have seen that rights to human services are subject in practice to limits, complexities and contradictions. But to understand such rights as articulations of human need allows us to appraise them as goods that are essential to the fabric of society.

8

RIGHTS OF REDRESS

Rights that remain unfulfilled or that are dishonoured do not necessarily cease to *be*. But to exist in any meaningful sense, rights must be effective. They cannot be effective unless they are asserted. To survive once established, rights must continue either to be specifically enforceable, or else it must be possible for people who have been denied rights to seek some form of redress. This applies as much to social rights as any other kind. If we are to understand social rights as articulations of need they are constituted through an ongoing interactive process of bottom-up claims making and top-down doctrinal prescription – of challenge and concession. We have seen that social rights are not the same as legal or civil rights, yet in a democratic-welfare-capitalist state they depend for their definition on the law-making process and in many instances they necessarily intersect with the civil law. The legal and administrative machinery of a welfare state will generally provide the individual with at least some means of redress if she cannot obtain or enforce those rights. When constituted as human rights, the enforceability of social rights is altogether less certain, though the international legal framework provides the context in which the interpretation and development of social rights can and does occur.

This chapter is in two parts. The first considers the relationship between social rights and the law. It will discuss the process by which social policy provision has been 'juridified'; the issue of access to legal expertise and the role of lawyers; and the enduring debate as to whether social rights can or should be justiciable. The second part examines the different levels at which redress in relation to social rights may be obtained, focusing on international monitoring arrangements, the role of the courts at the national level and the significance of administrative mechanisms of redress.

Social rights and the law

Albeit in different ways, the founding 'fathers' of the sociological tradition – Durkheim, Weber and Marx – had regarded the evolution of modern law and the administrative state in the post-Enlightenment period as integral to the emergence of capitalist societies (Hunt, 1978). But they had not foreseen the emergence of the welfare state and the manner in which social rights of citizenship might be framed. We have seen in Chapter 4 how contemporary theorists have adapted the Marxist critique of rights to an analysis of social rights, but other thinkers have also considered the relevance of law and jurisprudence to social rights in capitalist welfare states. The discretionary relief once administered under the Poor Laws assumed a new form: a legalised form, whereby official decisions were subjected 'to the governance of predetermined rules' (Jowell, 1975: 2). This legalisation and the consequent juridification of social administration presented what Teubner (1987) describes as a 'regulatory trilemma'. As a systems theorist, Teubner regards the law and social administration as separate 'autopoietic systems', each with its own integrity and distinctive self-regulatory knowledge. The framing of social rights as rights of welfare state citizenship brought these two systems into collision with one another and in the process three things could happen.

First, the systems might prove *incongruous*. In Britain, for example, even before the consolidation of the post–Second World War welfare state, policy makers had deliberately and systematically attempted to frame social policy provision in ways that insulated it from judicial scrutiny (Cranston, 1985: 287–288). Second, the process might lead to the *over-socialisation* of law. This was the outcome feared by lawyers adhering to the classical legal theory, famously exemplified by Dicey's (1885) insistence on judicial purity: the principle that the law must be kept above politics and policy making. The supposition was that the judiciary, far from being a constitutional check upon the legislature and the executive, might be reduced to an overstrained political instrument (Harden & Lewis, 1986; Luhmann, 1987). Third, the process might alternatively lead to the *over-legalisation* of social administration. This is the outcome identified by Habermas, who contends that juridification is part of the process by which technical welfare systems can colonise the life world of the individual subject (1987; and see Tweedie & Hunt, 1994). A related sociological interpretation is that the relationship between the state and the individual becomes 'fundamentally depoliticised – referenced in terms of welfare instead of power' (Garland, 1981: 43): social rights, in other words, become an expression of inviolable legal principles, not negotiable social policies. These three possible outcomes can be presented as a hypothetical trilemma, or simply as three ways of problematising the relationship between social rights and law. The reality, of course, is complicated. We shall consider the development of legal remedies in the second part of this chapter, but for now I shall discuss, on the one hand, how it is that lawyers have been drawn into the realm of social rights and, on the other, whether or not that is a realm that can appropriately be subject to judicial oversight.

Access to justice

When T. H. Marshall delivered the lectures on which the ground-breaking paper setting out his concept of social rights was based, he used the occasion to mark the publication of the Legal Aid and Advice Bill by which the British government was to extend the provision of state-funded legal aid, subject to a means-test, to civil legal matters (1950: 29–31). This he plainly regarded as an extension of social rights. Legal aid might alternatively be regarded as a civil right, since it guarantees effective access to the courts; as a foundational right that is 'conservative of all other rights' (e.g. Durbach, 2008: 59); or even as a 'fourth right of citizenship' (NCC, 1977). In practice, as we shall see, legal aid is not necessarily available directly to support litigation in relation to disputes concerning *social* rights, but it is worth a moment to discuss the provenance and development of legal aid. As with other social services, the origins of legal aid are to be found in philanthropic provision and, for example, the 'dock brief' system by which litigants and defendants coming before the court without means might have counsel assigned from any willing to take on their cases free of charge (Zander, 1978: ch. 1). Public funding for the defence of criminal prosecutions in which the liberty of the subject was at stake has become a human rights obligation (Article 14 of the ICCPR of 1966), though it is a right extended in several jurisdictions to assistance in civil cases involving, for example, risks of domestic violence or homelessness (Durbach, 2008). However, legal aid systems generally direct state funds to underwrite the costs of lawyers in private practice, to whom the poorest and least advantaged in society are unlikely to turn (e.g. Mameli, 1997). Additionally, statutory provision for civil legal aid has been or is being curtailed in some jurisdictions (especially in England – see Boon, 2001; The Alliance for Legal Aid, 2014).

In the area of social rights, however, provision of *specialist* legal assistance remains very much the provenance of the voluntary sector. The beginnings of a welfare rights movement can be traced back to the 1960s, and such developments as the pioneering approach adopted by neighbourhood law firms in the US were staffed by radical young lawyers. This was in part, a self-funded activity fuelled by the civil rights movement, but also sponsored for a while under the Economic Opportunity Act of 1964 as part of President Johnson's 'War on Poverty'. The first director of the Office of Economic Opportunity had described these legal services as the 'heavy artillery' in the war on poverty (Carlin *et al.,* 1967). Britain, in the 1970s, witnessed the emergence – of its own law centre movement, based on the US example (Stephens, 1982): a variety of community-based projects undertaking welfare rights casework – often grant aided by local government – and campaigning charitable bodies, such as the Child Poverty Action Group, committed to 'test case strategies', whereby they would take social rights cases for rulings before the higher courts (Prosser, 1983).

It was an era in which the legal profession and an emerging breed of paralegal welfare rights experts went out into the world as 'secular missionaries . . . to do important ethical work' (Gearty, 2011: 34); to bring new 'counter-hegemonic strategies' to bear in support of the welfare rights movement (Hunt, 1990); and to empower the powerless. The secular missionaries were not without their critics. Neo-Marxist and 'critical' legal theorists agonised that far from being counter-hegemonic, such strategies channelled or co-opted working-class resistance into bureaucratic and legal modes of participation. The welfare rights movement, while seeking to undermine the abstract 'high bourgeois image' of the law, succeeded in bringing it closer to people (Bankowski & Mungham, 1976). In so doing lawyers and welfare rights workers, far from empowering their clients, were dehumanising them by negating people's own understanding and experience of how problems might be solved. Contemporary sceptics continue to express concern lest social rights activists carry with them a partiality for the law that eclipses the necessarily open-textured nature of social rights and the 'necessity of politics' (Gearty, 2011: 52). The risk was fully realised by at least one such secular missionary (this author) when he wrote:

> The illusion created by a society whose complex laws and bureaucratic procedures isolate and oppress the individual is that people's problems appear to be 'personal' and that the only possible solutions to those problems appear to be those that are that professionally administered.

> (Brixton Advice Centre, 1976: 13–14)

TABLE 8.1 The pros and cons of legal strategies in the field of social rights activism

Pros	Cons
• Empowers individuals and groups	• Can individuate and disempower
• Harnesses and extends social rights	• Cannot secure substantive resources
• Raises awareness and informs debate	• May unintentionally create inequality
• Delivers evidence of policy failure	• Victory can be negated by legislation

There are undeniably pros and cons to legalistic strategies in the field of social rights activism (see Table 8.1). These strategies can succeed in securing social security benefits for people who are entitled to them, in curbing bad employment practices and in improving local housing conditions. They can raise awareness of social injustice and/or demonstrate to policy makers where policy is failing. However, the improvements they can bring to the living conditions of poor people are likely to be marginal. This is first because individual casework cannot improve the levels at which social security benefits are set, and cannot create new jobs or homes. Second, when the resources required to fulfil social rights are scarce and must be rationed, those who exercise their rights successfully may do so at the expense of others. Third, the gains made as a result of ground-breaking test cases may be short-lived if the legislature has the power to change the law and effectively nullify the victory.

The justiciability debate

This leads us to what has been called the 'justiciability' debate (Gearty & Mantouvalou, 2011; Hunt, 1996; Langford, 2008a). Is it possible – is it right – that social rights should be subject to judicial scrutiny? We might argue that social rights, though equal in standing to civil and political rights, are different in character. It is not simply that they are self-executing or ill-suited to processes of judicial scrutiny, but that as articulations of human need the transactions they entail are not legal but fundamentally social. This is an issue to which I shall return in Chapter 10. In the meantime, let us consider the established contours of the debate.

The first problem is that the judicial process is primarily framed as the resolution of contests between disputing parties. The roots of this problem may be traced back to the ancient practice of trial by combat. This is, perhaps, less manifest in legal systems based on the Roman legal tradition (premised on inquisitorial procedures and legal codification) than in those now based on the English tradition (premised on adversarial procedures and common-law principles) (e.g. Watson, 1990). In the contemporary world there is considerable overlap between systems, and the concept of the *inter partes* trial has universal symbolic significance. Though the judicial duel could assume a variety of forms, its most pertinent manifestation entailed a petition to the king by nobles requiring a resolution to some dispute between them. Resolution was achieved through armed combat, presided over by the king, between the appointed champions of the contesting parties. The king would specify the rules of combat and determine which of the champions had won. The dispute was thereby settled, without regard to substantive considerations of truth or justice, in favour of the party whose champion was declared the victor. Combat now takes place by way of formal argument between appointed advocates on behalf of the disputing parties, and the role of the judge is not to intervene in the contest, but – like a sovereign of old – to ensure the rules of combat are observed and (except in jury trials) determine who has won. Even with the safeguards that can be provided by according the judge a more active inquisitorial role in the proceedings, any dispute resolution procedure is likely to disadvantage weaker parties at the expense of the powerful. Parties without access to expert advice and assistance are likely to suffer some element of disadvantage relative to those with the resources to hire the best. We shall see in the second part of this chapter that legal justice and social justice are not inevitably incommensurable, but there is a fundamental issue about framing the pursuit of justice as the resolution of a dispute. Social rights disputes by their nature are likely to pitch vulnerable citizens against powerful governmental agencies, and the strategic role of the welfare lawyer or social rights advocate becomes that of 'party upgrading' (Galanter, 1976) – of compensating for the inherent inequality of the contest.

The second problem lies with, on the one hand, the expertise of the judiciary and its attitudes on the other. The charge made against the judiciary has been that it is ill-equipped to consider matters of social policy (Harden & Lewis, 1986; Luhmann, 1987) and that its members are likely to be drawn from a privileged stratum of society with little understanding of, or sympathy for, the problems of the most needy in society (Griffiths, 1997). These tendencies are clearly more evident and more entrenched in some countries than in others, but in principle, both problems are remediable. Judges' principal expertise, axiomatically, is in matters of law. Nevertheless, procedural rules could be adapted better to harness that expertise (Lewis & Birkinshaw, 1993). And there is no reason why judges should not be advised as occasion demands by social policy experts or why they should not receive specialist training as they might in relation to any specialist area of jurisdiction (e.g. Alston, 1990). Certainly there is evidence, for example, of extreme conservatism and inconsistency on the part of the British judiciary in the era when social rights cases were first brought before them (Griffiths, 1997), but there is more recent evidence from around the world where judges have displayed considerable understanding and sympathy for the plight of people in need (Mantouvalou, 2011: 118–121; and see Sachs, 2009). What is more, steps can be taken to ensure that judges are not necessarily drawn only from the upper echelons of society (see, for example, Neuberger, 2010).

The next problem has to do with the legitimacy and the supposedly undemocratic nature of judicial intervention. Checks and balances on the exercise of power within a liberal democracy are supposedly provided by the division of powers between the legislature, the executive and the judiciary. We have already seen that judicial purists were afraid that allowing the judiciary to adjudicate on social rights risked drawing them into tasks more properly fulfilled by the executive, particularly with regard to the allocation of public resources. The concern arises because social rights, unlike civil rights, are costly and it is not for the judiciary to impose costs on the government. However, as Plant (1992), among others, has argued, civil rights entail costs as well. Judicial decision making imposes costs on the criminal justice system, which is in principle no different from imposing legitimate costs on social security, healthcare and education systems. But related to this is the extent to which an unelected and unaccountable judiciary ought not to be allowed to tread on the toes of the democratically elected legislature. This is especially the case in jurisdictions using the English common-law system, where principles of interpretation established by higher courts set precedents for lower courts to follow and can so 'make' law independently of the legislature, for example, by reinterpreting its meaning and effect. In some jurisdictions, such as the US, the courts have the power to strike down legislation as unconstitutional. Constitutionality and democracy can be uneasy companions. The judiciary is accountable for overseeing the conduct of the executive and the legislature, and if within a majoritarian electoral democracy it should act to protect the social rights of powerless or unpopular minorities, it can fulfil a significant democratic function (e.g. Mantouvalou, 2011: 125).

Finally, I have already alluded to the possibility that social rights activism can have unintended effects and may even fuel inequalities. This is a criticism that can be aimed at such judicial decision making as results from such activism, though it is as much a criticism of unequal access to the courts, which can result in sharp-elbowed middle classes using the courts to secure access to public goods and services unavailable to their poorer compatriots: an issue of recent concern, for example, in Brazil (Piovesan, 2008). The extension of provision for collective complaints and class actions has a part to play in this respect (see below). Nevertheless, whatever the limitations of the remedies available through judicial scrutiny, litigation can be a means of providing a voice to the voiceless. Though Schiengold (1974/2004) had once dismissed as a 'myth' the very idea that social rights can be defined or realised through the pursuit of legal enforcement, he nevertheless conceded that recourse to litigation and individual rights can be a *tactic* within a broader mobilisation for change.

The juridification debate has generated a great deal of heat, but its importance lies in the light it casts on those mechanisms of redress that are available in relation to social rights matters.

Levels of redress

We therefore turn to relevant rights of redress. Rights of redress in themselves have a long history and to tell a chronological story of their relationship with social rights we would need to revert to the beginnings of the capitalist welfare state. In this instance, however, it is more sensible to consider social rights in a global context and to consider the different levels at which redress may be sought. The human rights framework has provided supranational monitoring mechanisms; nation states have provided a variety of mechanisms for judicial supervision through the courts; and finally, given the peculiar nature of social rights there is also, apart from the courts, a myriad of specialised, quasi- or non-judicial administrative mechanisms of redress.

International mechanisms

The effective cornerstone of social rights within the international human rights framework is the ICESCR of 1966 (Craven, 1995; and see Hunt, 1996: ch. 1). In Chapter 2, I briefly drew attention to two fundamental differences between the ICESCR and its sister document, the ICCPR. First, the latter required states parties immediately to take steps to ensure that their constitutional and legislative arrangements complied with the covenant; the former required that countries take steps within their available resources progressively to realise compliance with the covenant. Second, whereas the ICCPR established the Human Rights Committee, an independent body of experts, to oversee the implementation of the covenant and receive complaints about violations, the ICESCR entrusted oversight to the standing UN body, the ECOSOC, composed of government representatives, a responsibility that ECOSOC initially delegated to a sessional working group. It was not until 1985 that ECOSOC appointed a specialist committee of independent experts (prominent lawyers and human rights specialists), the CESCR, to function in parallel with the Human Rights Committee.

The CESCR receives quinquennial reports from states parties as to their progress in real-ising social rights. The reports are subject to pre-sessional scrutiny, followed by plenary discussion with state representatives. The committee is empowered to undertake missions to visit countries in the event that it should wish further to investigate particular concerns, as occurred twice in the 1990s in the case of alleged housing rights violations in Panama and the Dominican Republic. The committee seeks to characterise its engagement with states parties as a 'constructive dialogue' (Hunt, 1996: 20). Since 1992, the committee has invited submis-sions from NGOs in order that they might contribute to its deliberations, but the response from NGOs has been described as 'disappointing' (Hunt, 1996: 234). Nevertheless in 2008, following a process of consultation and debate that had gone on for 18 years, an Optional Protocol to the ICESCR was adopted to allow the committee to consider individual com-plaints by or on behalf of persons aggrieved by violations of social rights. The protocol finally came into force in 2013 and at the time of writing it remains to be seen how far its role may now develop. The CESCR has an advisory jurisdiction, with no power to make enforceable orders against states parties. It is able to issue general comments as to the interpretation of states parties' obligations under the ICESCR, and though these represent a form of jurispru-dence, they do not have the status of case law.

The 'linchpin' (Craven, 1995: 107) of the ICESCR and, arguably, its critical weakness, is the progressive realisation principle contained in Article 2. The International Commission of Jurists has twice convened groups of experts to consider the meaning and scope of Article 2, giving rise to the promulgation in 1986, of the Limburg Principles and in 1996, the Maas-tricht Guidelines (both are reproduced as appendices in Eide *et al.,* 2001). The Limberg Prin-ciples are broadly reflected in the CESCR's General Comment No. 3 of 1991, which sought to define the core obligations of states parties to ensure minimal essential levels of social provi-sion; the widest possible enjoyment of such provision as can be achieved; and that particular attention be paid to the needs of vulnerable members of society. The subsequent Maastricht Guidelines included a call for lawyers, judges and the legal community generally to 'pay far greater attention' to violations of social rights (para. 28). The principle that social rights are to be progressively realised signals that social rights may not in practice be inviolable; it is a principle born of political pragmatism, not legal exactitude. And yet the legal community has laboured valiantly to provide a coherent understanding of the principle (Alston & Quinn, 1987; Langford & King, 2008). But, harking back to the justiciability debate, one can see that critics might object that in the process, the lawyers have rather taken ownership of the principle and its interpretation (Gearty, 2011).

This is the context in which three regional supranational systems of adjudication in rela-tion to social rights have also developed – each instituted under the terms of one of the three regional charters identified in Chapter 2 of this volume. The Council of Europe under the Social Charter of 1961 created the European Committee of Social Rights with parallel functions to the UN's CESCR (Conant, 2010; Khaliq & Churchill, 2008). The charter was revised in 1996 to include provision for collective complaints from trades unions and NGOs regarding alleged social rights violations. The complaints procedure eventually came into force in 2007 and the committee has, for example, considered complaints on behalf of Roma minorities and disability groups (Harris, 2009), but, like the CESCR, it lacks the power to make binding judgements. Nevertheless, the Social Charter's sister document, the European Convention on Human Rights of 1950, had constituted the European Court of Human Rights which, though it ostensibly has jurisdiction only in civil and political rights matters,

TABLE 8.2 Illustrations of the 'integrated approach': Reading across from civil rights to social rights

The civil right:	*Potential relevance to social rights:*
• to life itself	• where – in extreme circumstances – a person is systematically denied any means of livelihood
• of equality between men and women	• where men and women may be treated differently with regard to social benefits (for example, carers' allowances or pensions)
• to protection against inhumane or degrading treatment	• where, for example, asylum seekers or prisoners are denied the means of basic subsistence or necessary healthcare
• to private and family life	• where a person is denied the means to maintain herself independently of others and/or the opportunity to share an adequate home with members of her family

Note: These are loosely based on specific legal cases cited in jurisprudential literature referenced throughout this chapter, but it is important to stress that they are drawn from diverse civil rights jurisdictions – both national and supranational – and are based on unique and often complex individual circumstances, which cannot here be fully explained. These should therefore be regarded as illustrative instances, not as statements of universal principle.

has on occasion ruled in matters where social rights could be 'read across' from civil rights, in accordance with the 'integrated approach', explained in Table 8.2 (Mantouvalou, 2011; Palmer, 2007). Additionally, elements of the European Social Charter have been incorporated into the European Union's Charter of Fundamental Rights of 1989 and 2000 (now incorporated in a protocol to the Lisbon Treaty of 2009), in relation to which the European Court of Justice has jurisdiction.

The other two regional supranational systems are those relating to the American Convention on Human Rights of 1969 (and its Additional Protocol of San Salvador) and the African Charter on Human and People's Rights of 1981. The former is overseen by the Organisation of American States' Inter-American Commission on Human Rights and the Inter-American Court on Human Rights (Melish, 2008), and the latter by the Organisation of African States' African Commission on Human Rights and the African Court on Human Rights (Chirwa, 2008). In each instance the commission was entrusted, broadly speaking, with an advisory jurisdiction and the court with an adjudicative role. In the African context, this is further complicated by the intersecting jurisdiction of the African Union's Court of Justice (now set to be superseded by the African Court of Justice and Human Rights). It has been suggested that 'the needs of the peoples of Africa seem to have been rather lost in the designing of successive frameworks of ever grander human rights architecture' (Gearty, 2011: 45).

Some of the supranational bodies identified above have made important contributions to the interpretation and development of social rights. They are, however, remote from the everyday workings of rights workers and the everyday experiences of the world's most vulnerable people. Additionally, treaty-related complaints procedures can only be implemented against countries that are full parties to the relevant treaty and such protocols as may apply. There is insufficient scope in this book to detail the many instances of countries which have not signed or ratified social rights treaties, or the protocols relating to complaints procedures, or which have done so subject to reservations. Significantly, some established welfare states are not full parties to all such treaties and protocols. For example, neither the UK nor the US has signed the Optional Protocol to the ICESCR; the UK has opted out of the social rights protocol to the EU Lisbon Treaty and has not signed up to the complaints procedure under the Council of Europe's revised Social Charter; the US never fully ratified the American Convention on Human Rights and is not a party to the social rights provisions of the San Salvador Protocol. Though it was, paradoxically, a US president and his widow (Franklin and Eleanor Roosevelt) who were so vitally instrumental in ensuring the incorporation of social rights into the international human rights framework, the US has consistently resisted attempts to make such rights binding (Sunstein, 2005).

The Human Rights Commission, whose oversight extended to all the rights proclaimed in the UDHR, had operated a confidential complaints procedure, until the commission was superseded by the UN Human Rights Council (UNCRC) in 2006. The council operates an open complaints and representations procedure, which may encompass complaints that cannot otherwise be addressed to a treaty body or similar regional complaints procedure in the field of human rights. However, the council is concerned with investigating only such cases as appear to reveal a consistent pattern of gross and reliably attested violations of human rights. The council also has the power to appoint and receive reports from special rapporteurs, and this non-judicial mechanism is one we shall mention again in Chapter 10. For now, we shall consider mechanisms of redress that operate closer to the citizens of nation states.

National courts

It will be clear from our discussion of the justiciability debate that the role of the courts in relation to social rights has been controversial and, unsurprisingly, there is considerable variation between countries as to the extent to which courts can or do in practice engage with social rights matters. The basis of a court's jurisdiction may depend on whether social rights arise from a national constitution, or from specific social legislation. And in either case, the role of the courts in interpreting social rights may vary depending on legal traditions (e.g. whether a country operates with a predominantly common-law or a civil/codified law system). The account that follows is general and much simplified: I shall mention the role of constitutional courts on the one hand and ordinary courts on the other, and I shall offer a brief discussion of judicial discretion.

Most countries have a written constitution, though a few (including the UK) do not (Gordon, 1999). Most national constitutions incorporate at least some social rights, such as a right to education, but the inclusion of a comprehensive range of social rights is rare (Jung et al., 2013). Of those constitutions that include social rights, there is a distinction to be drawn between, on the one hand, those that regard them as aspirational or express them to be 'directive principles' (e.g. India and Ireland) and, on the other, those that explicitly provide for the justiciability of social rights (e.g. South Africa and Finland). Broadly speaking, post-communist and Latin American countries are rather more likely than Western European and North American countries to make social rights justiciable, though there appears to be little by way of regional norms in other parts of the world. Several developing countries have established separate constitutional courts to adjudicate on alleged constitutional violations (Gargarella, et al., 2006; Gauri & Brinks, 2008), but in other jurisdictions it may fall to a supreme court to oversee the interpretation and observance of the constitution. And in Germany, for example, there is a specialist Federal Social Court to oversee provision for social rights specifically provided under the national constitution.

Social rights, however, are the rights of everyday life and it is in the ordinary courts that they are likely most frequently to surface. Long before the concept of social rights was established, courts of law exercised a role in relation to dealings between employers and employees, or landlords and tenants, that had bearing on what we might now identify as the social rights of the employees or tenants. In capitalist welfare states this has continued, albeit subject to social legislation that may have developed, modified or circumscribed the workings of the law or conferred particular responsibilities on the courts. In some instances, as we shall see, specialist areas of jurisdiction have been removed or withheld from the courts and conferred on quasi-judicial or administrative bodies or tribunals. Nevertheless, the decisions of these bodies and tribunals will usually remain subject to appeal or review by the courts. And in liberal democratic societies, decisions by administrative and executive bodies ought in any event to be susceptible to judicial review, whether governed by prerogative or constitutional convention.

From a positivist perspective, the fundamental significance of rights is that they are ostensibly determinate. The significance of social rights as conceptualised by T. H. Marshall was that they constituted the transition from the Poor Law to the modern welfare state; from capricious charity to guaranteed support; from discretionary poor relief to defined rights. In practice, however, social rights are seldom rigidly defined. Specified as human rights they are loosely defined, as we have seen. Specified as rights of citizenship they may appear to be precisely defined, but, as Dworkin (1977; and see Chapter 4, this volume) has argued, however exactly framed a statute or regulation might seem to be, it will always leave some space for discretion as to its implementation or interpretation. This is the space within which administrative and judicial decision makers alike may exercise their power. In the judicial context they may have room to decide whether or not to intervene in response to a complaint, or else to decide just how a specified right is to be interpreted.

I have already mentioned how in Britain in the 1960s and '70s social rights activists first began to take test cases before the ordinary courts (Prosser, 1983). The outcomes revealed trends in just how the judiciary exercised their discretionary power. In social security cases, when asked to review the decisions of administrative tribunals, the judges would decline to intervene in cases of claimants whom they appeared to regard as undeserving, while sympathetically invoking principles of administrative justice in support of claimants whom they appeared to regard as deserving. In housing cases they used their power to protect property owners against the claims of tenants on the one hand, and the interventions of public authorities on the other, while sympathetically defending public authorities against the claims of those whom they appeared to regard as the undeserving homeless (Griffiths, 1997). Nevertheless, there are many examples from around the world where judicial innovation has played an important role in advancing social rights. I have also mentioned above the 'integrated approach' whereby judges – when constrained to adjudicate solely on the basis civil and political rights charters but confronted by a social injustice – have read across from those charters in support of social rights (see Table 8.2 above). Such a practice has been important even in the British context where the Human Rights Act of 1998 'domesticated' the civil and political rights provisions of the European Convention on Human Rights on terms that allowed British courts to comment on whether British laws were compliant (King, 2008; Mantouvalou, 2011: 142).

It has been suggested that in the past two decades social rights jurisprudence has been 'emerging from the shadows' (Langford, 2008a: 1), and most certainly there is a considerable volume of reported cases from around the world (Langford, 2008b). This book is not a legal text, however, and I shall refrain from citing an array of illustrative cases. But I shall mention what has become one of the most celebrated cases – celebrated not least because it arose in an era of promise in post-apartheid South Africa. It is known as the Grootboom case, the story of which I tell in Box 8.1. The story speaks to a number of issues concerning the role that courts can play, most particularly regarding the limitations imposed by the progressive realisation principle, not just in housing cases, but in relation to all social rights.

BOX 8.1   THE GROOTBOOM CASE

[Official report reference: *Government of the Republic of South Africa and Others v. Grootboom and Others* [2000] ZACC 19, 2001 (1) SA 46 (CC), 2000 (11) BCLR 1169 (CC)]

The background

Irene Grootboom lived in Wallacedene, an informal squatter settlement in the eastern suburbs of Cape Town in South Africa. The settlement had been established during the 1980s after a relaxation of the apartheid pass laws made it easier for rural populations to migrate to urban areas. The residents of Wallacedene lived in severe poverty and without basic services. Many Wallacedene residents had their names on a waiting list for low-cost housing. Eventually, a group of about 900 people, including Irene Grootboom, began to move from Wallacedene onto adjacent, vacant, privately owned land that had been ear-marked for low-cost housing. The landowner obtained an eviction order, and the sheriff was ordered to dismantle and remove any of the makeshift structures remaining on the land. The magistrate granting the order said the community and the municipality should negotiate in order to identify alternative land for the community to occupy on a temporary or permanent basis. In 1999, having nowhere to go, the community moved onto the Wallacedene sports field and began to erect temporary structures.

In the high court

With legal assistance, the community demanded that the municipality provide temporary accommodation. In the absence a satisfactory response, the community – in the name of 'Irene Grootboom and 900 others' – applied to the Cape High Court, arguing first, that on the basis of the South African Constitution of 1996 everyone had a right of access to adequate housing and the state had a duty to take reasonable measures, within its available resources, to make sure that right was progressively realised; second, they argued that under the constitution their children had an absolute right to shelter. The high court rejected the first argument, asserting that the government's housing programme was reasonable and fulfilled the requirements of the constitution. It was conceded, however, that there was an obligation on the state to provide shelter for the children, and it was in the best interests of the children that they should not be separated from their families.

In the constitutional court

Unhappy with this decision, the government appealed against it before South Africa's Constitutional Court. Hearing the case afresh in 2000, the court concluded, unlike the Cape High Court, that in fact the government's housing programme had fallen short of the state's obligation to provide relief to people in need, and that an insufficient proportion of national housing budget had been devoted to that purpose. The court's judgment set out the state's obligations to devise and implement a comprehensive and coordinated short-, medium- and long-term programme for the provision of adequate housing, ensuring along the way that this would not exclude any significant segment of society. An order was made in terms then agreed between the parties, by which the national and provincial governments were to provide for the needs of Irene Grootboom and the 390 adults and 510 children in the informal settlement.

The aftermath

It should be noted, however, that the constitutional court also ruled that Irene Grootboom had no right to demand immediate housing and, notwithstanding their intolerable living conditions, that the Wallacedene squatters had no right to resort to land invasion, a form of self-help the court found to be unacceptable. In the event, Irene Grootboom was never rehoused and later left Wallacedene. Eight years later, in 2008, at the age of just 39, she died penniless and living in a shack. It has become an iconic case. Its significance is that it was the first clear ruling by a national constitutional court in support of a claim based on social rights. However, the case also illustrates the limitations of social rights premised on the progressive realisation principle. Irene Grootboom, despite the fame the case brought her as a housing rights activist, never benefited from the court's ruling.

Administrative mechanisms

More important still than the courts, perhaps, in terms of their day-to-day impact on people's lives are the various administrative and quasi-judicial mechanisms and procedures by which social rights are, or might be, safeguarded or promoted. Inevitably, there is enormous variation between countries as to the nature and extent of the mechanisms that may be deployed. It is also quite difficult to summarise the different types of redress that may be available. There is a spectrum, ranging from specialised tribunals chaired by lawyers, which are courts in all but name, to processes by which disputed decisions are merely double checked by administrative officials. However, it is not simply a question of the degree to which a mechanism is legal or administrative in character. It is a question of just how social rights are conceived and where the focus of the procedure lies. A taxonomy of the different forms and mechanisms of redress is presented in Table 8.3. It may be seen that this draws, on the one hand, on the distinction initially explained in Chapter 1 between doctrinal and claims-based conceptions of rights and, on the other, a distinction between procedures which are focused on the obligations of the state, as opposed to those focused on the demands of the individual.

TABLE 8.3 Forms of administrative redress

Conception of rights	Focus of redress	Form of redress	Implied status of the individual	Typical mechanism of redress
Doctrinal	Obligations of the state	Appeal	Juridical subject	Tribunal (quasi-judicial forum)
	Demands of the individual	Personal complaint	Heroic consumer	Complaints procedure (managerial process)
Claims-based	Obligations of the state	Petitionary complaint	Aggrieved citizen	Ombudsperson (*or* public forum)
	Demands of the individual	Review	Passive client	Case committee/Panel (*or* supervisory check)

The resulting model draws out the different ways in which the form of redress and the status of the individual may be constituted. The specific mechanisms or fora for redress may be variously described, using terms such as 'tribunal', 'ombudsperson', 'complaints procedure' or 'case committee', though such terms can be misleadingly applied; my purpose is to explore the underlying logic informing processes of redress.

Redress in the form of an *appeal* is premised on a doctrinal conception of rights and a concern that the state should properly meet its obligations. The individual is constituted as a juridical subject and the classic forum or mechanism is a tribunal, which may or may not be chaired by a lawyer, but which performs a formal function that is quasi-judicial. Tribunals can also be introduced for the social regulation of private disputes (e.g. between employees and employers, or between tenants and landlords) and case-review committees (such as might deal, for example, with school admissions appeals) that do not necessarily operate under formal adjudicative procedures and may be mis-described as tribunals. But our particular concern is with tribunals that adjudicate on claims against the state. This can briefly be illustrated with reference to the development of social security tribunals in Britain, a process that began with the introduction of unemployment insurance in 1911. The concern at that time was that the ordinary courts had proved themselves to be ill-suited to the handling of industrial injury claims brought against employers by unrepresented workers and that a different sort of adjudicative forum was required. The government introduced a three-member 'Court of Referees' chaired by a lawyer, but sitting with lay trades-union and local business representatives. The sporting nomenclature symbolised the hope that this would be received by the working classes as a mechanism to ensure 'fair play' on terms they would understand (Wraith & Hutchinson, 1973). In the 1930s another tribunal was introduced to adjudicate on social assistance benefits for unemployed people, though the government's motive for this was to provide a safety valve that might deflect public resentment against the increasingly unpopular household means-test associated with the benefit (Lynes, 1975). Tribunals for the adjudication of different benefits thereafter proliferated, but were then, by stages, consolidated and increasingly 'judicialised' as social security law became ever more complex (Leggatt, 2001; Thomas & Genn, 2013). What this story illustrates is an enduring tension between the need for accessible redress and a desire for technical rigour.

Redress in the form of a *petitionary complaint* is premised on a claims-based conception of rights but, once again, a concern that the state should properly meet its obligations. The individual is constituted as an aggrieved citizen and the classic remedy is that of an ombudsperson. The mechanism is petitionary in the sense that it entails a process by which public attention may be drawn to a grievance. And there are instances of other forms of public or democratic community fora, established expressly to enable citizens to channel their disapproval or demand a 'social response' (McCarthy *et al.*, 1992; Mulcahy & Lloyd-Bostock, 1992). The ombudsperson, however, had its origins in Scandinavian tradition, dating back more than two centuries (Stacey, 1978). It provides a model based on the idea of a people's champion, specifically empowered to challenge state authority using investigatory powers to 'dig where the courts and tribunals cannot trespass' (Lewis & Birkinshaw, 1993: 78). The substantive process, unlike that before a tribunal, is not adversarial, but entirely inquisitorial. In the Nordic tradition, ombudspersons have been allowed to point out systemic weaknesses in policy and administration and propose improvements. The ombudsperson model – or at least the 'ombudsman' term or label – has been adopted in various forms by governments around the world (in Australia, Austria, Canada, France, New Zealand and the UK), and incidentally, within different private business sectors as part of a variety of both voluntary and regulatory schemes. The model can be applied in a social rights context as a mechanism for challenges to government departments and agencies in respect to social security, health and social care, education and housing. It is rare, however, for it to be implemented on terms that live up to the Nordic ideal. For example, in the case of the UK's Parliamentary Commissioner for Administration (a sort of ombudsperson) s/he can only be accessed through a citizen's Member of Parliament, can only investigate restrictively defined instances of 'maladministration' (rather than substantive decisions), and has no power to enforce her/his public recommendations. The effectiveness of any ombudsman scheme or public complaints forum depends largely on the willingness of governments to allow themselves to be subject to such scrutiny.

Redress in the form of a *personal complaint* is premised on a doctrinal conception of rights and a concern with satisfying or appeasing the demands of the individual. The individual is constituted as a 'heroic consumer' (Warde, 1994), and the classic remedy is a formal complaints procedure. The process is informed by managerialist doctrine that regards citizens as potentially vocal consumers of social services, the provision of which may be regarded as a business like any other (see Chapter 1, this volume). Customer grievances must be turned into complaints, and the information they generate must be regarded as a management tool by which to enhance the efficacy of the service (Pfeffer & Coote, 1991). Staff in health and social care, social security and educational institutions must share the mission of the institution and must be trained to deal proactively and expeditiously with complaints, to disarm aggrieved consumers and to ensure the institution's mission is achieved. The doctrinal fiction on which this depends assumes parity of power between welfare professionals and administrators on the one hand and their potentially vulnerable or disadvantaged patients, clients, claimants, parents or students on the other. And it assumes that the latter are 'consumers' through 'choice' rather than necessity. The object is more akin to the satisfaction of civil rights than the fulfilment of social rights. The trend towards the development of formal complaints procedures is characteristic of the managerial trend to which capitalist welfare states have lately been subject. Such procedures can be sophisticated in design and entail, for example, specialist staff and independently chaired complaints panels. In the British case, complaints procedures, particularly in relation to health and social care provision have lately become increasingly complex and fragmented following reforms aimed at driving competitive local commissioning, such that at the time of writing, one watchdog has declared the system to be 'utterly bewildering' (Healthwatch England, 2014). The effectiveness of individual complaints procedures in the social rights context is potentially limited if the focus is on the resolution or containment of the complaints, rather than the satisfaction of complainants' needs (Brewer, 2007).

Redress in the form of a *review* is premised on a claims-based conception of rights and, once again, a concern with satisfying or appeasing the demands of the individual. The individual is constituted as a passive client or helpless supplicant, and the remedy might be a case committee or review panel, or failing that, some kind of administrative double check. The internal review represents the oldest means by which administrative review may be sought. In the days before the modern welfare state, the recipients of poor relief, like the eponymous hero of Charles Dickens's novel *Oliver Twist,* might dare to ask for more – or to have their cases looked at again. Where elements of discretion persist in relation to the provision of social assistance or social care, it may still be common practice for case conferences, committees or panels to review the cases of clients who express dissatisfaction. Even where citizens have rights to social assistance, medical treatment, education, social care or rehousing, the form this takes may very well entail the exercise of discretion and deliberation, not with regard to a client's entitlement, but the most appropriate form of help, treatment or placement. Where funds for particular forms of relief, facilities for particular kinds of treatment or care, places in particular schools, or the provision of housing of a particular specification are subject to budgetary limits or practical constraints, special panels may need to consider or perhaps re-consider to whom these should go. And even when rules of entitlement to a social benefit may be clear, if no right of appeal to an independent tribunal is provided, it is to be expected that some form of internal process of administrative or supervisory review of the facts of a case might be undertaken. The extension and development of social rights, even within the most developed welfare states, do not extinguish the use of such mechanisms, though of course the quality and consistency of the resultant decision making will always be problematic and subject to challenge. In such circumstances, front-line welfare professionals and administrators as decision makers become ad hoc policy makers, rather than rights adjudicators (Lipsky, 1980/2010).

Summary/conclusion

This chapter, in part, has been about what happens when rights go wrong. Yet it is also about more than that, since rights of redress can be the means by which social rights are affirmed and thereby realised.

The relationship between social rights and the law has been and perhaps always will be in some respects problematic. Legal systems and administrative state welfare systems have a different functional logic and underlying purpose and do not necessarily rub along together so easily. The reality, however, is that social citizenship rights find expression in statutory legal form, and citizens, especially vulnerable or disadvantaged citizens, may require legal advice and assistance in order to obtain their social rights. The development of a right to such assistance has been slow and uneven, and where it has been fulfilled, the benefits, some would argue, have been ambiguous. The debate at the heart of this chapter is the so-called justiciability debate: can and should social rights be susceptible to legal interpretation and adjudication? We have considered arguments from either side of the debate, but have not necessarily settled on a definite conclusion.

The chapter has also substantively examined the different levels at which mechanisms or processes of redress may function. This has first entailed consideration of the international human rights framework and specific machinery for the monitoring of social rights. The critical and enduring issues here have been the principle of progressive realisation that has been applied to social rights, and just how this has been interpreted. The issue remains pertinent when we consider social rights as rights of citizenship, when specified by national constitutions or through domestic social legislation. Provision for social rights has until relatively recently been developed largely beyond the gaze of the courts, and yet the courts have demonstrated their power to either foster or frustrate social rights. Finally, developed welfare states have created a variety of mechanisms for administrative redress, which reflect different conceptions of social rights and which constitute the bearers of rights in different ways. The processes by which social rights can be enforced disclose just how elusive social rights can be, both conceptually and in practice.

PART THREE

Re-thinking social rights

9

SOCIAL RIGHTS AND SOCIAL DEVELOPMENT

At the beginning of Chapter 5, I touched on the relationship between social rights and human development and the important distinction between the economic and social components of human development. My purpose then was to set the scene for an exploration of the different ways in which social rights have evolved around the world. And in Chapter 2, readers may recall, when discussing the relationship between needs and rights, I discussed the concept of poverty and the extent to which social rights succeed or fail to counter poverty. In this short chapter I shall return to consider more specifically the role of social rights in relation to social development and, in particular, to the alleviation of poverty. My purpose now is to reflect on the different ways in which social rights are, or ought to be, a part of the social development process.

The poverty-rights-development triad incorporates a combination of links (see Figure 9.1) and these I shall explore. The link between development and rights is associated with a particular discourse concerning rights to self-determination or 'freedom'. The link between poverty and development is associated with an essentially technocratic discourse as to how a rights-based or 'rights standards' approach can alleviate poverty. The link between rights and poverty is associated with a normative or humanistic discourse that regards poverty as an unnecessary and unacceptable violation of rights. There are connections and intersections between these discourses, but for the purposes of discussion we shall consider each in turn.

Self-determination and the right to development

Civil and political rights have together been characterised as 'first-generation' rights, and social rights as 'second-generation' rights. In 1986, the UN General Assembly's Declaration on the Right to Development (DRtD) gave expression to a central plank within a 'third generation' of human rights. Third generation rights are widely represented as collective, group or solidarity rights: as rights to peace, to a healthy environment and to 'development'. Central to the concept of development was the principle of 'self-determination' (Rosas, 2001).

Agitation for a more holistic understanding of human rights had begun in the 1960s with the peace movement, the green movement and the anti-racist/anti-apartheid movement. The

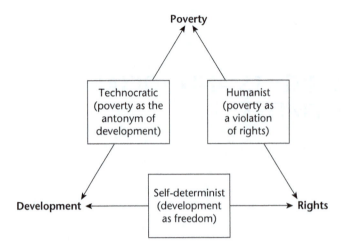

FIGURE 9.1 The links between poverty, development and rights: Contrasting understandings

instigation of the demand for a right to development is widely attributed to a call articulated by the Senagalese delegate to the UN, Justice Keba M'Baye, when he called not only for the right to live, but for 'the right to live better' (1972). The agenda for the DRtD was driven largely from the global South, with some resistance from parts of the global North, especially the US (Marks, 2004). The declaration did not give rise to legally binding covenants and remains aspirational in nature. Nevertheless, it had considerable symbolic significance. Its advocates contend that it transcended the unfortunate schism between civil and political rights on the one hand and the social rights agenda on the other (Sengupta, 2000, 2010) and set them in a broader context. The declaration itself:

- expresses the right of 'every human person and all peoples . . . to participate in, contribute to, and enjoy economic, social, cultural and political development', which implies 'the full realization of the right of peoples to self-determination', including 'the exercise of their inalienable right to full sovereignty over all their natural wealth and resources' (Article 1);
- asserts that 'the human person is the central subject of development', but also that 'all human beings have a responsibility for development, individually and collectively' and should 'promote and protect an appropriate political, social and economic order for development' (Article 2 [1] and [2]); and
- holds that states:
  - ○ 'have the right and the duty to formulate appropriate national development policies that aim at the constant improvement of the well-being of the entire population and of all individuals' (Article 2 [3]);
  - ○ 'have the primary responsibility for the creation of national and international conditions favourable to the realization of the right to development' (Article 3 [1]);
  - ○ 'have the duty to co-operate with each other in ensuring development and eliminating obstacles to development' (Article 3[3]);
  - ○ 'have the duty to take steps, individually and collectively, to formulate international development policies' (Article 4); and

o   ensure 'equality of opportunity for all in their access to basic resources, education, health services, food, housing, employment and the fair distribution of income' (Article 8).

The declaration therefore reiterated rights proclaimed in existing treaties and instruments, including the right to self-determination. In seeking to reframe them in terms of an overarching right to development, there were some elements of ambiguity. The DRtD proclaimed the right of peoples (in the plural), but stressed that the human person (in the singular) is the central subject. It proclaimed the duty of nation states to formulate national policies, but required all states to co-operate in the formulation of international policies. Is the right to development the right of individual subjects, exercisable against nation states, or a right of nation states to international co-operation? The declaration adds nothing to the exposition of social rights already contained in the UDHR and ICESCR, other than perhaps to call for international assistance in realising them.

The implicit premise is that self-determination cannot be achieved without international co-operation. If first generation rights were about freedom and democracy, and second generation rights were about substantive equality and wellbeing, then third generation rights were supposed to be about international solidarity and co-operation. The battle lines drawn between the interests of the 'non-aligned' nations of the global South who championed the right to development, and those of the global North (especially the US), revolved substantially around the challenges posed by a right to development to the structural economic and political imbalances of the status quo (Marks, 2004) and the prevalence of the neo-liberal pro-market ideological assumptions represented by the so-called Washington consensus (see Chapter 4, this volume). The right to self-determination expressed in the DRtD may be thought of as the combination of first generation rights to freedom and democracy scaled up to the international level. Aristotle's famous reservation concerning democratic governance was that 'in democracies the poor have more sovereign power than the rich; for they are more numerous' (1981: 363). In the current context of extreme global inequalities, democracy between nations premised on an effective right to national self-determination would require a revolutionary upheaval to the global capitalist world order. Unsurprisingly, that hasn't happened. The editors of a collection of papers first presented at the 2003 Nobel Symposium on the Right to Development and Human Rights in Development lamented that 'the operationalization of the right [to development] has not kept up with theory' (Andreassen & Marks, 2010: xxix).

The impetus for the elusive idea of a right to development has been sustained – paradoxically perhaps – by Amartya Sen's (1999) liberal-individualist framing of 'development' as *freedom*. This has been important, not least because it explicitly connects with the issue of poverty (discussed in Chapter 2, this volume). Sen, though no supporter of solidarity rights, can be credited with inflecting UN agencies away from strict adherence to the Washington consensus, and for shaping certain elements of the work of the UNDP. There is an implicit resonance, I would argue, between Sen's framing of human development and certain underlying purposes of the DRtD. For Sen, human rights provide the means to guarantee basic human freedoms. But it is human development that enhances human capabilities so as to give the full expression to freedom. Freedom is constituted through human development, not rights: rights are but a means to an end, not an end in themselves. The capabilities approach prioritises 'individual freedom as a social commitment' (1999: ch. 12). It fits with what I am characterising for the purposes of this chapter as a 'self-determinist' approach in that it is more of an approach *to,* than a theory *of* development; it expressly *challenges* top-down theories based on welfare utilitarianism and Rawlsian social justice; it attempts simultaneously to embrace potentially contradictory notions of freedom (freedom of individual opportunity and freedom of systemic process); and yet it supports a role for competitive markets (see Prendergast, 2005). It is an elusive approach which, it might be noted, does not fit easily within the taxonomy of perspectives outlined in Figure 3.1 (in Chapter 3, this volume), save as a hybrid that pragmatically – if not contrarily – synthesises elements of competitive individualism from the β perspective with elements of radical communitarianism from the γ perspective: demands for personal freedom with expectations of collective support. It does not necessarily or expressly lay claim to do so, but it does lend some sense to the ambiguities inherent within the UN's generally somewhat neglected DRtD.

Development and the technical means to alleviate poverty

Though the DRtD itself may have slipped rather from prominence, the preoccupations of the UN with the monitoring of human development and of global poverty have not. The initial debate around the DRtD had coincided with a realisation that attempts by the World Bank and the IMF to address poverty in the global South though crude structural adjustment programmes were failing (Deacon *et al.,* 1997; Yeates, 2001). The conditions attached to aid and the loans provided to developing countries in the 1980s imposed free-market solutions that, far from alleviating poverty, served to exacerbate it. The result in the 1990s was a partial shift towards a 'Post Washington Consensus': while still favouring free markets and restricted public spending, this espoused a social safety net approach to poverty alleviation (Deacon, 2007; World Bank, 1991). The emphasis was on 'getting the institutions right' (Yeates, 2008: 287); on promoting both private sector reform and good governance; on social risk management; on partial re-regulation and the use of 'smart' conditionalities; and on the tailored use of social funds to promote community-level initiatives (e.g. Braathen, 2005).

The high point, perhaps, of this technocratic turn was the publication of the UN's MDGs, already discussed in Chapter 5. Insofar as the MDG initiative had been partly inspired by Amartya Sen, it is important to stress that the apparent softening of the Washington consensus did not extend to an accurate understanding of his concept of human capabilities. The first chapter of the *Human Development Report 2000* (UNDP, 2000), which had been penned personally by Sen, included a careful discussion of the capabilities concept. But in the rest of the report, other authors picked up the pen, and the notion of human capabilities was deftly appropriated as a malleable concept akin to that of human capital, notwithstanding that Sen himself is quite clear that human capabilities and human capital are *not* the same thing (1999: 292–297). Capabilities are concerned with substantive freedoms, not productive capacity. Development, the UNDP still assumed, self-evidently requires economic growth, while rights require liberal democracy. Both require a pluralistic and apolitical social context in which NGOs and civil society groups can play a role as much as government. Lip service is paid to the importance of social rights, but their enforcement, according to UNDP, requires regulatory mechanisms akin to those by which global trade is governed. As it identified the gaps that exist in the global order, the UNDP's 2000 report began to draw on language bearing all the hallmarks of new public managerialist doctrine (see Chapter 1, this volume; and e.g. Porter & Craig, 2004). It spoke of the need for incentive structures, self-assessment techniques, benchmarking and culture change – and for poorer countries to avail themselves of the *opportunities* that globalisation offers (UNDP, 2000: 9). Although this report was written a few years before the global financial crisis of 2008–11, it failed to acknowledge that though powerful people might interpret the risks of a globalised capitalist economy in terms of new opportunities, the world's vulnerable people might experience such risks in terms of chronic insecurity (Vail, 1999). The significance of the language of the UNDP in this era – and that in a parallel report from the World Bank (Braathen, 2000; World Bank, 2001) – was that it reflected the context in which the UN's MDGs had been framed: their purpose was to urge upon the members of the UN the meeting of *goals,* not the realisation of *rights.*

Nevertheless there had been an attempt to formulate a human rights approach to poverty reduction. In 2001, the UN's CESCR had asked the OHCHR to develop draft guidelines on integrating human rights into poverty reduction strategies. The OHCHR appointed consultants – two lawyers (Paul Hunt and Manfred Nowak) and an economist (Siddiq Osmani) – who produced and consulted on a first draft in 2002 before presenting a revised draft and a conceptual framework document in 2004 (Hunt *et al.,* 2004). The draft guidelines were finally adopted and published as a set of *Principles and Guidelines for a Human Rights Approach to Poverty Reduction Strategies* (OHCHR, 2006). The authors, in their conceptual framework document, suggest that Sen's capability approach provides a useful conceptual 'bridge' between poverty and human rights (Hunt *et al.,* 2004: 6). What is meant by this is not especially clear. It is argued that the non-fulfilment of human rights counts as poverty if the rights involved 'correspond to the capabilities that are considered basic by a given society' (Hunt *et al.,* 2004: 10). This contention seems to suggest that capabilities (as substantive individual freedoms) can be equated with, or read across from, agreed and established understandings of rights. For my part, I'm not entirely sure that that is what Sen meant. For Sen, human rights can create the space in which human capabilities may be realised. Be that as it may, the principles on which the OHCHR guidelines are premised require:

- specific and prioritised norms and defined standards;
- accessible mechanisms of accountability (that may or may not entail justiciability);
- democratic participation of poor people in the development of strategy;
- that particular attention be paid to the well-being of especially vulnerable social groups;
- the identification of immediate, intermediate and long-term targets; [and]
- the use of indicators and benchmarks to monitor progress. (Hunt *et al.,* 2004: 21)

The end result (see Box 9.1) is a set of 'rights standards' (cf. Mishra, 1999), with ordered targets. The approach embraces the principle of progressive realisation and the methods of public managerialism. The document is to all intents and purposes a sister document to the MDGs. It may be noted that social rights to work, food, housing, healthcare and education are included and clearly outlined, but the right to social security is omitted. Apparently, it was felt that to include the right to social security would be counterproductive since in some parts of the world 'social security' is, at best, an unfamiliar or ambiguous term and, at worst, a disputed concept (Nowak, 2011).

The OHCHR document articulates the links between development and poverty, drawing on the language of rights, but the implied premise is that poverty and development are opposites. The document is a response to the UN agenda that assumes that economic development is the *sine qua non* of poverty alleviation. It offers a sophisticated, but primarily technical,

BOX 9.1 THE OHCHR *PRINCIPLES AND GUIDELINES FOR A HUMAN RIGHTS APPROACH TO POVERTY REDUCTION STRATEGIES* (2012)

Integrating specific human rights standards

Right to work

Target 1: Full employment
Target 2: All workers to be able to earn a minimum necessary income
Target 3: All workers to receive reasonable financial support during spells of unemployment
Target 4: To eliminate gender inequality in access to work
Target 5: To eliminate gender inequality in remuneration for work
Target 6: To eliminate child labour
Target 7: To eliminate bonded labour
Target 8: All workers should be able to work in safe and healthy working conditions
Target 9: No worker should be subject to unfair dismissal

Right to adequate food

Target 1: All people to be free from chronic hunger
Target 2: Eliminate gender inequality in access to food
Target 3: All people to be free from food insecurity
Target 4: All people to have access to food of adequate nutritional value
Target 5: All people to have access to safe food

Right to adequate housing

Target 1: All people to have a home
Target 2: All people to enjoy security of tenure
Target 3: All people to enjoy habitable housing
Target 4: All people to enjoy housing situated in a safe and healthy location
Target 5: All people able to afford adequate housing
Target 6: Adequate housing physically accessible to all
Target 7: All people to enjoy housing with access to essential services, materials, facilities and infrastructure

Right to health

Target 1: All people to have access to adequate and affordable primary health care
Target 2: To eliminate avoidable child mortality
Target 3: To eliminate avoidable maternal mortality
Target 4: All men and women of reproductive age to have access to safe and effective contraception
Target 5: To eliminate HIV/AIDS
Target 6: To eliminate the incidence of other communicable diseases
Target 7: To eliminate gender inequality in access to health care

Right to education

Target 1: To ensure universal primary education for boys and girls
Target 2: To make free primary education available to all children
Target 3: To implement compulsory primary education
Target 4: To eradicate illiteracy
Target 5: To ensure equal access for all to secondary education
Target 6: To make free secondary education available to all children
Target 7: To eliminate gender disparity in primary and secondary education
Target 8: To improve the quality of primary and secondary education

[i.e. in addition to civil and political rights, including the rights of equal access to justice]

answer to a human problem (an approach that seems broadly consistent with the α perspective in Figure 3.1 in Chapter 3).

Poverty as a violation of rights?

The process that led to the formulation of the MDGs had begun with the UN's Vienna Declaration of 1993 (UN, 1993), followed by the Copenhagen Social Summit of 1995 (UN, 1995). These events have been taken as landmarks: the first is credited with having declared that poverty was a violation of human rights (Lister, 2004: ch. 7); the second resulted in a commitment to social development. At both events the universality and indivisibility of human rights and the principles of the DRtD were ritually reaffirmed. What the Vienna Declaration of 1993 specifically affirmed was that 'the existence of widespread extreme poverty *inhibits* the full and effective enjoyment of human rights' (Article 14 [emphasis added]) and that 'extreme poverty and social exclusion constitute a violation of human *dignity*' (Article 25 [emphasis added] – an affirmation expressly restated by the UN General Assembly [2012]). In fact, neither affirmation states that poverty *of itself* is a direct violation of rights. The report from the Copenhagen summit commits itself to creating an environment that 'will enable people to achieve social development' (UN, 1995: 11), and to 'eradicating poverty in the world' (UN, 1995: 13). The means to such ends include provision for a stable legal framework; an enabling economic environment; and dynamic, open and free markets. The report added that the parties to the summit would 'reaffirm, promote and strive to ensure the realization of rights set out [in the UDHR, the ICESCR and the DRtD] . . . particularly in order to assist people living in poverty' (UN, 1995: 12).

Upon a close reading, therefore, it is clear that the UN was in no way retreating from the principle that social rights are progressively, not immediately, realisable and, in this sense, cannot be wholly inviolable. Poverty 'inhibits' the realisation of rights and it violates human 'dignity'. The Vienna Declaration of 1993 and the Copenhagen Social Summit of 1995 fall short of declaring a right not to be poor. It was accepted, certainly, that the scale of global poverty amounted to an injustice, giving rise to obligations on the part of the international community to prevent hindrance to, and facilitate the promotion of, the right to development (Salomon, 2007, 2010). However, in 2001 the UN's CESCR submitted unequivocally,

> The rights to work, an adequate standard of living, housing, food, health and education, which lie at the heart of the Covenant [the ICESCR], have a direct and immediate bearing upon the eradication of poverty. Moreover, the issue of poverty frequently arises in the course of the Committee's constructive dialogue with States parties. In the light of experience gained over many years, including the examination of numerous States parties' reports, the Committee holds the firm view that poverty constitutes a denial of human rights.
>
> (CESCR, 2001: para. 1)

The idea that poverty represents a violation of rights is an important and powerful one (Lister, 2004). It brings the symbolic and mobilising potential of rights discourse directly to bear on the issue of poverty. It can do so, broadly speaking, in two ways: through formal institutional approaches to combat global injustices and rein in the destructive forces that fuel and perpetuate poverty, or through substantive interventions that give expression to our universal humanity and/or acknowledge that people experiencing poverty are not passive victims or mere statistics, but human beings with their own agency.

Approaches inspired by institutional justice concerns

The author and activist who most clearly brings a human rights perspective to bear on global poverty issues is Thomas Pogge (2002, 2007: ch. 1). Pogge holds to an institutionalist conception of social rights, regarding them as 'moral claims on the organization of one's society' (2002: 64). His concern is with moral, not legal, rights and here he draws on the authority of the UDHR, Article 28: 'Everyone is entitled to a social and international order in which the rights and freedoms set forth in this Declaration can be fully realized'. On that basis, he contends that a global institutional order that continues to permit a foreseeable and extensive incidence of extreme poverty is in violation of human rights. By that standard, the commitment under the MDGs merely to halve the proportion of people living in extreme poverty by 2015 was simply not enough. The alternative, according to Pogge, depends first, on the entrenchment of democracy. Currently, he contends, the most affluent have shaped the world order to the disadvantage of the poorest and we must hold the powerful to account. At the very least it would be necessary to obtain international agreement that no kind of financial aid should be provided to non-democratic regimes. Second, he proposes the introduction of some form of international fiscal mechanism with which to fund development aid. One such mechanism would be a currency transfer tax (or Tobin tax – see Nissanke, 2003), which would entail a UN-administered tax (that might be set at anything between 0.005 and 1%) on the 2 or more trillion dollars-worth (US$) of speculative currency transfers that take place each day. Pogge's own preference would be for a global resources dividend, a tax that would redistribute from those in the world who make the greatest demands on the world's resources to those who make the least. It would work by raising a levy (US$2.00 per barrel of oil, for example) on those countries that use or sell limited natural resources extracted from their own territories.

The third of Pogge's proposals is for some form of cosmopolitan citizenship. There are similarities here with other proposals for cosmopolitan or global citizenship emanating from a spectrum of authors (Delanty, 2000; Dwyer, 2010: ch. 10; Falk, 1994; Held, 2010). The common core of these proposals is a form of institutional cosmopolitanism premised on generalised and universal equality between all individuals – forms of post-national inclusion at both sub- and supranational levels, but subject in the foreseeable future to an enduring role for the nation state within a system of multilateral global governance. David Held, in particular, has suggested that the initial stages in a transition to cosmopolitan governance might centre on a further reshaping of the Washington consensus in the direction of a social democratic agenda (Held, 2004, 2010). It is striking, however, that none of these proposals contain much, if any, explicit detail as to the role of social rights. The assumption appears to be that the realisation of social rights is somehow assured on the basis of generic cosmopolitan principles that include a commitment to social justice. It is possible to envisage reforms to the apparatuses of the UN that might facilitate such an agenda, though none of these currently seem feasible. Proposals here include the ideas of strengthening ECOSOC by giving it charter powers and a proper infrastructure, and of creating a UN 'People's Assembly' or even a 'World Parliament' (Patomäki & Teivainen, 2004).

Institutional justice approaches, incidentally, may be broadly consistent with the **δ** perspective in Figure 3.1 in Chapter 3, albeit that their concerns for abstract notions of justice may also draw upon socially inflected liberal individualistic influences from the **α** perspective.

Approaches inspired by concerns for humanity

An approach distinguishable from, though not necessarily unsympathetic to, that of Pogge is that of Tom Campbell (2007). Campbell, who once attempted to explore the idea of socialist rights (1983), regards poverty as a violation of rights, not so much because it is unjust, as because it is an affront to the humanity of the people who experience it. He contends that all human rights derive from the existence of needs (2007: 59), though, puzzlingly, he associates needs with Sen's concept of capabilities, rather than – as a socialist might – with Marx's concept of species characteristics. Nonetheless, he conceives of social rights as rights to the resources required for a truly human life. Poverty therefore violates human rights in the same sense as torture or slavery might. Poverty should be eradicated or indeed abolished out of humanity by enforcing the rights of the poor. Campbell himself is somewhat philosophically preoccupied with competing utilitarian and deontological justifications, but I would take the broad implication of his argument, if we refer back to Chapter 3 in this volume, to be that a eudaimonic/humanitarian ethic should prevail over a hedonic/justice-based ethic.

On this basis, Campbell would prefer a global humanitarian levy to Pogge's global resource dividend. A global humanitarian levy would replace existing bilateral and multilateral overseas aid arrangements with an international system under which all national governments would levy a hypothecated tax of, Campbell suggests, 2 per cent on all personal incomes in excess of $50,000 (US$) (or the equivalent) and 2 per cent on all personal wealth above $500,000. Such a mechanism, according to Campbell, would ensure the fulfilment of subsistence rights that are 'grounded primarily in the universal humanitarian obligation to participate in the relief of extreme suffering' (2007: 67).

It is possible to conceive of mechanisms – whether based on the taxation of currency transactions, natural resource usage or personal income/wealth (Atkinson, 2004; Zedillo, 2001) – by which to garner resources for poverty eradication, but this leaves aside the question of just how such resources should be distributed. Peter Townsend has argued that such funding should provide the basis for establishing an international welfare state (Townsend, 2002, 2007, 2009: chs. 1 & 2; Townsend & Donkor, 1996). Townsend's demand was founded on a lifetime of scholarship and campaigning around poverty and was deeply rooted in Fabian socialism. His argument was that provision for a broadly construed right to social security was already internationally enshrined through the UDHR and the ICESCR and should be realised by building on the experiences of the richer OECD countries in developing social security systems. Elements of his argument are (albeit posthumously) reflected in the ILO's Social Protection Floor initiative (Batchelet, 2011; ILO, 2012b). This is an approach that contrasts radically with that of the OHCHR's guidelines for a rights-based approach (see above). A concrete and practicable first step in the construction of an international social security system, according to Townsend, would be the introduction of an international universal child benefit, funded by a Tobin tax, and rolled out globally, merging with and/or succeeding existing schemes as appropriate (including, for example, the conditional cash transfer schemes currently being developed in parts of the global South) (2009: ch. 7).

It remains to be seen whether it will ever be possible to pursue such ideas through the established institutional machinery of the UN. In the meantime, however, agitation for rights–based action against poverty can be detected at other levels. Callinicos (2003), for example, has suggested that through global networks such as the World Social Forum it might be possible to build campaigns drawing upon diverse constituencies for rights–based demands for basic incomes, reduced working hours and better public services. Some of these demands are also expressed in proposals by Guy Standing for the extension, globally, of a new form of 'occupational citizenship' (Standing, 2009). These are issues to which I shall return in Chapter 10, but for now it is worth mentioning approaches taken by a campaign organisation in which poor people themselves are directly involved.

ATD Fourth World is a human rights-based, anti-poverty organisation that was founded in 1957 in France by Joseph Wresinski, a Catholic priest. It now has a presence in over 30 countries around the world, and it will be discussed again in Chapter 10. Wresinski made himself famous both in France and at the UN by promoting the claim that extreme poverty is a form of violence and a violation of human rights. It is fundamentally a campaigning and educational organisation that aims to give a voice to people in poverty and to promote poor people's participation in policy making. As a contribution to the debate about the UN's post-2015 development agenda, the organisation has published a report, drawing on a cross-national participatory evaluation. The evaluation was based on a well-developed methodology by which ATD Fourth World has for some years been seeking to empower people living in poverty to communicate and 'to build a collective understanding of their situation as well as construct a sense of pride that counteracts their stigmatisation and isolation' (2014: 14). The principal thrust of the report and other recent publications is that whatever happens, poor people should not be 'left behind'. The rights it asserts are not specific social rights, but the rights to be heard, to equal participation and not to be discriminated against. The concern is to combat not only poverty, but 'poverty-ism' (Davies, 2008). Povertyism is a form of discrimination that may be equated with sexism, racism, disablism and ageism.

Poverty is an assault on a person's humanity as much through stigma and discrimination as it is through material deprivation (Dean, 1992; Lister, 2004). When people fight for their rights on the basis of a common identity, they characteristically mobilise and take pride in their shared identity: their class, their gender, their sexuality or their ethnicity, for example. But it is not possible for a person to take pride in their poverty – at least not in the same way. ATD Fourth World attempts to organise at a national level, but few other national or local organisations effectively mobilise poor people to speak for themselves, rather than speaking on their behalf. Such organisations tend to be transient. The US welfare rights movement of the 1960s is a case in point (Piven & Cloward, 1977), though there was a more recent attempt to build a Poor People's Economic Human Rights Campaign in the US to oppose the introduction of harsh welfare reforms in the 1990s (Baptiste & Bricker-Jenkins, 2002). The latter was significant for the way in which it sought explicitly to equate the struggle against poverty with the historic struggle against slavery. Both struggles had confronted class interests that demanded 'a flexible, contingent – and terrified – work force and the substitution of mandatory work activity for real jobs'. The organisers' objective was to produce

> a populace that questions, that demands, that moves. In those circumstances concessions might be possible. But we believe that this is a new period of history in which ending poverty is eminently possible. If we educate and organize around the realities

and possibilities of this moment, the [welfare reforms] could have the same galvanizing effect as the Dred Scott decision of 1857 [by which the US Supreme Court ruled that a slave by virtue of his African descent could not be a citizen and had no right to sue for his freedom]. It is worth remembering that the abolition movement did eventually prevail. Poverty is no more inevitable or permanent than slavery.

(Baptiste & Bricker-Jenkins, 2002: 200)

In a similar vein, Tom Campbell concluded that 'we need to work for the emergence of moral progress of a kind that led to a universal acknowledgement that the once time-honoured practice of slavery is morally heinous' (2007: 74). The idea that poverty is as much a rights violation as slavery is especially powerful, but its mobilising potential requires a different kind of solidarity among those it afflicts than that of a cause constructed around the celebration of an identity. Poverty, like slavery, is something to abolish, not celebrate.

Nonetheless, approaches inspired by concerns for humanity will be solidaristic in nature, though in terms of their place within the taxonomy of perspectives outlined in Figure 3.1 in Chapter 3 of this volume, they are currently, perhaps, more likely to exhibit elements from the δ perspective than the common-interest elements typified by the γ perspective.

Summary/conclusion

This chapter has been concerned with locating social rights in relation to recent international measures intended to promote social development and alleviate global poverty. In an attempt to illuminate some rather complex, if not confusing, debates the chapter has focused on three broad approaches.

The first is that framed through the idea of a *right to development*. The idea found expression through the UN's DRtD, but received an incidental fillip through the influential (but often misinterpreted) work of Amartya Sen, whose widely celebrated capabilities approach is encapsulated in the slogan 'development as freedom'. The idea rests on a holistic outlook that seeks to transcend the distinction between first and second generation human rights by prioritising a right to development. Its focus is on the principle of self-determination and a normative commitment to personal freedom facilitated as necessary through social co-operation. The individual human subject must be allowed and enabled to survive on her own terms. It may be argued that this holistic approach provides a context in which social rights might come into their own, or alternatively, that it is a distraction from a concerted and effective promotion of social rights.

The second approach is that framed through the idea of the *development agenda:* the main-stream technocratic approach to social development. The idea assumes that human development is both the antonym and the answer to global poverty. Its managerial focus is on the setting of goals and the monitoring of performance. A rights-based approach can be incorporated into this agenda, but on the basis of 'rights standards'. This entails an element of compromise in the sense that progressively realisable rights are not inviolably vested in the human subject, but set in terms of the achievable metrics of the development process.

The third approach is framed through the idea of *poverty as a rights violation*. The idea itself is often equivocally expressed: poverty may be seen as causing, contributing to, or providing the context for, the violation of human rights. Such interpretations result in advocacy in the cause of institutional justice – in calls for mechanisms that will hold the powerful to account and/or create a new global framework for cosmopolitan justice. However, the idea can also be interpreted in terms of a right not to be poor and/or as reason for enforcing the already existing social rights of people experiencing poverty. A rights–based approach in this context might well focus on the substantive realisation of social rights, though it can also focus on the rights of poor people to have their voices heard.

What emerges is that social rights have tended sometimes (though not necessarily always) to be marginalised within the social development process; to be denied a distinctive purpose or a leading role; to be reduced to standards, not imperatives; or to be deployed as primarily rhetorical devices in support of demands for global justice. Where a role for substantive social rights has been proposed, the proposals have arguably been either too tentative or ostensibly, perhaps, too unrealistic. But that is a matter for discussion in my concluding chapter.

10

THE FUTURE OF SOCIAL RIGHTS

This book has introduced two rather different ways in which our understanding of social rights has come about. The idea of social rights first crystallised with the development of capitalist welfare states in the global North and through an account of this process furnished – largely after the event – by T. H. Marshall. Marshall suggested that social rights had emerged as the culmination of the story by which modern citizenship had evolved. Social rights were a tangible product of capitalist development: we had *made* them. A related but different idea of social rights crystallised on the international stage as the world emerged from the second of the two world wars that had occurred during the first half of the twentieth century. Social rights, it was decided, were an essential component of our human rights, and they are necessary to peace and social order: we had *discovered* them.

However, the underpinning argument in this book has been that social rights may be understood as articulations of human need. Human beings are and have always been by definition both needy and social. By socially negotiating the ways in which we together satisfy our needs, we constitute customary expectations and practices. Insofar as we can construct the claims we make upon one another through a discourse of rights and shared responsibilities, we might recognise that we have always had social rights. Their existence is neither the unique achievement of capitalist civilisation, nor a revelatory insight of twentieth-century policy makers, jurists and ethicists. But we have now invented the discourse of rights and extended it to encompass the process by which human beings articulate and claim mutual recognition for their needs. It is a conflicted and elusive discourse on the one hand – but an evolving and powerful one on the other. Gathering together some of the unfinished threads from previous chapters, this chapter will consider the future for social rights as meaningful and effective social constructs.

It will do so in three stages. The first stage is theoretical: it will return to a critique of the Marshallian concept of social citizenship and argue for a more open understanding of the chaotic, multi-layered processes by which social rights are constructed. The second stage is normative: it will return to a critique of the dominant human rights paradigm by which social rights are held to be progressively realisable and argue that, as an approach to the recognition of human vulnerability, it is not sufficient. The third stage is practical and will offer a critical account of proposals and ideas for different approaches to the development of social rights.

A post-Marshallian theory of social rights

Informing much of this book and other recent work by this author (Dean, 2010, 2013) is what might be called a post-Marshallian concept or account of social rights. It is post-Marshallian in the following ways: first, in the sense that we live increasingly in a post-national or global era to which the Marshallian account is no longer fully suited; second, in the sense that it has a different story to tell from that told by Marshall; and third, because it defines social rights not in terms of what they prescribe, but in terms of their social essence and the extent to which they are socially constituted. Social rights are most certainly central to social policy. They are articulated *through* social policy and are widely framed by social legislation. But they were not invented by the welfare state; they are socially negotiated expressions of human need. The 'Stone Age Economics' (Sahlins, 1974) of pre-historic hunter-gatherer societies determined how to align wants with means. But clearly such societies must also have contrived customs and practices (social policies and processes) by which they organised how resources should be shared; how their members should care for each other; and who should look to whom for what. Douglas and Ney (1998) make the point that contemporary social scientific analysis can be paradoxically asocial: the whole person, as the locus of human transactions and the creator of meaning, goes missing! It is a charge that can be laid against Marshall, for whom social rights were institutional rather than social constructs. The issue is expressed in similar terms by Isin *et al.* (2008), when they speak of 'recasting the social in citizenship'.

I would argue that if we are now to think about social rights and social citizenship differently, we must nonetheless accept that social rights are part of human history. They have been and are now negotiated or 'disputed' (see Clarke *et al.,* 2014) in all sorts of different ways, at diverse sites and at a multiplicity of levels. The normative premises on which social rights may be negotiated are hugely variable. If it were ever possible to reconstruct and evaluate the basis of Stone Age social policy, we might – who knows – be either impressed or appalled by the inclusiveness/exclusivity and fairness/unfairness of the social rights to which it implicitly gave expression in comparison to social policies under contemporary welfare regimes. In Chapter 3 and Figure 3.1 I presented a taxonomy or theoretical model by which to represent competing perspectives on the connections between social rights, human needs and ethical responsibility. Each perspective was and is imbued with a different logic and normative underpinning. We can extend and reconstitute that model in order to provide a further overarching model that describes different 'modes' of social citizenship. These are different ways in which it is possible for social rights to evolve. Central to this model are two dimensions: sociality and negotiation.

Sociality is a constitutive characteristic of our 'species being' (Marx, 1844). Human beings are vulnerable, interdependent creatures who are nevertheless uniquely and purposefully social. The character of their sociality not only marks them out from other species, but it defines the conscious identity of every member of the species and the basis on which human beings recognise and communicate with each other (Honneth, 1995). It defines what it means to be human. However, the form, the depth and the orientation of human sociality may vary over time and in different social contexts. Human interdependency can be managed in different ways. Human individuals may be enabled, or aspire, to be more or less self-sufficient or more or less mutually supportive.

Negotiation is a fundamental component of everyday life and communicative action (Habermas, 1987). However, negotiation can take place at a variety of levels and in the context of differing relations of power. It may occur in the context of the intimate personal relationships, or at the level of high-powered international diplomacy. It may be informally governed through relations of trust, or formally circumscribed by rules of procedure. It can be instigated by bottom-up demands, or by top-down impositions – by popular resistance, or by governmental intervention. Negotiation is the warp and weft of social existence. It is by no means confined to face-to-face dialogue, explicit argument or political debate, but it can take the form of subtly waged battles for hearts, minds or for popular approval; of struggles for hegemonic ascendancy between dominant and subaltern discourses (Gramsci, 1971); and of artful strategies of resistance (Scott, 1985). Negotiation is axiomatically a dialogic and dialectical process, though it may be more or less powerfully directed or shaped by hegemonic frames of reference.

Social rights are expressions of sociality, and they are negotiated. If we take sociality and negotiation as intersecting dimensions that define differing modes of social citizenship, it is possible to construct the model represented in Figure 10.1. In this model the sociality dimension runs from weak (on the left of the diagram) to strong (on the right): 'weaker' sociality in this sense implies a form of sociality inclined to individual self-sufficiency within a competitive social environment, while 'stronger' sociality implies a form of sociality inclined to mutual support in a co-operative social environment. It must be acknowledged however that sociality, though it may assume a different character and orientation, has significance at both extremes of this spectrum. The negotiation dimension runs from hegemonically weakly framed negotiation (at the bottom) to hegemonically strongly framed negotiation (at the top). More 'weakly' framed negotiation in this sense implies a form of negotiation motivated by emotional affect (e.g. respect or resentment) and expressed through subaltern or everyday demands, while more 'strongly' framed negotiation implies a form of negotiation shaped or constrained by the conventions of rational argument and informed by dominant or systemic prescription. It should be noted that relations of power are operative at both extremes of this spectrum: strong hegemonic framing will entail argument in the context of a heavily one-sided ideological agenda, while weak hegemonic framing might imply resistance to paternalistic or even coercive methods of persuasion. However, it is the actual modes of social citizenship that I describe using this model that may be of more immediate interest to some readers than the theoretical method by which I seek to define them.

The idea of a 'mode' of social citizenship is intended to capture something about the ways in which citizens embrace the justice, or tolerate the injustice, of the social arrangements around them. Human societies have to accommodate demands and resistances, inequalities and divisions. A classic account of the 'social bases of obedience and revolt' has been provided by Barrington Moore, who endeavoured through an insightful anthropological and social historical analysis to tease out recurring elements in the 'moral codes' (1978: ch. 1) by which all human societies have sought – whether successfully or unsuccessfully – internally to co-ordinate the exercise of authority, the division of labour and the distribution of resources. His central observation is that every social order has both beneficiaries and victims and for a social order to be sustainable, its victims must apparently submit to a form of 'social anaesthesia'. Moore's chosen task was that of determining 'how people awake from anaesthesia,

---

BOX 10.1   POPULAR NOTIONS OF SOCIAL JUSTICE

People will accommodate to an unequal distribution of resources in society, provided it is in the context of:

- **Just reward:** they must be persuaded there is broad equality of reward in relation to skill and effort.
- **Just restraint:** they must be persuaded that nobody is hoarding scarce resources or free loading.
- **Just advantage:** they must be persuaded that those who are privileged fulfil their social obligations.
- **Just shares:** they must be persuaded that social risks and responsibilities are equally shared.

---

how they overcome a sense of inevitability and how a sense of injustice may take its place' (1978: 460–461). Along the way, however, he throws out a number of hints about how human beings accommodate to different notions of justice. Box 10. 1 provides not so much a paraphrase of Moore's argument as a somewhat selective interpretation.

Figure 10.1 contrasts four ideal typical ways in which social rights might attract popular support as rights of social citizenship. Each mode of social citizenship equates, or can be aligned, with one of the social rights perspectives identified earlier in Chapter 3, and they have accordingly been labelled **α, β, γ** and **δ,** respectively:

- The **α** mode reflects both meritocratic and utilitarian concerns. The rights it claims are rights to just rewards; to equal chances, not equal outcomes; to guaranteed opportunities and equal treatment, albeit with a reliable social safety net in case of misfortune. In contemporary terms it is recognisable as a liberal–individualist mode of social citizenship and powerfully hegemonic.

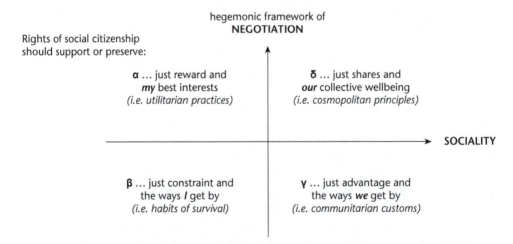

FIGURE 10.1 Modes of social citizenship and the basis on which they have popular support

- The β mode reflects what Moore (1978: 38) characterises as the 'dog in the manger taboo'. The rights it claims are ambiguously 'social', since their priority is to preserve the habits by which the individual and her/his individual family survives, while ensuring that the individual should not be disadvantaged by the greed of others. It is recognisable as a moral authoritarian mode of citizenship that supports just constraints on greed and idleness and is accepting of law and order and punitive forms of poor relief.

- The γ mode reflects communitarian concerns for the maintenance of social cohesion or stability. Moore makes the point that in a hierarchical society 'a secure but lowly status is much easier to bear than no position at all . . . [because] . . . the individual can trade obedience and loyalty for security if the relationship has some colour of justice and affection' (1978: 463). The advantage of those with wealth and high status is just or tolerable so long as they observe the principles of *noblesse oblige* and their responsibilities to the poor. This is recognisably consistent with certain elements of a conservative mode of social citizenship.

- The δ mode reflects a cosmopolitan understanding of equality and a concern for universal human welfare. It is consistent with a rule of equality characterised by Moore (1978: 38) as 'a form of general social insurance against misfortune'. Social insurance provides a mechanism for the sharing of risks and responsibilities, and in a contemporary context (provided it achieves universal coverage – see Chapters 6 and 7, this volume) it is, or can be, consistent with a social democratic mode of social citizenship.

This is the last of the heuristic conceptual models that will be presented in this book, though it is in many respects merely a differently inflected iteration of the previous models. Its function is to cast further insight into the conflicting influences and ambitions that may be at work in the construction of social rights at different moments in history, within different populations and under different regimes. If it is accepted that social rights are the outcome of the struggle to achieve recognition for human needs, it may be grasped first, that this is a *continuous* struggle that occurs at a variety of sites and levels and it is likely that it will sometimes give rise to rights that are objectively suboptimal or unsustainable; second, it is a *dynamic* struggle and it is unlikely that the form and substance of the rights that emerge will conform or even approximate to just one of the modes of social citizenship defined above.

The idea that social rights may be understood as 'sites of social struggle' or 'sites of dialogue' is prefigured, for example, by Nedelsky and Scott (1992: 62). In part this is a reaffirmation of the argument that all rights are socially constructed (e.g. Schiengold, 1974/2004; Travers, 2010; Waters, 1996), though Nedelsky and Scott were also affirming the specific argument that is central to this book, namely that social rights are the means by which we structure relationships of interdependency: they are 'rights in relationship' (1992: 69). Such dialogue can take place at an infinite variety of sites, within and between households, communities, nations and global institutions. It can entail 'conversations' between combinations of individual actors and collective actors. At one level, a subsistence farmer (perhaps with the assistance of a community elder) may, through dialogue, establish customary rights for members of her household to access a water source on a neighbour's land. At another level, the rights of HIV/AIDS sufferers to antiretroviral drug treatment may be developed through a 'constructive constitutional conversation' between the judiciary and the government – as occurred in the celebrated case of *Cruz Bermudez v. Ministerio de Sanidad y Asistencia Social* (1999) before the Venezuelan Supreme Court (discussed, for example, in O'Mathúna *et al.,* 2005: 40). Or at a global level, complex multi-party negotiations may entail conversations within or across the boundaries of conflicting orthodoxies (e.g. the characteristically **α** mode Washington consensus of the World Bank and the characteristically **δ** mode Social Protection Floor initiative of the ILO).

I have said from the outset that though they are socially constructed, social rights have real effects. Another way of putting this is to say that they are or can be 'constitutive' of social practice (Schiengold, 2004: xxi). In Chapter 8, I cited the first edition of Stuart Schiengold's book *The Politics of Rights,* which was in many ways a foundational text of the socio-legal studies tradition of 'legal realism'. Its contention was that although legally framed rights are top-down mythical constructions, they provide a discursive resource that can be deployed as a bottom-up political tactic. In the second, 40th anniversary edition of his book, Schiengold has added a preface in which he suggests a new politics of rights that would 'decentre' law in an even more radical sense. He presents 'a vision of the interpenetration of multiple levels of legality' (2004: xxii) and of a role for law and 'cause lawyering' (see also Sarat & Schiengold, 2001) within a context where rights can be accorded not fixed meanings, but a plurality of everyday meanings. By my reading, that implies that when it comes to social rights, legal meanings are only one kind of meaning (albeit an important kind) within that plurality.

I shall address the normative and practical implications later in this chapter, but I am at present attempting to ground a post-Marshallian conception of social citizenship that encompasses competing modalities and that is negotiated at a multiplicity of levels. Although I have characterised the non-dominant **δ** social citizenship 'mode' as cosmopolitan in a normative and practical sense, I am here concerned with a *theory* that is cosmopolitan in an overarching methodological sense (Beck, 2002, 2003). It is because the era of methodological nationalism is largely (though by no means entirely) spent that the Marshallian conception of social citizenship must be transcended in order to account for social rights as a global human phenomenon. A cosmopolitan methodological perspective begins potentially to blur the boundaries between citizenship rights and human rights. Arguing for a cosmopolitan social theoretical outlook, Robert Fine revisits those critiques of the human rights agenda that draw a strict distinction between top-down rights as imperialistic instruments of social control and redemptive bottom-up rights as instruments of emancipation, arguing that in reality 'everything interesting occurs in the in-between' (2007: 141). This would seem to chime with my contention that social rights are made at the points where competing modalities collide.

Challenging the normative foundations of the human rights agenda

In Chapter 3 I drew a distinction between the dominant and (after Woodiwiss, 2005) the 'minor' traditions in prevailing human rights discourse: the former being essentially individualistic, and the latter essentially solidaristic. Central to the dominant tradition is the totemic concept of dignity. The term appears in nearly all international instruments pertaining to human rights. The preamble to the UDHR calls at its outset for the recognition of the 'inherent dignity . . . of all members of the human family'. Such recognition may be normatively interpreted as a claim to equal integrity and personal autonomy amidst a family of atomistic, self-seeking individuals, though, potentially, it might also be interpreted as a claim to inclusion and ontological security within a diverse and interdependent human family. It is the former interpretation that overwhelmingly dominates although, in Chapter 3, we noted the excoriating critique of Hannah Arendt, for whom the claim to some kind of *inborn* human dignity – if indeed that is what 'inherent' dignity means – is hubris: an 'arrogant myth'.

Arendt's argument needs to be understood in context. Her scholarship revolved around a critical analysis of totalitarianism. The immense significance claimed for the post–Second World War human rights agenda was that it could address the rights of stateless persons and those who had been denied citizenship, and, in a fundamental sense, the rights of those whose experiences of war and atrocity had stripped them of their very humanity. Reflecting on such horrors as the Nazi concentration camps, Arendt concluded:

> The assumption of human rights, based upon the assumed existence of a human being as such, broke down at the very moment when those who professed to believe in it were for the first time confronted with people who had indeed lost all other qualities and special relationships – except they were still human. The world saw nothing sacred in the abstract nakedness of being human.

> (1951: 295)

For Arendt, humanity was not an abstract quality; it arises through membership of a concrete political community. Her complaint was that 'today we consider both history and nature alien to the essence of man' (1951: 435). An appeal to inherent or intrinsic human dignity was for her a negation of the reality of the human condition. Paradoxically, although Arendt was supremely critical of Marx, she shared with him the belief that humanity is defined not only by human biology, but also essentially by human history and community. In different ways, Arendt and Marx each recognised the constitutive character of human interdependence, though in both analyses there was some ambiguity as to the place of social rights. Arendt drew a distinction between public rights and private interests (1977) – a distinction that, confusingly and perhaps perversely, appears to correspond pretty much to the now familiar distinction between on the one hand, civil and political rights (which she saw as 'public') and, on the other, social rights (which she saw as 'private') (Parekh, 2008: 93). For Arendt our humanity is defined through participation in the public sphere, while the means by which human beings satisfy their biological needs are seen as a private, not a social, matter. Nevertheless, she conceded that the meeting of what she called private interests is a necessary foundation for the exercise of public freedom and 'public happiness'. Poverty, she argues, must be overcome for the sake of political life (Parekh, 2008: 27). There is a sense in which Arendt's conception of the private and public realms equates with the Aristotelian notions of hedonic wellbeing (private existence) and eudaimonic wellbeing (public existence) (see Chapters 2 and 3, this volume). The fullness of our humanity is realised through public participation in a political community – in other words, through civic virtue.

This is, up to a point, consistent with an alternative definition of dignity: a dignity that is not inherent, but achieved. Jones (2012) suggests three broad definitions of dignity: the 'intrinsic' dignity assumed by human rights discourse; the 'attributed' dignity associated with high social status and/or with dignitaries; and the kind of dignity that may be defined on the basis of a virtue ethics approach (see Chapter 4, this volume). Differently inflected versions of the latter view may be seen, for example, in the work of MacIntyre (1999 – discussed in Jones, 2012) or Harris (1997). It is a view that looks for dignity in interdependence. Since humans are all vulnerable creatures there is as much dignity in receiving as in giving care and support; and there is a complementarity between awareness of one's human limitations (humility) and one's willingness to help others (compassion). Here we are concerned with everyday virtues, including and especially those associated with a public service ethic: with, for example, the vocational commitment of healthcare professionals and welfare administrators in their deal-ings with vulnerable individuals, and with the public spiritedness entailed when people take part in public deliberation and lend support to the collective provision of social services. However, this is, perhaps, too tenuous a defence of the use of the word dignity to define a foundational human right. If dignity is a virtue or a spiritual quality, it may be admirable or desirable, but it is not innate. Dignity 'in practice' (Wright *et al.*, 2014: 60–61) is socially constructed and realised or experienced through interdependence and solidarity with others.

Yet we have seen in Chapter 9 that one of the principal justifications for social rights and social development has been that poverty is held to be a violation of human dignity. Rela-tive poverty is widely understood as something more than material deprivation, but rather in terms of its relational and symbolic aspects: the humiliation, the shame and the loss of dignity with which it is associated (Lister, 2004; Smith, 1776; Walker *et al.*, 2013). Poverty in this sense is socially constructed, as are the social rights by which we might lay claim to counter poverty. The right not to be poor can be a right, provided it is effectively asserted. But I would argue that this is not best achieved by appeals to inherent dignity. People can be so anaesthetised to suffering that they accept their lot and suffer *with dignity*. As Barrington Moore has put it: 'The human capacity to withstand suffering and abuse is impressive, tragi-cally so' (1978: 13). The international anti-poverty organisation ATD Fourth World, which I mentioned in Chapter 9, seeks to promote the dignity of poor people. The ATD acronym originally stood for '*Aide à Toute Détresse*' (help for all in distress), but it has recently been anglicised so as to stand for 'All Together in Dignity'. This was not simply a concession to the forces of linguistic imperialism, but an acknowledgement of the organisation's philoso-phy, which focuses on enabling people experiencing poverty to fight stigma and prejudice by establishing a sense of shared dignity. Just as Alcoholics Anonymous requires members publicly to confess their alcoholism, ATD Fourth World requires its members publicly to acknowledge their own poverty. The difference is that alcoholics must struggle throughout their lives to cope with their addiction, but people experiencing poverty should surely be enabled to escape from poverty, rather than to find dignity in poverty. Is there not a contra-diction here? (I'm honestly not sure.)

Other social movements seek to foster not dignity, but indignation. The most spectacular example is the worldwide Occupy movement that sprang up in opposition to the austerity measures and associated curtailment of social rights following the global financial crisis that began around 2008 and whose ramifications rumble on (Kerton, 2012; Pickerill & Krin-sky, 2012). The Spanish wing of that movement is known as *Indignados* (Castañeda, 2012), which translated to English means 'outrage', a name directly influenced by a manifesto enti-tled *Indignez-Vous* in the original French language edition, by the former resistance fighter, human rights campaigner and supporter of myriad radical causes, Stéphane Hessel (2011). As a loosely networked global movement, Occupy (and/or *Indignados*) is concerned with a range of discontents within which social rights do not always feature that explicitly, but the move-ment's potential impact, it might be argued, stems from a refusal to suffer with what might conventionally be described as 'dignity'.

Attempts to connect abstract notions of human dignity with the pragmatic business of realising social rights are rather scarce. A notable exception is a thoughtful account provided by Chan & Bowpitt (2005), though this is very much concerned with welfare *systems,* rather than explicitly with social rights and discourses of rights. For Chan and Bowpitt, human dig-nity 'resides in our possession of intrinsic capacities which strive for autonomy and mutuality'

(2005: 22). If human dignity can be said to equate with personal autonomy (Doyal & Gough, 1991), it may be argued that this should amount to far more than mere self-sufficiency (Williams, 1999). And as for mutuality, it is a slippery concept. It may refer to a narrow contractarian calculus of reciprocity, rather than to inclusive social relations of interdependency. In Chan and Bowpitt's case, mutuality is addressed in a teleological manner by drawing on the psychological literature, which demonstrates that social interaction is necessary to personal development and self-identity. The focus remains on what is allegedly intrinsic to the individual rather than the constitutive character of her sociality.

Let us return for a moment to Tom Campbell's plea for humanity before justice (see Chapter 9, this volume): poverty is a violation of human rights because it amounts to inhumanity, not injustice (2007). This humanitarian approach, as I read it, found the idea of human rights on tangible human solidarity, not on imagined inborn dignity. I am not suggesting, as do some (e.g. Macklin, 2003), that we should banish the term 'dignity' from public discourse. Bioethicists remind us that we live in era when, as a result of new technologies, the definition of what it is in biological terms to be human is quite literally in question, and it behoves us in the wider context 'to understand and acknowledge the variations in [the] meanings [of human dignity]' (Pellegrino *et al.*, 2009: 535). However, just as we can now manipulate the genetics of the human organism, we have long had the capacity to eradicate poverty, which –though it may be a condition symbolically devoid of dignity – is the objective result of a failure of human solidarity.

I would argue that at the very least this requires a recalibration of our understanding of human rights in favour of what I have been referring to as the minor tradition. If the object of social rights is not so much to underwrite some abstract standard of human dignity, as to respond to humanitarian indignation, the principle that social rights may be 'progressively realised' is to be questioned: it is not good enough. The assertion of this book is that social rights are constituted through the naming and claiming of needs – at a multiplicity of sites and levels. The idea of what would be 'good-enough' is suggested by Fiona Williams's reflections on 'good-enough principles for welfare' (1999) (and mentioned in Chapter 3, this volume). Drawing on Winnicott's (1953) notion of 'good-enough parenting', Williams suggests that ' "good-enough" indicates a morality grounded in the relational conditions of everyday life sufficient for the recognition of moral worth' (1999: 675). Williams's principles of welfare cover issues of interdependence; care; intimacy; bodily integrity; identity; transnationality; and voice. A full exposition warrants more space than is available in this chapter, but here lies the basis of a bid for the kind of social rights where human subjects

> are sustained through interdependence, through striving for the mutual recognition of worth and a tolerance of diversity, and whose capacity for self-interested action is mediated through bonds of belonging and meanings of identity and structured by local, national and international relations of power and inequality.
>
> (1999: 685)

Notions of dignity remain wholly relevant, but humanity is socially contextualised. Insofar as needs may be translated into rights, they are *social* rights. What they demand is more than dignity; they demand the recognition of needs and good-enough responses to need.

We have seen is that when social rights are translated into rights of citizenship within a welfare state, the right to social security provides some protection (or 'asylum' in its literal and non-pejorative sense) against the hazards of life, including the risks of an exploitative labour market and of poverty in old age; the right to housing provides some protection against the hazards of exclusive housing markets and the risks of homelessness; and the right to social care provides some protection against the risks of social exclusion and socially produced disability. Whether as human rights or citizenship rights, social rights as I wish to define them are concerned with the social negotiation of human needs. Their full realisation requires more than a defence of human dignity (however defined); it requires the expansion of human solidarity.

What is to be done?

I have presented a theoretical model through which to interpret the ways in which – whether for good or ill – social rights might unfold in future and a normative argument as to the direction in which I believe we should reframe, or at least rebalance, the social rights agenda. But what are the implications of this analysis in practical terms? I set out to make this book relevant to practice: to the practices of an entire spectrum of actors, including agitators, activists, community workers, aid workers, welfare rights workers, other welfare professionals and administrators, lawyers, policy commentators and, perhaps, policy makers. Of course, academics can be actors too. I am not proposing the formation of a revolutionary vanguard (*pace* Lenin, 1902), since it is for such actors continually to reflect, discuss and decide how best to proceed from within the multiplicity of contexts in which they find themselves. But I shall very briefly outline a few comments and suggestions, which fall under two headings. The first leans towards issues and disparate examples within the constitutional and legal sphere. The second is of greater relevance to informally grounded action, advocacy and campaigning. Inevitably, however, there is considerable potential overlap.

Legal and constitutional context

Should we seek to re-write the UDHR? Insofar as the UN has, in addition to the UDHR, generated an ostensibly impressive range of other social rights–related treaties and constitutional instruments (see Box 2.3 in Chapter 2, this volume), do we need more? The first possibility is not on the agenda and it is difficult to see the circumstances in which the international community might in the foreseeable future convene a legitimate forum through which to approach such a task. It would be interesting to contemplate just what kind of declaration might emerge from such a negotiation and to what extent it might differ from that agreed in 1948. In practice, the best that might be done is for alternative fora to develop and propose revised declarations.

The Spanish Society for International Human Rights Law has elaborated a Declaration on the Human Right to Peace, a final version of which was adopted in 2010 at an international congress convened in Santiago de Compostela under the auspices of the World Social Forum on Education for Peace (SSIHRL, 2010). On the premise that poverty and social exclusion are regarded as forms of structural, as opposed to armed, violence, the authors contend they are incompatible with peace. The declaration accordingly makes express provision for social rights to combat poverty, albeit that these amount to little more than a restatement or reaffirmation of existing provisions in the UDHR. Though it has no legal standing, this alternative declaration is significant first, as an attempt to situate social rights in a broader context, but also as a tactic through which to influence working groups reporting to the UNHRC. In 2012, the UNHRC considered, but could not agree to, a somewhat different version of a declaration on the right to peace (that nonetheless made mention of social rights). At the time of writing, attempts to formulate a draft that would attract international agreement have been signally unsuccessful.

If the scope for developing international treaties is limited, effort might be better devoted to making the existing international monitoring framework work better. Maximum use could be made of existing accountability mechanisms. Mention was made in Chapter 8 of the complaints procedures provided under the Optional Protocol to the ICESCR and, for example, the revised European Social Charter. There is a case for putting internal pressure on countries which have not opted in to such procedures to do so and for promoting the use of the fora created by such procedures. Special procedures (OHCHR, 2013) for the appointment of special rapporteurs, independent experts and working groups who report to the UNHRC also provide an opportunity for promoting social rights, and there are currently several special rapporteurs with investigative responsibilities in specific social rights–related fields (see Box 10.2). In 2006 the UNHRC introduced a process of universal periodic review (see www.ohchr.org/en/hrbodies/upr/pages/uprmain.aspx) under which, at four yearly intervals, UN member states are required to submit for critical examination national reports relating to their compliance with human rights obligations. Human rights bodies and NGOs have the opportunity to submit independent reports as a part of the periodic review process, providing yet another avenue by which failures to respect, protect or fulfil social rights may be highlighted.

More radical reforms to the machinery of the UN would require changes to its basic architecture. Brief mention of such possibilities was made in Chapter 9. The innovations necessary to establish institutions capable of administering global taxation mechanisms and redistribution though – for example, a global basic income (see www.globalincome.org) or an international social security system (Townsend, 2002) – would require a significant strengthening of the powers of ECOSOC relative to those of other organs of the UN and probably, therefore, amendments to the UN Charter. This would in turn be dependent on the democratisation of UN Security Council and General Assembly procedures (Patomäki & Teivainen, 2004). Nevertheless, enhanced co-ordination between and within existing UN agencies and further strengthening of regional supranational co-ordinating bodies clearly

---

BOX 10.2   UN SPECIAL RAPPORTEURS WITH SOCIAL RIGHTS–RELATED RESPONSIBILITIES

- Special rapporteur on adequate housing as a component of the right to an adequate standard of living
- Special rapporteur on the right to education
- Special rapporteur on extreme poverty and human rights
- Special rapporteur on the right to food
- Special rapporteur on the right of everyone to the enjoyment of the highest attainable standard of physical and mental health
- Special rapporteur on the human right to safe drinking water and sanitation

could have a part to play in the development and enforcement of social rights worldwide. There is scope for the promotion of some degree of 'global social reformist hegemony' in relation to social rights (Deacon, 2007: 189).

In an era of globalisation, with significant levels of international migration (Castles & Miller, 2009), one of the most enduring yet urgent challenges is that of establishing the social rights of migrants. This we touched upon in Chapter 4 when discussing anti-racist critiques of citizenship-based conceptualisations of social rights. The International Convention on the Protection of the Rights of All Migrant Workers and Members of Their Families of 1990 (which only came into force in 2003) provides rights to participate in contributory social security schemes (where these exist), to urgent medical care and to education for the children of migrants. But the convention has been neither signed nor ratified by any of the economically advanced countries of the world (albeit many of them do begrudgingly comply, more or less, with its main provisions). A form of global citizenship that would allow for migration without borders would seem to be a remote possibility, though it has been afforded serious consideration in a UNESCO report (Pecoud & de Guchteneire, 2005). The UDHR provides for a right to emigration under Article 13 (that is, a right to leave a country, including one's own) but no corresponding right to immigration (that is to enter any other country). To provide an open right of mobility – as broadly applied within the EU – would be logical, but opens up the question of the extent to which social rights can indeed be universal.

Entzinger (2007) has suggested that for established welfare states there are four possible solutions: speeding up integration of immigrants into the labour market; limiting safety net entitlements for established citizens and immigrants alike; allowing restricted entitlement for immigrants; and de-territorialising entitlements (i.e. allowing greater portability of entitlements 'earned' over the life course through working or residing in different countries). In practice, most developed welfare states employ a mixture of such solutions, but the underlying assumption is that there are limits to the human solidarity upon which provision of social rights depends (Alesina & Glaeser, 2004; Goodhart, 2006). This assumption has been challenged on empirical grounds (Banting & Kymlicka, 2006), but from an ethical perspective, the point made, for example, by Honneth (1995; and see discussion in Chapter 4, this volume), is that rights transcend feelings of solidarity: they are concerned with the recognition of the claims of distant strangers, without regard for territorial boundaries.

For the foreseeable future, nevertheless, social rights – whether for established citizens or recent migrants – will for the most part be framed in a national context, and here we might return for a moment to a discussion begun in Chapter 8, when we considered how some countries have written social rights into their constitutions, with or without provision for them to be justiciable. Debates have been promoted in the UK, which has no written constitution, for the adoption of some form of social charter to provide a framework through which to interpret or develop social legislation and/or to hold the executive more closely accountable in the sphere of social rights (Coote, 1992; Van Buerren, 2002). A commission was recently established to consider whether there should be a UK Bill of Rights, but its inconclusive report was generally opposed to the inclusion of social rights within any such a bill (Commission on a Bill of Rights, 2012), and the principal focus of its deliberations had lain elsewhere. The UK does have an Equalities and Human Rights Commission with investigative powers, but such powers do not in practice extend to direct engagement in the sphere of social rights; arguably, though, the commission's monitoring of social inequalities can serve to provide evidence of failures to protect social rights (Burchardt & Vizard, 2007).

In Australia, a similarly constituted Federal Human Rights Commission has in the past used its investigative powers, for example, to mount an inquiry into the impact of homelessness on children and young people (Hunt, 1996: 190–195).

With or without the context of a constitutional framework or national monitoring bodies, it is often through the ingenuity and determination of welfare rights workers and legal experts that pressure for observance, reform and further development of social rights is maintained. Though the limitations of legalistic strategies for advancing social rights were discussed in Chapter 8 it is important to acknowledge the contribution that legal activism can play as a tactic within wider strategies (cf. Schiengold, 1974/2004). Such work may proceed out of moral conviction, but the quotidian reality is that social legislation is but the means, not an end. It may provide, for example, for the administration of a particular social security scheme and do nothing more and no less than assign or regulate the responsibilities and conduct of officials appointed to fulfil particular tasks (Hirst, 1980). When benefit is withheld under such a scheme, a welfare rights worker or lawyer who assists a legal appeal is not so much upholding a right to social security as challenging the propriety of a particular administrative ruling or regulation. As a UK Social Security commissioner, rejecting one such appeal, once said: 'At the end of the day, the supplementary benefit scheme [the then prevailing social assistance scheme] is not something to which there is a divine right: it is nothing more than an arbitrary compromise, sanctioned by Parliament, between the demand for benefits on the one hand and the availability of public funds to finance it' (case R(SB)55/83 – reported in *Welfare Rights Bulletin,* Issue No. 60 (July 1984) p. 8 – see Figure 10.2).

Substantive social rights do indeed arise from more or less arbitrary compromises between competing interests. But they can also be the outcome of campaigns for less conditionality and for more generous provision (in short, for better compromises): campaigns in which welfare rights casework and cause lawyering can play a supporting role. To those who press the cause of social rights, the nation state that currently governs most of our social rights may appear

> . . . as a link in a chain of historical development. Hence it by no means constitutes 'man's natural environment' but merely a real fact whose actual power must be reckoned with but which has no inherent right to determine our actions. The state and the laws shall be seen as having no more than an empirical validity. In the same way as a yachtsman must take exact note of the direction of the wind without letting the wind determine his course; on the contrary, he defies it and exploits it in order to hold fast to his original course.
>
> (Lukács, 1971: 262)

Local/informal context

The constitutional and legal context matters, but of equal and in some respects greater importance is the everyday context of the life world, of local struggles and informal demands.

That world is by no means disconnected from the systemic legal and constitutional sphere, since it exists in continual communication with it: reacting to, resisting and informing it. Political activity of various kinds spans the divide between these contexts. The post-Marshallian conception of social citizenship that I have outlined enables us to understand that the social negotiation of social rights permeates every level of human existence, from

FIGURE 10.2 'You do not have a divine right to your benefit . . .'
Reproduced by kind permission of Child Poverty Action Group

the local to the global. At the level of everyday relations of interdependency, we can see that the realisation of social rights might entail the 'publicising' of 'privately' experienced needs. This is the essence of the 'politics of needs interpretation' espoused by Nancy Fraser (1989: ch. 8), and upon which I have expanded elsewhere (Dean, 2010). Fraser's original argument was that needs discourse is generated in three spheres: the political, the economic and the domestic. Fraser's particular idea of a politics of needs interpretation is of a struggle to project the needs associated with everyday livelihoods and household survival from the domestic to the political sphere and to prevent the subordination of such needs to the demands of the economic sphere. This entails a notion of 'private' and 'public' realms quite similar to that of Hannah Arendt (see above), albeit that Fraser is seeking to erode the barriers between them so as to achieve a fundamental 'rebalancing' of democracy.

The implication, to my mind, is that this opens up the possibilities for negotiating social rights; for translating hidden or neglected needs – especially those experienced by women and marginalised social groups – into rights-based claims-making; and for expanding our understanding of social rights, not least as rights that can be 'enjoyed' without necessarily being formally implemented through legislation (Davy & Pellissery, 2013). Practical instances of something like this may be seen, for example, in the resistance practices of the Malaysian peasants studied by Scott (1985) – practices Scott refers to as a form of 'infra-politics'. Resistance can be seen in the practices adopted within informal settlements that can amount, according to Holston (2009), to a form of 'insurgent citizenship'. Such social practices may well be far from perfect in terms of the levels of equality and inclusion that they achieve, and they may or may not lead to the realisation of more formal forms of social citizenship. But as sites of social citizenship, they matter. They are grass-roots sites within which struggles for gender equality, sustainable living standards and social justice can be fomented.

Grass-roots sites can now, of course, be global as well as local. Infra-politics can be virtually as well as physically located. The power and penetration of social media based on new information technologies dissolve the significance of territorial boundaries and facilitate communication within virtual communities with shared needs and interdependencies (Williams, 2007). It is this that has made possible the resistances of the Occupy and *Indignados* movements mentioned above. The potential of movements such as these for the promotion of social rights has still, perhaps, to be realised. At one stage the emergence of the World Social Forum had been regarded as the foundation through which global resistance to global capitalist hegemony might be articulated (Callinicos, 2003; Kaldor, 2003), though it has since been criticised, for example, by Bob Deacon for resolving 'not to fashion a manifesto, preferring instead a thousand voices to bloom' (2007: 190).

However, one example of a popular manifesto that could perhaps be globally promoted through such channels would be Guy Standing's proposed charter for the 'precariat' (2014). This is an informal charter that gives expression to Standing's call for a form of global occupational citizenship (mentioned in Chapter 9, this volume). A summary of the charter is presented in Box 10.3. Critics suggest that this perhaps falls between two stools: it seeks on the one hand to popularise the concept of the precariat, as a growing and increasingly disadvantaged global class, but on the other it depends on some quite esoteric terminology and reasoning (Harris, 2014). I mention it here for its potential as a campaigning tool that draws on the language of rights – as an alternative to more formal attempts to develop or amend human rights treaties and conventions.

Returning for a moment from global to local sites for grass-roots social rights activism, these need not be insurgent in origin. They can, after a fashion, be manufactured, though their effectiveness may be limited. In England, for example, there were experiments in the 1970s with non-statutory urban neighbourhood councils (Cockburn, 1977: ch. 5); with local community relations councils (created under Race Relations Act of 1968, but discontinued after 1976); and locally elected community health councils (statutorily created in 1974, but eventually abolished in 2003). In this author's experience, such bodies could be effective, if

---

BOX 10.3   THE DEMANDS CONTAINED IN GUY STANDING'S
***PRECARIAT CHARTER* (2014)**

- Redefine work as productive and reproductive activity
- Reform labour statistics (to account for all forms of useful work)
- Make recruitment practices brief encounters (to limit burden on precariously employed workers)
- Promote associational freedom
- Reconstruct occupational communities (to strengthen their bargaining power)
- Stop class-based migration policy
- Ensure due process for all
- Remove poverty traps and precarity traps
- Make a bonfire of benefit assessment tests
- Stop demonising disabled people
- Stop workfare now!
- Regulate payday loans and student loans
- Institute a right to financial knowledge and advice
- De-commodify education
- Make a bonfire of subsidies
- Move towards a universal basic income
- Share capital via sovereign wealth funds
- Revive the commons
- Revive deliberative democracy
- Re-marginalise charities

---

only marginally and on occasion, in mobilising local rights-based demands. For example, the Brazilian Constitution of 1988 made specific provision for social rights and sought to embed principles of citizen participation. This has led to the creation of an extensive federal and local network of social policy management councils, with responsibility for formulating and managing policy in areas such as education, health and welfare, with parity of representation from community representatives on the one hand, and representatives of government and service providers on the other (Coelho, 2004). Admittedly, the ability of such councils at a local level to effectively mobilise people is extremely variable. However, a much-hailed example of such a process has been the participatory budget-making process in Porto Allegre (Wainwright, 2003). Elsewhere in Latin America, in Venezuela from 2005 onwards the Chavez regime sought to create a 'new geometry of power' (Massey, 2008) through the promotion of communal councils, autonomous from existing local government structures and governed by citizens assemblies. These self-organising councils could be locally instigated and established by between 200 and 400 families in urban areas, 20 in rural areas and 10 in indigenous areas (Marcano, 2009). It was intended that they would incorporate local grass-roots committees concerned, *inter alia*, with health, education, water and energy provision, and that they should establish a communal bank and bid for government funds for infrastructural and housing projects. Some 44,000 such councils have been established across the country (Azzellini, 2013). Their impact, it would seem has, in practice, been modest and their functioning compromised by the persistence of social inequalities, as well as by resistance from career bureaucrats and the Venezuelan right wing, but as a model for bottom-up engagement having the potential for the framing of social rights, the initiative sets an interesting precedent.

Among the proposals contained in a draft social charter proposed by the Canadian Anti-Poverty Organisation in 1992 (Nedelsky & Scott, 1992; Hunt, 1996 pp. 185–190) was provision for a national social rights council that would evaluate compliance with the charter, conduct investigations and make representations for reform or improvements in social rights provision. The council would function according to 'dialogic' principles – that is to say, it would embrace the idea that social rights are constituted through negotiation. The social charter was never adopted, but the idea of a social rights council remains attractive, albeit that I would argue not for national social rights councils, but for *local* social rights councils. The Brazilian social policy management councils provide a model of sorts, but their essential feature should be that they would provide a bottom-up forum through which to conduct a politics of needs interpretation. There is inevitably a danger that local fora of this nature might co-opt as much as empower local people and that, however constituted, they would be insufficiently socially inclusive. Their aim, however, should be to attract significant participation and provide a site for debate relating specifically and immediately to the needs of local people. They would provide fora in which not only would grievances be aired, but vernacular discourses of need could be promoted, and rights-based demands could be framed. Such bodies are unlikely to be entrusted with direct executive powers, but they could be accorded some measure of influence over local human service providers and a voice in national policy-making processes.

A life-first principle?

Such ideas are presented not as blueprints, but as suggestions. More important, I would argue, is the need to reframe the terms of debate through which we think about social rights. I have spoken of how we might inflect the approach to social rights from the dominant to the minor tradition. Another way of expressing this is to speak of a 'life-first' approach. The term first emerged in the context of a critical study of labour market activation policy in England (Dean, 2003) and a suggestion that by inverting and combining the policy expressions 'work-first' (the premise that people should be forced to labour before their longer term interests are considered) and 'work-life balance' (the premise that people might nevertheless be allowed to combine labour with other aspects of their lives), one could attract support for an approach that would be more accommodating to people with complex needs. This initially somewhat facile idea has since acquired greater depth (e.g. Dean, 2014a) and can be used to capture a more general conception concerning the nature of human welfare or wellbeing, and of social citizenship as an open process of social negotiation. Social rights are a requirement of a good life: of a life lived in pursuit of not only hedonic, but eudaimonic wellbeing (Aristotle, c. 350 BCE), and of an ethical life during which we seek mutual recognition not only through love and solidarity, but also through rights (Honneth, 1995). A life-first principle means accepting collective responsibility for the attainment of good lives.

This is an idea that can be inflected in a variety of different ways. Within the realms of conventional political discourse the life-first principle is a challenge to narrow utilitarian and managerial thinking, since it recognises that life's meaning precedes the things that people might choose, or be made, to do. From within the spectrum of liberal thinking, social liberals and 'reluctant collectivists' (George & Wilding, 1985: ch. 3) are likely – implicitly or explicitly – to subscribe to some brand of Kantian deontological ethics (see Chapter 3, this volume) that can accommodate elements of collective responsibility and which may be attracted, for example, to a Rawlsian conception of social justice, on the one hand, or Sen's capability approach, on the other. Similarly, inheritors of the civic republican tradition, radical democrats and left-communitarians, might rally in various ways around a life-first approach that emphasises the significance of life-guarantees through risk sharing and social insurance. There is scope for discussion of the life-first principle within contemporary liberal and communitarian discourses.

The life-first principle resonates most strongly with a Marxian theory of human need (see, again, Chapter 2, this volume). Marx defined human needs in relation to human beings' species characteristics: the things that define what it is to be human. And he espoused a concept of 'radical' needs (Heller, 1974), by which he was alluding to the ultimate potential of humanity. His vision was of a society that might succeed from capitalism: a society in which the measure of things would flow from inclusive understandings of *need* (premised on fully human lives), rather than from fetishised conceptions of *value* (premised on the commodity form). There is no immediate prospect of capitalism's revolutionary overthrow, but we can envisage how a life-first emphasis upon the development of social rights and democratic social planning might constitute the beginnings of what Soper (1981) has alluded to as a politics of human need. Essentially the same insight is captured by de Sousa Santos's conceptualisation (which I briefly mentioned in Chapter 5) of an 'axiology of care' (de Sousa Santos, 2006: 31): a theory that values care, not economic progress or commodities. De Sousa Santos was suggesting that as a means to challenge the orthodoxies of global capitalism we might explore alternative ways of thinking that emanate from the global South. In Chapter 7 I briefly touched on the ideas of Ivan Illich (1973, 1977) and Paulo Freire (1972), who have each radically challenged the professionalised premises on which human service provision imported by the global South from the global North are founded, arguing instead for rights to health and educational provision to be premised on 'conviviality' and shared consciousness-raising. There is also an important connection that can be made with the feminist ethic of care that was discussed in Chapter 3 – an ethic which, once again, puts care centre stage, emphasising the extent to which human wellbeing depends on the social negotiation of responsibilities and relationships. The point about the life-first principle is that it construes the human individual's need for autonomy not in terms of self-sufficiency, but in the context of social interdependency; it prioritises the integrity of the human being as a living social actor, rather than as a competitive, utility-maximising individual and agent of economic production.

Whether in the context of conventional ideological discourse or more radical interpretations of human need, the life-first principle provides a foundation for a politics that prioritises the articulation of human need – that it is to say, which prioritises social rights.

Summary/conclusion

This concluding chapter has endeavoured to consider the future for social rights. It does not offer a crystal ball vision for the future. But it has, first of all, distilled from the preceding chapters what amounts to a post-Marshallian account of social citizenship. In so doing it deconstructs one of the two principal sources from which we have hitherto drawn our understanding of social rights, namely T. H. Marshall's theory of welfare state citizenship under twentieth-century capitalism. The central argument is that human beings were social beings before they ever invented civic and political institutions. Human beings socially negotiate the basis on which they recognise each other's needs and establish social processes by which to provide for such needs. Such social processes are what we may now define as social citizenship. Social citizenship will continue as a feature of human society, but it has always and will continue to manifest itself and evolve in a variety of modes. Drawing once again on material from previous chapters, this final chapter has presented a theoretical model through which to interpret those different modes. Central to this model is the dialogical nature of social rights and the idea that they are negotiated within relations of interdependency, at a variety of sites and levels. It is at the site and level of nation states that social rights and social citizenship continue for the most part to be framed, but this is almost certainly changing. Social citizenship can be local or global.

Second, the chapter has turned to the other principal source from which we have drawn our understanding of social rights, namely the international human rights framework. In doing so it has developed a critique of the normative foundations of that agenda, and its emphasis on an essentially liberal-individualist construction of the rights-bearing human subject: a construction primarily premised on a notion of individual dignity, rather than social solidarity. The chapter contends that the future development of social rights will require a rebalancing of the normative foundations and associated assumptions about the character of the human condition.

Finally, the chapter considers what in practice is to be done in order to advance the cause of social rights. It touches briefly on a disparate range of strategies: some situated at the level of constitutional mechanisms and legal practices – others at the level of informal mechanisms and informal practices. The discussion is not prescriptive, though it seeks to put into broad perspective the different contributions that different actors might make. It concludes by suggesting a unifying principle – the life-first principle: an ethical principle that prioritises and justifies collective action in support of good lives. The life-first principle is capable of differing inflections and interpretations, but it entails a core commitment to social rights and human welfare. The concept and discourses of social rights present a range of strategic possibilities and can be expanded and utilised in a variety of ways. But the key argument of this book is that social rights may be understood as articulations of human need. The concept of human need is elastic, but so too are the social rights through which we may struggle to express our needs and bring fulfilment to human lives.

BIBLIOGRAPHY

Alcock, P. (2006). *Understanding Poverty* (3rd edition). Basingstoke: Palgrave Macmillan.

Alesina, A., & Glaeser, E. (2004). *Fighting Poverty in the US and Europe*. Oxford: Oxford University Press.

Alinsky, S. (1969). *Reveille for Radicals*. New York: Random House.

Alkire, S., & Santos, M. (2010). *Acute Multidimensional Poverty: A new index for developing countries (Working Paper No. 38)*. Oxford: Oxford Poverty and Human Development Initiative (OPHI), Oxford Department of International Development.

Allen, G. (2011). *Early Intervention: The next steps*. London: Cabinet Office.

Alston, P. (1990). US ratification of the Covenant on Economic, Social and Cultural Rights: The need for an entirely new strategy. *American Journal of International Law, 84*(2), 365–393.

Alston, P., & Quinn, G. (1987). The nature and scope of states parties' obligations under the International Covenant on Economic, Social and Cultural Rights. *Human Rights Quarterly, 9*(1), 156–229.

Amin, S. (1997). *Capitalism in the Age of Globalization*. London: Zed Books.

Andreassen, B., & Marks, S. (Eds.). (2010). *Development as a Human Right: Legal, political and economic dimensions* (2nd edition). Antwerp: Intersentia.

Annetts, J., Law, A., McNeish, W., & Mooney, G. (Eds.). (2009). *Understanding Social Movements and Social Welfare*. Bristol: The Policy Press.

Apel, K. (1980). *Towards the Transformation of Philosophy*. London: Routledge.

Apel, K. (1991). A planetary macro-ethics for humankind. In E. Deutsch (Ed.), *Culture and Modernity: East-West philosophical perspectives*. Honolulu: University of Hawaii Press.

Arendt, H. (1951). *The Burden of Our Time*. London: Secker & Warburg.

Arendt, H. (1977). Public rights and private interests. In M. Mooney & F. Stuber (Eds.), *Small Comforts for Hard Times: Humanists on public policy*. New York: Columbia University Press.

Arendt, H. (1978). *The Origins of Totalitarianism*. New York: Meridian Books.

Aristotle. (c. 350 BCE). *Eudemian Ethics – Books I, II and VIII* (1982 edition, translated by M. Woods). Oxford: Clarendon Press.

Aristotle. (1981). *The Politics* (revised by T. Saunders, translated by T. Sinclair). Harmondsworth: Penguin.

Ashton, E. (2011). The alleged dichotomy between positive and negative rights and duties. In C. Beits & R. Goodin (Eds.), *Global Basic Rights*. Oxford: Oxford University Press.

ATD Fourth World. (2014). *Challenge 2015: Towards sustainable development that leaves no one behind*. Paris: ATD Fourth World.

Atkinson, A. (Ed.). (2004). *New Sources of Development Finance, UNU-WIDER*. Oxford: Oxford University Press.

Azzellini, D. (2013). The communal state: Communal councils, communes and workplace democracy. *NACLA Report on the Americas, 46*(2), 25–30.

Bagilhole, B. (2009). *Understanding Equal Opportunities and Diversity*. Bristol: The Policy Press.

Baker, J., Lynch, K., Cantillon, S., & Walsh, J. (2004). *Equality: From theory to action*. Basingstoke: Palgrave Macmillan.

Ball, S. (2008). *The Education Debate*. Bristol: The Policy Press.

Balloch, S., & Hill, M. (Eds.). (2007). *Care, Community and Citizenship*. Bristol: The Policy Press.

Bankowski, Z., & Mungham, G. (1976). *Images of Law*. London: Routledge & Kegan Paul.

Banting, K., & Kymlicka, W. (2006). *Multiculturalism and the Welfare State*. Oxford: Oxford University Press.

Baptiste, W., & Bricker-Jenkins, M. (2002). A view from the bottom: Poor people and their allies respond to welfare reform. In R. Albelda & A. Withorn (Eds.), *Lost Ground*. Cambridge, MA: South End Press.

Barnes, C., & Mercer, G. (2010). *Exploring Disability* (2nd edition). Cambridge: Polity.

Barr, N. (2010). Long-term care: A suitable case for social insurance. *Social Policy & Administration, 44*(4), 359–374.

Barrientos, A. (2001, 1–2 March). *Welfare regimes in Latin America*. Paper presented at the Social Policy in Developing Contexts workshop, University of Bath, UK.

Barrientos, A. (2004). Latin America: Toward a liberal-informal welfare regime. In I. Gough, G. Wood, A. Barrientos, P. Bevan, P. Davis & G. Room (Eds.), *Insecurity and Welfare Regimes in Asia, Africa and Latin America: Social policy in development contexts*. Cambridge: Cambridge University Press.

Barry, A., Osborne, T., & Rose, N. (Eds.). (1996). *Foucault and Political Reason*. London: UCL Press.

Bastagli, F. (2009). *From Social Safety Net to Social Policy? The role of conditional cash transfers in welfare state development in Latin America*. Brasilia: UNDP International Policy Centre for Inclusive Growth.

Batchelet, M. (2011). *Social Protection Floor for a Fair and Inclusive Globalization*. Geneva: International Labour Office.

Bauman, Z. (1987). *Legislators and Interpreters*. Cambridge: Polity.

Bauman, Z. (1998). *Work, Consumerism and the New Poor*. Buckingham: Open University Press.

Beck, U. (1992). *Risk Society: Towards a new modernity*. London: Sage.

Beck, U. (2002). The cosmopolitan society and its enemies. *Theory, Culture and Society, 19*(1–2), 17–44.

Beck, U. (2003). Toward a new critical theory with a cosmopolitan intent. *Constellations, 10*(4), 453–468.

Beck, U., & Beck-Gernsheim, E. (1995). *The Normal Chaos of Love*. Cambridge: Cambridge University Press.

Beck, W., Van der Maesen, L., & Walker, A. (Eds.). (1997). *The Social Quality of Europe*. Bristol: The Policy Press.

Bell, D. (1973). *The Coming of Post-Industrial Society*. London: Heinemann.

Bennett, F., & Lister, R. (2010). *The 'Living Wage': The right answer to low pay?* London: The Fabian Society.

Bentham, J. (1789). An introduction to the principles and morals of legislation. In M. Warnock (Ed.), *Utilitarianism* (1962 edition). Glasgow: Collins.

Berlin, I. (1967). Two concepts of liberty. In A. Quinton (Ed.), *Political Philosophy*. Oxford: Oxford University Press.

Bevan, P. (2004). The dynamics of Africa's in/security regimes. In I. Gough & G. Wood (Eds.), *Insecurity and Welfare Regimes in Asia, Africa and Latin America*. Cambridge: Cambridge University Press.

Beveridge, W. (1942). *Social Insurance and Allied Services* (Cmd. 6404). London: Her Majesty's Stationery Office (HMSO).

Billis, D., & Glennerster, H. (1998). Human services and the voluntary sector: Towards a theory of comparative advantage. *Journal of Social Policy, 27*(1), 79–98.

Bochel, H. (2005). Ethics, risk and social policy. In C. Bochel, H. Bochel, R. Page & R. Sykes (Eds.), *Social Policy: Issues and developments*. Harlow: Pearson Education.

Boon, A. (2001). Cause lawyers in a cold climate. In A. Sarat & S. Schiengold (Eds.), *Cause Lawyering and the State in a Global Era*. Oxford: Oxford University Press.

Boratav, K., & Özuğurlu, M. (2006). Social policies and distributional dynamics in Turkey. In M. Karshenas & V. Moghadam (Eds.), *Social Policy in the Middle East*. Basingstoke: Palgrave/United Nations Research Institute for Social Development (UNRISD).

Bornat, A., Pereira, C., Pilgrim, D., & Williams, F. (Eds.). (1993). *Community Care: A reader*. Basingstoke: Macmillan.

Bottomore, T. (1992). Citizenship and social class, forty years on. In T. Marshall & T. Bottomore (Eds.), *Citizenship and Social Class*. London: Pluto.

Boyle, A. (2007). *Human Rights or Environmental Rights? A reassessment*. Edinburgh: University of Edinburgh, School of Law.

Braathen, E. (2000). New social corporatism: A discursive-comparative perspective on the World Development Report 2000/2001. In Comparative Research on Poverty (CROP) (Ed.), *A Critical Review of the World Development Report 2000/2001, Attacking Poverty*. Bergen: CROP.

Braathen, E. (2005). Social funds in Africa: A technocratic-clientalistic response to poverty? In A. Cimadamore, H. Dean & J. Siqueira (Eds.), *The Poverty of the State: Reconsidering the role of the state in the struggle against global poverty*. Buenos Aires: Consejo Latinamerico de Ciencias Socialses (Latin American Council of Social Sciences)/Comparative Research on Poverty (CLACSO/CROP).

Bradshaw, J. (1972, 30 March). The concept of social need. *New Society*.

Brewer, B. (2007). Citizen or customer? Complaints handling in the public sector. *International Review of Administrative Sciences, 73*(4), 549–556.

Brixton Advice Centre. (1976). *Tenth Annual Report*. London: Brixton Advice Centre.

Burchardt, T. (1997). *Boundaries between Public and Private Welfare: A typology and map of services (CASE Paper 2)*. London: Centre for the Analysis of Social Exclusion, London School of Economics (LSE).

Burchardt, T. (2013). *Re-visiting the Conceptual Framework for Public/Private Boundaries in Welfare – Social Policy in a Cold Climate Research Note 2*. London: LSE.

Burchardt, T., & Vizard, P. (2007). *Definition of Equality and Framework for Measurement: Final recommendations of the Equalities Review Steering Group on Measurement (CASE Paper 120)*. London: Centre for the Analysis of Social Exclusion/Suntory Toyota and International Centres for Economics and Related Disciplines (CASE/STICERD).

Burrows, R., Pleace, N., & Quilgars, D. (Eds.). (1997). *Homelessness and Social Policy*. London: Routledge.

Bynum, W. (2008). *The History of Medicine: A very short introduction*. Oxford: Oxford University Press.

Cahill, M. (2002). *The Environment and Social Policy*. London: Routledge.

Callender, C. (2010). Bursaries and institutional aid in higher education in England: Do they safeguard access and promote fair access? *Oxford Review of Education, 36*(1), 45–62.

Callinicos, A. (2003). *An Anti-Capitalist Manifesto*. Cambridge: Polity.

Callinicos, A. (2007). *Social Theory: A historical introduction* (2nd edition). Cambridge: Polity.

Callinicos, A. (2010). *Bonfire of Illusions: The twin crises of the liberal world*. Cambridge: Polity.

Campbell, T. (1983). *The Left and Rights*. London: Routledge & Kegan Paul.

Campbell, T. (1988). *Justice*. Basingstoke: Macmillan.

Campbell, T. (2006). *Rights: A critical introduction*. London: Routledge.

Campbell, T. (2007). Poverty as a violation of human rights: Inhumanity or injustice? In T. Pogge (Ed.), *Freedom from Poverty as a Human Right: Who owes what to the very poor?* Oxford: UNESCO/Oxford University Press.

Carlin, J., Howard, J., & Messinger, S. (1967). *Civil Justice and the Poor*. New York: Russell Sage.

Carter, M. (2003). *T. H. Green and the Development of Ethical Socialism*. Exeter: Imprint Academic.

Castañeda, E. (2012). The *Indignados* of Spain: A precedent to Occupy Wall Street. *Social Movement Studies: Journal of Social, Cultural and Political Protest, 11*(3–4), 309–319.

Castells, M. (1983). *The City and the Grassroots*. London: Edward Arnold.

Castles, F. (1982). *The Impact of Parties*. London: Sage.

Castles, F., & Mitchell, D. (1993). Worlds of welfare and families of nations. In F. Castles (Ed.), *Families of Nations: Patterns of public policy in Western democracies*. Aldershot: Dartmouth.

Castles, S., & Miller, M. (2009). *The Age of Migration* (4th edition). Basingstoke: Macmillan.

Cerami, A. (2013). *Permanent Emergency Regimes in Sub-Saharan Africa: The exclusive origins of dictatorship and democracy*. Basingstoke: Palgrave.

Cerami, A., & Vanhuysse. (2009). *Post-Communist Welfare Pathways: Theorizing social policy transformations in Central and Eastern Europe*. Basingstoke: Palgrave.

Chambers, R., & Conway, G. (1992). Sustainable rural livelihoods: Practical concepts for the 21st century. In Institute of Development Studies (Ed.), *Discussion Paper 296*. Brighton: Institute of Development Studies.

Chan, C.-K., & Bowpitt, G. (2005). *Human Dignity and Welfare Systems*. Bristol: The Policy Press.

Chan, C.-K., Ngok, K.-L., & Phillips, D. (2008). *Social Policy in China*. Bristol: The Policy Press.

Chan, J. (1999). A Confucian perspective on human rights for contemporary China. In J. Bauer & D. Bell (Eds.), *The East Asian Challenge for Human Rights*. Cambridge: Cambridge University Press.

Chant, S. (2008). The feminization of poverty and the feminisation of anti-poverty programmes. *Journal of Development Studies, 44*(2), 165–197.

Children's Rights Alliance for England (CRAE). (2013). *State of Children's Rights in England: Review of government action on UN recommendations for strengthening children's rights in the UK*. London: CRAE.

Chirwa, D. (2008). African regional human rights system. In M. Langford (Ed.), *Social Rights Jurisprudence: Emerging trends in international and comparative law*. Cambridge: Cambridge University Press.

Chitty, C. (2009). *Education in Britain* (2nd edition). Basingstoke: Palgrave Macmillan.

Clarke, J. (1999). Coming to terms with culture. In H. Dean & R. Woods (Eds.), *Social Policy Review 11*. Luton: Social Policy Association.

Clarke, J., Coll, K., Dagino, E., & Neveu, C. (2014). *Disputing Citizenship*. Bristol: The Policy Press.

Clarke, J., & Newman, J. (1997). *The Managerial State*. London: Sage.

Clarke, P. (1996). *Deep Citizenship*. London: Pluto.

Coates, D. (2007). *The National Minimum Wage: Retrospective and prospect*. London: The Work Foundation.

Cockburn, C. (1977). *The Local State: Management of cities and people*. London: Pluto Press.

Coelho, V. (2004). Brazil's Health Councils: The challenge of building participatory political institutions. *IDS Bulletin, 35*(2), 33–39.

Commission on a Bill of Rights. (2012). *A UK Bill of Rights? The choice before us*. London: Ministry of Justice.

Comola, M., & de Mello, L. (2010). *Enhancing the Effectiveness of Social Policies in Indonesia (OECD Economics Department Working Papers), Paper No. 810*, doi: 10.1787/18151973.

Conant, L. (2010). Regional legal frameworks for human rights and social policy in Europe. In A. Nevile (Ed.), *Human Rights and Social Policy: A comparative analysis of values and citizenship in OECD countries*. Cheltenham: Edward Elgar.

Coote, A. (Ed.). (1992). *The Welfare of Citizens: Developing new social rights*. London: Rivers Oram/ Institute for Public Policy Reesearch (IPPR).

Craig, G. (2008). The limits of compromise? Social justice, 'race' and multiculturalism. In G. Craig, T. Burchardt & D. Gordon (Eds.), *Social Justice and Public Policy: Seeking fairness in diverse societies*. Bristol: The Policy Press.

Craig, G., Atkin, K., Chattoo, S., & Flynn, R. (Eds.). (2012). *Understanding 'Race' and Ethnicity*. Bristol: The Policy Press.

Cranston, M. (1976). Human Rights, Real and Supposed. In N. Timms & D. Watson (Eds.), *Talking about Welfare*. London: Routledge & Kegan Paul.

Cranston, R. (1985). *Legal foundations of the welfare state*. London: Weidenfeld and Nicholson.

Craven, M. (1995). *The International Covenant on Economic, Social and Cultural Rights*. Oxford: Clarendon Press.

Crompton, R. (2008). *Class and Stratification* (3rd edition). Cambridge: Polity.

Crosland, A. (1956). *The Future of Socialism*. London: Jonathan Cape.

Cutler, T., Williams, K., & Williams, J. (1986). *Keynes, Beveridge and Beyond*. London: Routledge & Kegan Paul.

da Silva, J.-G., Belik, W., & Takagi, M. (2005). The challenges of a policy of food security in Brazil. In A. Cimadamore, H. Dean & J. Siqueira (Eds.), *The Poverty of the State: Reconsidering the role of the state in the struggle against global poverty*. Buenos Aires: Consejo Latinamerico de Ciencias Socialses (Latin American Council of Social Sciences)/Comparative Research on Poverty (CLACSO/CROP).

Daly, M. (2002). Care as a good for social policy. *Journal of Social Policy, 31*(2), 251–270.

Daly, M. (2011). *Welfare*. Cambridge: Polity.

Daniel, P., & Ivatts, J. (1998). *Children and Social Policy*. Basingstoke: Macmillan.

Davidova, N., & Manning, N. (2009). Russia: State socialism to marketised welfare. In P. Alcock & G. Craig (Eds.), *International Social Policy: Welfare regimes in the developed world* (2nd edition). Basingstoke: Palgrave.

Davies, M. (2008). Stigma, shame and sense of worth. In J. Strelitz & R. Lister (Eds.), *Why Money Matters: Family income, poverty and children's lives*. London: Save the Children.

Davis, K., & Moore, W. (1945). Some principles of stratification. *American Sociological Review, 10*(2), 242–249.

Davis, P. (2004). Rethinking the welfare regime approach in the context of Bangladesh. In I. Gough & G. Wood (Eds.), *Insecurity and Welfare Regimes in Asia, Africa and Latin America*. Cambridge: Cambridge University Press.

Davy, B. (2012). *Land Policy*. Farnham: Ashgate.

Davy, B., & Pellissery, S. (2013). The citizenship promise (un)fulfilled: The right to housing in informal settings. *International Journal of Social Welfare, 22*(Supplement 1), S68–S84.

Davy, U. (2013). Social citizenship going international: Changes in the reading of UN-sponsored economic and social rights. *International Journal of Social Welfare, 22*(Supplement 1), S15–S31.

de Schweinitz, K. (1961). *England's Road to Social Security*. Perpetua: University of Pennsylvania.

de Sousa Santos, B. (2001). *Toward a New Legal Common Sense* (2nd edition). London: Butterworths.

de Sousa Santos, B. (2006). *The Rise of the Global Left: The World Social Forum and Beyond*. London: Zed Books.

Deacon, B. (1993). Developments in East European social policy. In C. Jones (Ed.), *New Perspectives on the Welfare State in Europe*. London: Routledge.

Deacon, B. (2007). *Global Social Policy and Governance*. London: Sage.

Deacon, B., Hulse, M., & Stubbs, P. (1997). *Global Social Policy*. London: Sage.

Dean, H. (1991). *Social Security and Social Control*. London: Routledge.

Dean, H. (1992). Poverty discourse and the disempowerment of the poor. *Critical Social Policy, 12*(35), 79–88.

Dean, H. (2003). Reconceptualising welfare-to-work for people with multiple problems and needs. *Journal of Social Policy, 32*(3), 441–459.

Dean, H. (Ed.). (2004). *The Ethics of Welfare: Human rights, dependency and responsibility*. Bristol: The Policy Press.

Dean, H. (2007). The ethics of welfare-to-work. *Policy and Politics, 35*(4), 573–589.

Dean, H. (2009). Critiquing capabilities: The distractions of a beguiling concept. *Critical Social Policy, 29*(2), 261–273.

Dean, H. (2010). *Understanding Human Need*. Bristol: The Policy Press.

Dean, H. (2011). The ethics of migrant welfare. *Ethics and Social Welfare, 5*(1), 18–35.

Dean, H. (2012a). The experience of welfare: The life course and the welfare state. In J. Baldock, L. Mitton & S. Vickerstaff (Eds.), *Social Policy* (4th edition). Oxford: Oxford University Press.

Dean, H. (2012b). *Social Policy* (2nd edition). Cambridge: Polity.

Dean, H. (2012c). Welcome relief or indecent subsidy? The implications of wage top-up schemes. *Policy and Politics, 40*(3), 305–21.

Dean, H. (2013). The translation of needs into rights: Reconceptualising social citizenship as a global phenomenon. *International Journal of Social Welfare, 22*(Supplement 1), S32–S49.

Dean, H. (2014a). Life-first welfare and the scope for a 'eudemonic ethic' of social security. In M. Keune & A. Serrano (Eds.), *Deconstructing Flexicurity and Developing Alternative Approaches: Towards new concepts and approaches for employment and social policy*. New York: Routledge.

Dean, H. (2014b). Social rights and natural resources. In T. Fitzpatrick (Ed.), *International Handbook on Social Policy and the Environment*. Cheltenham: Edward Elgar.

Dean, H., & Khan, Z. (1997). Muslim perspectives on welfare. *Journal of Social Policy, 26*(2), 193–209.

Dean, H. with M. Melrose (1999). *Poverty, Riches and Social Citizenship*. Basingstoke: Macmillan.

Dean, H., & Rodgers, R. (2004). Popular discourses of dependency, responsibility and rights. In H. Dean (Ed.), *The Ethics of Welfare*. Bristol: The Policy Press.

Delanty, G. (2000). *Citizenship in a Global Age*. Buckingham: Open University Press.

Deneulin, S. (2006). *The Capability Approach and the Praxis of Development*. Basingstoke: Palgrave Macmillan.

Destremau, B. (2000). Poverty, exclusion and the changing role of the state in the Middle East. In H. Dean, R. Sykes & R. Woods (Eds.), *Social Policy Review 12*. Newcastle: Social Policy Association.

Dicey, A. (1885). *Introduction to the Law of the Constitution* (1939 edition, edited by E. Wade) London: Macmillan.

Donnelly, J. (2003). *Universal Human Rights in Theory and Practice* (2nd edition). Ithaca, NY: Cornell University Press.

Donzelot, J. (1979). *The Policing of Families: Welfare versus the state*. London: Hutchinson.

Doogan, K. (2009). *New Capitalism? The transformation of work*. Cambridge: Polity.

Douglas, M. (1977). *Natural Symbols*. Harmonsworth: Penguin.

Douglas, M., & Ney, S. (1998). *Missing Persons: A critique of the social sciences*. Berkeley: University of California Press.

Doyal, L. (1979). *The Political Economy of Health*. London: Pluto.

Doyal, L., & Gough, I. (1991). *A Theory of Human Need*. Basingstoke: Macmillan.

Drakeford, M. (2000). *Privatisation and Social Policy*. Harlow: Longman.

Drescher, S. (2009). *Abolition: A history of slavery and anti-slavery*. Cambridge: Cambridge University Press.

Duncan, S., & Edwards, R. (Eds.). (1997). *Single Mothers in an International Context*. London: UCL Press.

Durbach, A. (2008). The right to legal aid in social rights litigation. In M. Langford (Ed.), *Social Rights Jurisprudence: Emerging trends in international and comparative law*. Cambridge: Cambridge University Press.

Dutta, P., Murgai, R., Ravallion, M., & van de Walle, D. (2012). Does India's employment guarantee scheme guarantee employment? *Economic & Political Weekly, XLVII*(16), 55–64.

Dworkin, R. (1977). *Taking Rights Seriously*. London: Duckworth.

Dwyer, P. (2000). *Welfare Rights and Responsibilities: Contesting social citizenship*. Bristol: The Policy Press.

Dwyer, P. (2004). Creeping conditionality in the UK. *Canadian Journal of Sociology, 25*(2), 261–283.

Dwyer, P. (2010). *Understanding Social Citizenship* (2nd edition). Bristol: The Policy Press.

Easterlin, R. (2005). Building a better theory of well-being. In L. Bruni & P. Porta (Eds.), *Economics and Happiness*. Oxford: Oxford University Press.

Edmonds, E., & Pavcnik, N. (2005). Child labor in the global economy. *Journal of Economic Perspectives, 19*(1), 199–220.

Eide, A. (2001). Cultural rights as individual human rights. In A. Eide, C. Krause & A. Rosas (Eds.), *Economic, Social and Cultural Rights*. Dordrecht: Martinus Nijhoff.

Eide, A., Krause, C., & Rosas, A. (Eds.). (2001). *Economic Social and Cultural Rights: A textbook* (2nd edition). Dordrecht: Martinus Nijhoff.

Elliott, B., & McCrone, D. (1987). Class, culture and morality: A sociological analysis of neo-conservatism. *Sociological Review, 35*(3), 485–515.

Ellis, K. (2000). Welfare and bodily order: Theorising transitions in corporeal discourse. In K. Ellis & H. Dean (Eds.), *Social Policy and the Body*. Basingstoke: Macmillan.

Elsinger, P. (1998). *Toward an End to Hunger in America*. Washington, DC: Brookings Institution.

Entzinger, H. (2007). Open borders and the welfare state. In A. Pecoud & P. de Guchteniere (Eds.), *Migration without Borders: Essays on the free movement of people*. Paris: UNESCO/Berghahn Books.

Equalities Review. (2007). *Fairness and Freedom: The final report of the Equalities Review*. London: Cabinet Office.

Escobar, A. (2012). *Encountering Development: The making and unmaking of the Third World* (2nd edition). Princeton, NJ: Princeton University Press.

Esping-Andersen, G. (1990). *The Three Worlds of Welfare Capitalism*. Cambridge: Polity.

Esping-Andersen, G. (1999). *The Social Foundations of Post-Industrial Economies*. Oxford: Oxford University Press.

Esping-Andersen, G. (2002). *Why We Need a New Welfare State*. Oxford: Oxford University Press.

Etzioni, A. (1995). *The Spirit of Community*. London: Fontana.

Fairbairns, Z. (1985). The cohabitation rule: Why it makes sense. In C. Ungerson (Ed.), *Women and Social Policy*. Basingstoke: Macmillan.

Falk, R. (1994). The making of a global citizenship. In B. van Steenbergen (Ed.), *The Condition of Citizenship*. London: Sage.

Falkingham, J., & Hills, J. (1995). *The Dynamic of Welfare: The welfare state and the life-cycle*. Hemel Hempstead: Prentice Hall/Harvester Wheatsheaf.

Fanon, F. (1967). *The Wretched of the Earth*. Harmondsworth: Penguin.

Felice, W. (1999). The viability of the United Nations approach to economic and social human rights in a globalized economy. *International Affairs, 75*(3), 563–598.

Fenger, H. (2007). Welfare regimes in Central and Eastern Europe: Incorporating post-communist countries in a welfare regime typology. *Contemporary Issues and Ideas in Social Science, 3*(2).

Ferguson, C. (1999). *Global Social Policy: Human rights and social justice*. London: Department for International Development.

Finch, J. (1989). *Family Obligations and Social Change*. Cambridge: Polity.

Finch, J., & Mason, J. (1993). *Negotiating Family Responsibilities*. London: Routledge.

Fine, B. (1984). *Democracy and the Rule of Law: Liberal ideals and Marxist critiques*. London: Pluto Press.

Fine, B. (2002). Marxism and the social theory of law. In R. Banakar & M. Travers (Eds.), *An Introduction to Law and Social Theory*. Oxford and Portand, OR: Hart Publishing.

Fine, R. (2007). *Cosmopolitansim*. London: Routledge.

Fitzpatrick, P. (1992). Law as resistance. In I. Grigg-Spall & P. Ireland (Eds.), *The Critical Lawyers' Handbook*. London: Pluto Press.

Fitzpatrick, S., & Stephens, M. (2007). *An International Review of Homelessness and Social Housing Policy*. London: Department for Communities and Local Government.

Fitzpatrick, T. (1999). *Freedom and Security: An introduction to the basic income debate*. Basingstoke: Macmillan.

Fitzpatrick, T. (2008). *Applied Ethics and Social Problems*. Bristol: The Policy Press.

Forder, A. (1974). *Concepts in Social Administration: A framework for analysis*. London: Routledge & Kegan Paul.

Forster, W. (1870). Speech introducing Elementary Education Bill, House of Commons. In S. Maclure (Ed.), *Education Documents* (1996 edition). London: Methuen.

Foucault, M. (1977). *Discipline and Punish*. Harmondsworth: Penguin.

Foucault, M. (1991). Govermentality. In G. Burchell, C. Gordon & P. Miller (Eds.), *The Foucault Effect*. Chicago: University of Chicago Press.

Foweraker, J., & Landman, T. (1997). *Citizenship Rights and Social Movements: A comparative and statistical analysis*. Oxford: Oxford University Press.

France, A. (1894). *Le Lys Rouge*. Paris: Calmann Lévy.

Frank, A. (1971). *Capitalism and Underdevelopment in Latin America*. Harmondsworth: Penguin.

Fraser, D. (2003). *The Evolution of the British Welfare State* (3rd edition). Basingstoke: Palgrave Macmillan.

Fraser, I. (2011, 10 May). Fidelity is confident its MINTs won't suck. *Bloomsbury Information QFINANCE*.

Fraser, N. (1989). *Unruly Practices: Power, discourse and gender in contemporary social theory*. Minneapolis: University of Minnesota Press.

Fraser, N. (2010). *Scales of Justice: Reimagining political space in a globalizing world*. New York: Columbia University Press.

Freeman, G. (1986). Migration and the political economy of the welfare state. *Annals of the American Academy of Political and Social Science, 485*(May), 51–63.

Freeman, M. (2000). The future of children's rights. *Children & Society, 14*(4), 277–293.

Freeman, M. (2002). *Human Rights.* Cambridge: Polity.

Freire, P. (1972). *Pedagogy of the Oppressed.* Harmondsworth: Penguin.

Fromm, E. (Ed.). (1965). *Socialist Humanism.* London: Allen Lane.

Fukuyama, F. (1992). *The End of History and the Last Man.* New York: Basic Books.

Gaia, E., Hujo, K., & Bennett, F. (Eds.). (2011). The use of conditions in social welfare programmes (Guest edited issue). *The Journal of Poverty and Social Justice, 19*(1).

Galanter, M. (1976). Delivering legality: Some proposals for the direction of research. *Law and Society Review, 11*(2), 225–246.

Galbraith, K. (1992). *The Culture of Contentment.* Harmondsworth: Penguin.

Garfinkel, I., Miller, C., McLanahan, S., & Hanson, T. (1998). Deadbeat dads or inept states? A comparison of child support enforcement systems. *Evaluation Review, 22*(6), 717–750.

Gargarella, R., Domingo, P., & Roux, T. (Eds.). (2006). *Courts and Social Transformation in New Democracies: An institutional voice for the poor?* Burlington, VT: Ashgate.

Garland, D. (1981). The birth of the welfare sanction. *British Journal of Law and Society, 8*(1), 29–45.

Garnham, A., & Knights, E. (1994). *Putting the Treasury First: The truth about child support.* London: Child Poverty Action Group.

Gauri, V., & Brinks, D. (Eds.). (2008). *Courting Social Justice: Judicial enforcement of social and economic rights in the developing world.* Cambridge: Cambridge University Press.

Gearty, C. (2011). Against judicial enforcement. In C. Gearty & V. Mantouvalou (Eds.), *Debating Social Rights.* Oxford: Hart Publishing.

Gearty, C., & Mantouvalou, V. (2011). *Debating Social Rights.* Oxford: Hart Publishing.

George, V. (1988). *Wealth, Poverty and Starvation: An international perspective.* Hemel Hempstead: Harvester Wheatsheaf.

George, V. (1993). Poverty in Russia: From Lenin to Yeltsin. In R. Page & J. Baldock (Eds.), *Social Policy Review 5.* Canterbury: Social Policy Association.

George, V. (2010). *Major Thinkers in Welfare: Contemporary issues in historical perspective.* Bristol: The Policy Press.

George, V., & Howards, I. (1991). *Poverty Amidst Affluence.* Aldershot: Edward Elgar.

George, V., & Page, R. (Eds.). (1995). *Modern Thinkers on Welfare.* Hemel Hempstead: Prentice Hall/Harvester Wheatsheaf.

George, V., & Wilding, P. (1985). *Ideology and Social Welfare.* London: Routledge & Kegan Paul.

George, V., & Wilding, P. (1994). *Welfare and Ideology.* Hemel Hempstead: Harvester Wheatsheaf.

Giddens, A. (1998). *The Third Way.* Cambridge: Polity.

Gilbert, B. (1966). *The Evolution of National Insurance in Great Britain.* London: Michael Joseph.

Gilbert, N. (2004). *Transformation of the Welfare State.* Oxford: Oxford University Press.

Gittens, D. (1993). *The Family in Question* (2nd edition). Basingstoke: Macmillan.

Glasby, J. (2012). Social care. In P. Alcock, M. May & S. Wright (Eds.), *The Student's Companion to Social Policy* (4th edition). Chichester: Wiley-Blackwell.

Goldthorpe, J., Llewellyn, C., & Payne, C. (1982). *Social Mobility and Class Structure in Modern Britain* (2nd edition). Oxford: Clarendon Press.

Goodhart, D. (2006). *Progressive Nationalism: Citizenship and the Left.* London: Demos.

Goodman, R., & Peng, I. (1996). The East Asian welfare states: Peripatetic learning, adaptive change and nation-building. In G. Esping-Andersen (Ed.), *Welfare States in Transition.* London: Sage.

Gordon, S. (1999). *Controlling the State: Constitutionalism from ancient Athens to today.* Cambridge, MA: Harvard University Press.

Gough, I. (1979). *The Political Economy of the Welfare State.* Basingstoke: Macmillan.

Gough, I. (1997). Social aspects of the European model and its economic consequences. In W. Beck, L. van der Maesen & A. Walker (Eds.), *The Social Quality of Europe.* Bristol: The Policy Press.

Gough, I., & McGregor, J. (Eds.). (2007). *Wellbeing in Developing Countries: From theory to research.* Cambridge: Cambridge University Press.

Gough, I., Wood, G., Barrientos, A., Bevan, P., Davis, P., & Room, G. (2004). *Insecurity and Welfare Regimes in Asia, Africa and Latin America: Social policy in development contexts*. Cambridge: Cambridge University Press.

Gramsci, A. (1971). *Selections from the Prison Notebooks*. London: Lawrence & Wishart.

Griffin, J. (2008). *On Human Rights*. Oxford: Oxford University Press.

Griffiths, J. (1997). *The Politics of the Judiciary* (5th edition). London: Fontana.

Grover, A. (2011). *Thematic Study on the Realization of the Right to Health of Older Persons by the Special Rapporteur on the Right of Everyone to the Enjoyment of the Highest Attainable Standard of Physical and Mental Health*. Geneva: Human Rights Council.

Haartmann, C., Haartmann, D., Shindonola-Mote, H., Nattrass, N., van Niekerk, I., & Samson, M. (2009). *Making the Difference! The BIG in Namibia – Basic Income Grant Pilot Project Assessment Report*. Windhoek, Namibia: Basic Income Group Coalition.

Habermas, J. (1987). *The Theory of Communicative Action: Vol 2: Lifeworld and System*. Cambridge: Polity.

Habermas, J. (1996). *Between Facts and Norms*. Cambridge: Polity.

Hadley, R., & Hatch, S. (1981). *Social Welfare and the Failure of the State*. London: Allen and Unwin.

Hall, S., & Held, D. (1989). Citizens and citizenship. In S. Hall & M. Jacques (Eds.), *New Times: The Changing Face of Politics in the 1990s*. London: Lawrence & Wishart.

Halmos, P. (1973). *The Faith of the Counsellors*. London: Constable.

Harden, I., & Lewis, N. (1986). *The Noble Lie: The British Constitution and the rule of law*. London: Hutchinson.

Hardoy, J., & Satterthwaite, D. (1989). *Squatter Citizen*. London: Earthscan Publications.

Hardt, M., & Negri, A. (2000). *Empire*. Cambridge, MA: Harvard University Press.

Harris, D. (2009). Collective complaints under the European Social Charter: Encouraging progress? In K. Kaikobad & M. Bohlander (Eds.), *International Law and Power: Perspectives on legal order and justice – Essays in honour of Colin Warbrick*. Netherlands: Koninklijke Brill NV.

Harris, G. (1997). *Dignity and Vulnerability: Strength and quality of character*. Oakland: University of California Press.

Harris, J. (2014, 9 April). A Precariat Charter: From denizens to citizens – review. *The Guardian*.

Hayek, F. (1976). *Law, Legislation and Liberty: Vol.2 – The Mirage of Social Justice*. London: Routledge & Kegan Paul.

Hayter, T. (1971). *Aid as Imperialism*. Harmondsworth: Penguin.

Healthwatch England. (2014). Health and care complaints system is 'utterly bewildering' for people. Retrieved 1 April 2014 from www.healthwatch.co.uk/news/health-and-care-complaints-system-is-utterly-bewildering-people

Hegel, G. (1821). *Elements of the Philosophy of Rights* (1991 edition, edited by A. Wood). Cambridge: Cambridge University Press.

Held, D. (1987). *Models of Democracy*. Cambridge: Polity.

Held, D. (2004). *Global Covenant: The social democratic alternative to the Washington consensus*. Cambridge: Polity.

Held, D. (2010). *Cosmopolitanism: Ideals and realities*. Cambridge: Polity.

Held, D., & McGrew, A. (2007). *Globalization/Anti-Globalization* (2nd edition). Cambridge: Polity.

Heller, A. (1974). *The Theory of Need in Marx*. London: Alison & Busby.

Heller, A. (1980). Can 'true' and 'false' needs be posited? In K. Lederer (Ed.), *Human Needs: A contribution to the current debate*. Cambridge, MA: Oelgeschlager, Gunn & Hain.

Helliwell, J., Layard, R., & Sachs, J. (2012). *World Happiness Report*. New York: Sustainable Development Solutions Network.

Henman, P., & Fenger, M. (Eds.). (2006). *Administering Welfare Reform: International transformations in welfare governance*. Bristol: The Policy Press.

Hessel, S. (2011). *Time for Outrage! (Indignez-vous!)*. London: Quartet Books.

Hewitt, M. (1993). Social movements and social need: Problems with post-modern political theory. *Critical Social Policy, 13*(37), 52–71.

Hill, M. (2006). *Social Policy in the Modern World: A comparative text.* Oxford: Blackwell.

Himmelfarb, G. (1995). *The De-Moralisation of Society.* London: Institute of Economic Affairs.

Hindess, B. (1987). *Freedom, Equality and the Market.* London: Tavistock.

Hirsch, F. (1977). *The Social Limits to Growth.* London: Routledge & Kegan Paul.

Hirst, P. (1980). Law, socialism and rights. In P. Carlen & M. Collison (Eds.), *Radical Issues in Criminology.* Oxford: Martin Robertson.

Hirst, P., & Thompson, G. (1996). *Globalization in Question: The international economy and the possibilities of governance.* Cambridge: Polity.

Hobbes, T. (1651). *Leviathan* (1991 revised student edition, edited by R. Tuck, R. Guess & Q. Skinner). Cambridge: Cambridge University Press.

Hobsbawm, E. (1962). *The Age of Revolution: 1789–1848.* New York: Mentor.

Hohfeld, W. (1946). *Fundamental Legal Conceptions as Applied in Judicial Reasoning.* New Haven, CT: Yale University Press.

Holden, C. (2008). International trade and welfare. In N. Yeates (Ed.), *Understanding Global Social Policy.* Bristol: The Policy Press.

Holliday, I. (2000). Productivist welfare capitalism: Social policy in East Asia. *Political Studies, 48*(4), 706–723.

Hollifeld, J. (1992). *Immigrants, Markets and States.* Cambridge, MA: Harvard University Press.

Holloway, J., & Picciotto, S. (Eds.). (1978). *State and Capital: A Marxist debate.* London: Arnold.

Holston, J. (2009). Insurgent citizenship in an era of global urban periperies. *City and Society, 21*(2), 245–267.

Holzmann, R., & Hinz, R. (2005). *Old-Age Income Support in the 21st Century: An international perspective on pension systems and reform.* Washington, DC: World Bank.

Honneth, A. (1995). *The Struggle for Recognition: The moral grammar of social conflicts.* Cambridge: Polity.

Hood, C. (1991). A public management for all seasons? *Public Administration, 69*(1), 3–19.

Howe, D. (2009). *A Brief Introduction to Social Work Theory.* Basingstoke: Palgrave Macmillan.

Hulme, R., & Hulme, M. (2008). The global transfer of social policy. In N. Yeates (Ed.), *Understanding Global Social Policy.* Bristol: The Policy Press.

Humpage, L. (2010). Revisioning comparative welfare state studies: An indigenous dimension. *Policy Studies, 31*(5), 539–557.

Hunt, A. (1978). *The Sociological Movement in Law.* Basingstoke: Macmillan.

Hunt, A. (1990). Rights and social movements: Counter-hegemonic strategies. *Journal of Law and Society, 17*(3), 309–328.

Hunt, P. (1996). *Reclaiming Social Rights.* Aldershot: Dartmouth/Ashgate.

Hunt, P. (2006). *Report of the Special Rapporteur on the Right of Everyone to the Enjoyment of the Highest Attainable Standard of Physical and Mental Health to the UN Economic and Social Council.* Geneva: UN Commission on Human Rights.

Hunt, P., Nowak, M., & Osmani, S. (2004). *Human Rights and Poverty Reduction: A conceptual framework.* Geneva: Office of the High Commissioner for Human Rights (OHCHR).

Ignatieff, M. (1984). *The Needs of Strangers.* London: Chatto and Windus.

Illich, I. (1971). *Deschooling Society.* London: Calder & Boyars.

Illich, I. (1973). *Tools for Conviviality.* London: Calder & Boyars.

Illich, I. (1977). *Towards a History of Needs.* New York: Bantam/Random House.

Illich, I., McKnight, J., Zola, I., Caplan, J., & Shaiken, H. (1977). *Disabling Professions.* London: Marion Boyars.

Inglehart, R. (1990). *Culture Shift in Advanced Industrial Society.* Princeton, NJ: Princeton University Press.

International Labour Organisation (ILO). (1995). *Protection Against Unjustified Dismissal (Report to International Labour Conference 82nd Session).* Geneva: ILO.

International Labour Organisation (ILO). (1999). *Report of ILO Director-General: Decent Work, International Labour Conference, 87th Session.* Geneva: ILO.

International Labour Organisation (ILO). (2009). *General Survey Concerning the Occupational Safety and Health Convention, 1981 (No. 155), the Occupational Safety and Health Recommendation, 1981 (No. 164), and the Protocol of 2002 to the Occupational Safety and Health Convention, 1981.* Geneva: ILO.

International Labour Organisation (ILO). (2010). *World Social Security Report 2010/11.* Geneva: ILO.

International Labour Organisation (ILO). (2011). *Equality at Work: The continuing challenge (Global Report under the follow-up to the ILO Declaration on Fundamental Principles and Rights at Work).* Geneva: ILO.

International Labour Organisation (ILO). (2012a). *Global Wage Report 2012/13.* Geneva: ILO.

International Labour Organisation (ILO). (2012b). *Social Protection Floors Recommendation, 2012 (No. 202): Recommendation concerning National Floors of Social Protection.* Geneva: ILO.

Ishkanian, A., & Szrerter, S. (Eds.). (2012). *The Big Society Debate: A new research agenda for social policy.* Cheltenham: Edward Elgar.

Isin, E., Brodie, J., Juteau, D., & Stasiulis, D. (2008). Recasting the social in citizenship. In E. Isin (Ed.), *Recasting the Social in Citizenship.* Toronto: University of Toronto Press.

Jackson, T. (2009). *Prosperity without Growth.* London: Sustainable Development Commission.

Jacobs, H. (2013). Private property and human rights: A mismatch in the 21st century? *International Journal of Social Welfare, 22* (Supplement 1), S85–S101.

James, S. (2008, 26–28 June). *A forgotten right? The right to clothing in international law.* Paper presented at the Sixteenth Annual Australian and New Zealand Society of International Law (ANZIL) Conference, Canberra, Australia.

Jessop, B. (2002). *The Future of the Capitalist State.* Cambridge: Polity.

Jo, Y., & Walker, R. (2014). Self-sufficiency, social assistance and the shaming of poverty. In E. Gubrium, S. Pellissery & I. Lodemel (Eds.), *The Shame of It: Global perspectives on anti-poverty policies.* Bristol: The Policy Press.

Johnson, N. (1987). *The Welfare State in Transition: The theory and practice of welfare pluralism.* Brighton: Wheatsheaf.

Jones, C. (1993). The Pacific challenge: Confucian welfare states. In C. Jones (Ed.), *New Perspectives on the Welfare State in Europe.* London: Routledge.

Jones, D. (2012, 18 June). *Human dignity in healthcare: A virtue ethics approach.* Paper presented at the Anscombe Bioethics Centre Conference on 'Human Dignity', Blackfriars Hall, Oxford, UK.

Jones, P. (1994). *Rights.* Basingstoke: Macmillan.

Jordan, B. (1973). *Paupers: The making of the claiming class.* London: Routledge & Kegan Paul.

Jordan, B. (1996). *A Theory of Poverty and Social Exclusion.* Cambridge: Polity.

Jordan, B. (1998). *The New Politics of Welfare.* London: Sage.

Jordan, B. (2008). *Welfare and Well-Being: Social value in public policy.* Bristol: The Policy Press.

Jowell, J. (1975). *Law and Bureaucracy: Administrative discretion and the limits of legal action.* New York: Dunellan.

Jung, C., Hirschl, R., & Rosevar, E. (2013). Economic and social rights in national constitutions. *Social Science Research Network.* Retrieved 23 January 2015 from http://dx.doi.org/10.2139/ssrn.2349680

Kabeer, N. (2004). Globalization, labor standards, and women's rights: Dilemmas of collective (in) action in an interdependent world. *Feminist Economics, 10*(1), 3–35.

Kaldor, M. (2003). *Global Civil Society: An answer to war.* Cambridge: Polity.

Kamenka, E., & Tay, A. (1975). Beyond bourgeois individualism: The contemporary crisis in law and legal ideology. In E. Kamenka & R. Neale (Eds.), *Feudalism, Capitalism and Beyond.* London: Edward Arnold.

Kananen, J. (2014). *The Nordic Welfare States in Three Eras: From emancipation to discipline.* Farnham: Ashgate.

Kant, I. (1785). *Groundwork of the Metaphysics of Morals* (1991 edition). London: Routledge.

Karshenas, M., & Moghadam, V. (2006). *Social Policy in the Middle East.* Basingstoke: Palgrave Macmillan.

Kelly, A. (1994). *The National Curriculum: A critical review.* London: Paul Chapman.

Kendall, J., & Knapp, M. (1995). A loose and baggy monster. In J. Davis Smith, C. Rochester & R. Hedley (Eds.), *An Introduction to the Voluntary Sector.* London: Routledge.

Kerton, S. (2012). Tahrir, here? The influence of the Arab uprisings on the emergence of Occupy. *Social Movement Studies: Journal of Social, Cultural and Political Protest, 11*(3–4), 302–308.

Khaliq, U., & Churchill, R. (2008). The European Committee on Social Rights. In M. Langford (Ed.), *Social Rights Jurisprudence: Emerging trends in international and comparative law.* Cambridge: Cambridge University Press.

Kim, S.-Y. (2011). *The Politics of Struggle in a State-Civil Society Partnership: A Case Study of a South Korean Workfare Partnership Programme,* PhD thesis, London School of Economics and Political Science.

King, D. (1999). *In the Name of Liberalism: Illiberal social policy in the United States and Britain.* Oxford: Oxford University Press.

King, J. (2008). United Kingdom. In M. Langford (Ed.), *Social Rights Jurisprudence: Emerging trends in international and comparative law.* Cambridge: Cambridge University Press.

Klug, F. (2000). *Values for a Godless Age: The story of the United Kingdom's new Bill of Rights.* London: Penguin.

Knijn, T., Martin, C., & Millar, J. (2007). Activation as a common framework for social policies towards lone parents. *Social Policy & Administration, 41*(6), 638–652.

Köhler, G., & Pogge, T. (2014, August). Big holes in the SDG draft. *CROP (Comparative Research on Poverty) Poverty Brief, 21.* Retrieved 1 December 2014 from www.crop.org

Korpi, W. (1983). *The Democratic Class Struggle.* London: Routledge & Kegan Paul.

Kuznets, S. (1955). Economic growth and income inequality. *American Economic Review, 45*(1), 1–28.

Kymlicka, W. (1995). *Multicultural Citizenship: A liberal theory of minority rights.* Oxford: Clarendon Press.

Langan, M., & Ostner, I. (1991). Gender and welfare: Towards a comparative framework. In G. Room (Ed.), *Towards a European Welfare State?* Bristol: School for Advanced Urban Studies (SAUS).

Langford, M. (2008a). The justiciability of social rights: From practice to theory. In M. Langford (Ed.), *Social Rights Jurisprudence: Emerging trends in international and comparative law.* Cambridge: Cambridge University Press.

Langford, M. (Ed.). (2008b). *Social Rights Jurisprudence: Emerging trends in international and comparative law.* Cambridge: Cambridge University Press.

Langford, M., & King, J. (2008). Committee on Economic, Social and Cultural Rights: Past, present and future. In M. Langford (Ed.), *Social Rights Jurisprudence: Emerging trends in international and comparative law.* Cambridge: Cambridge University Press.

Le Grand, J. (1982). *The Strategy of Equality.* London: Allen and Unwin.

Le Grand, J. (1990). *Quasi-Markets and Social Policy.* Bristol: School for Advanced Urban Studies (SAUS).

Le Grand, J., & Robinson, R. (Eds.). (1984). *Privatisation and the Welfare State.* London: Allen and Unwin.

Lederer, K. (Ed.). (1980). *Human Needs: A contribution to the current debate.* Cambridge, MA: Oelge-schlager, Gunn & Hain.

Lee, S., McCann, D., & Messenger, J. (2007). *Working Time Around the World: Trends in working hours, laws and policies in a global comparative perspective.* London: Routledge.

Leggatt, A. (2001). *Tribunals for users: One system, one service.* London: Lord Chancellor's Office.

Leibfried, S. (1993). Towards a European welfare state? On integrating poverty regimes into the European Community. In C. Jones (Ed.), *New Perspectives on the Welfare State in Europe.* London: Routledge.

Leisering, L., & Barrientos, A. (2013). Social ctizenship for the global poor? The worldwide spread of social assistance. *International Journal of Social Welfare, 22*(Supplement 1), S50–S67.

Lenaghan, J. (1997). Citizens' rights to health care in the UK. In J. Lenaghan (Ed.), *Hard Choices in Health Care.* London: British Medical Journal (BMJ) Books.

Lenin, V. (1902). *What Is to Be Done? Burning questions of our movement* (1934 edition). London: International Publishers.

Leung, J. (1994). Dismantling the 'Iron Rice Bowl': Welfare reforms in the People's Republic of China. *Journal of Social Policy, 23*(3), 341–362.

Levitas, R. (Ed.). (1986). *The Ideology of the New Right.* Cambridge: Polity.

Lewis, G., Gewirtz, S., & Clarke, J. (Eds.). (2000). *Rethinking Social Policy*. London: Sage.

Lewis, J. (2000). Work and care. In H. Dean, R. Sykes & R. Woods (Eds.), *Social Policy Review 12*. Newcastle: Social Policy Association.

Lewis, J. (2001). Family change and lone parents as a social problem. In M. May, R. Page & E. Brunsdon (Eds.), *Understanding Social Problems: Issues in social policy*. Oxford: Blackwell.

Lewis, J. (2006). Work/family reconciliation, equal opportunities and social policies: The interpretation of policy trajectories at the EU level and the meaning of gender equality. *Journal of European Public Policy, 13*(3), 420–437.

Lewis, J. (2009). *Work-family balance, gender and policy*. Cheltenham: Edward Elgar.

Lewis, J., & Surender, R. (Eds.). (2004). *Welfare State Change: Towards a Third Way?* Oxford: Oxford University Press.

Lewis, N., & Birkinshaw, P. (1993). *When Citizens Complain: Reforming justice and administration*. Buckingham: Open University Press.

Liddiard, M. (2001). Homelessness. In M. May, R. Page & E. Brunsdon (Eds.), *Understanding Social Problems: Issues in social policy*. Oxford: Blackwell.

Liebenberg, S. (2008). South Africa. In M. Langford (Ed.), *Social Rights Jurisprudence: Emerging trends in international and comparative law*. Cambridge: Cambridge University Press.

Lipset, M. (1963). *Political Man*. London: Mercury Books.

Lipsky, M. (1980/2010). *Street-level Bureaucracy: Dilemmas of the individual in public services*. New York: Russell Sage Foundation.

Lister, R. (1990). *The Exclusive Society: Citizenship and the poor*. London: Child Poverty Action Group.

Lister, R. (2003). *Citizenship: Feminist perspectives* (2nd edition). Basingstoke: Macmillan.

Lister, R. (2004). *Poverty*. Cambridge: Polity.

Lister, R. (2010). *Understanding Theories and Concepts in Social Policy*. Bristol: The Policy Press.

Lock, F. P. (1999). *Edmund Burke* (Vol. 1). Oxford: Clarendon Press.

Locke, J. (1690). *Two Treatises on Civil Government* (1960 edition, edited by P. Laslett). New York: Mentor.

Lockwood, D. (1996). Civic integration and class formation. *British Journal of Sociology, 47*(3), 531–550.

Lødemel, I., & Trickey, H. (Eds.). (2000). *'An Offer You Can't Refuse': Workfare in international perspective*. Bristol: The Policy Press.

Luhmann, N. (1987). The self-regulation of law and its limits. In G. Teubner (Ed.), *Dilemmas of Law in the Welfare State*. Berlin: Walter de Gruyter.

Lukács, G. (1971). *History and Class Consciousness*. London: Merlin Press.

Lund, F. (2008). *Changing Social Policy: The Child Support Grant in South Africa*. Cape Town: Human Sciences Research Council (HSRC) Press.

Lynes, T. (1975). Unemployment assistance tribunals in the 1930s. In M. Adler & A. Bradley (Eds.), *Justice, Discretion and Poverty*. Abingdon: Professional Books.

Lyotard, J. (1984). *The Postmodern Condition: A report on knowledge*. Manchester: Manchester University Press.

MacIntyre, A. (1999). *Dependent Rational Animals: Why human beings need the virtues*. Peru, IL: Carus Publishing.

MacIntyre, A. (2007). *After Virtue* (3rd edition). Notre Dame, IN: Notre Dame Press.

Macklin, R. (2003). Dignity is a useless concept. *British Medical Journal*. doi: http//dx.doi.org/10.1136/bmj.327.7429.1419

Mamdani, M. (1996). *Citizen and Subject: Contemporary Africa and the legacy of late colonialism*. Princeton, NJ: Princeton University Press.

Mameli, A. (1997). Poverty and group consciousness: The role of legal aid in social reforms. In A. Kjønstad & J. Veit-Wilson (Eds.), *Law, Power and Poverty*. Bergen: Comparative Research on Poverty (CROP).

Mann, M. (1987). Ruling class strategies and citizenship. *Sociology, 21*(3), 355–376.

Manning, N. (2007). Turkey, the EU and social policy. *Social Policy & Society, 6*(4), 491–501.

Mantouvalou, V. (2011). In support of legalisation. In C. Gearty & V. Mantouvalou (Eds.), *Debating Social Rights*. Oxford: Hart Publishing.

Marcano, C. (2009). From the neo-liberal barrio to the socialist commune. *Human Geography, 2*(3), 75–88.

Marcuse, H. (1964). *One Dimensional Man: Studies in the ideology of advanced industrial society.* Boston, MA: Beacon Press.

Marks, S. (2004). The human right to development: Between rhetoric and reality. *Harvard Human Rights Journal, 17,* 137–168.

Marks, S. (2013). The emergence and scope of the human right to health. In M. Zuniga, S. Marks & L. Gostin (Eds.), *Advancing the Human Right to Health.* Oxford: Oxford University Press.

Marmot, M. (2010). *Fair Society, Healthy Lives.* London: The Marmot Review.

Marshall, G. (1997). *Repositioning Class.* London: Sage.

Marshall, T. H. (1950). Citizenship and social class. In T. Marshall & T. Bottomore (Eds.), *Citizenship and Social Class* (1992 edition). London: Pluto.

Marshall, T. H. (1981). *The Right to Welfare and Other Essays.* London: Heinemann.

Marx, K. (1844). Economic and philosophical manuscripts. In L. Colletti (Ed.), *Early Writings* (1975 edition). Harmondsworth: Penguin.

Marx, K. (1848). *The Revolutions of 1848* (1973 edition, Vol. 2). Harmondsworth: Penguin.

Marx, K. (1859). Preface to a contribution to the critique of political economy. In *Marx and Engels Selected Works* (1969 edition, Vol. 1). Moscow: Progress.

Marx, K. (1887). *Capital* (1970 edition, Vol. 1). London: Lawrence & Wishart.

Marx, K. (1893). *Capital* (1956 edition, Vol. 2). London: Lawrence & Wishart.

Marx, K. (1894). *Capital* (1959 edition, Vol. 3). London: Lawrence & Wishart.

Marx, K., & Engels, F. (1848). *The Communist Manifesto* (1970 Merit Pamphlet edition). New York: Pathfinder Press.

Maslow, A. (1943). A theory of human motivation. *Psychological Review, 50*(4), 370–396.

Massey, D. (2008). Notas sobre la geometria del poder. *Dio-critica, 5,* 56–59.

Maxwell, S. (2005). *The Washington Consensus Is Dead! Long live the meta-narrative! (Working Paper 243).* London: Overseas Development Institute.

M'Baye, K. (1972). Le Droit au Développement comme un droit de l'Homme. *Revue des Droits de l'Homme, 5,* 503–505.

McCarthy, P., Simpson, B., Hill, M., Walker, J., & Corlyon, J. (1992). *Grievances, Complaints and Local Government: Towards the responsive local authority.* Aldershot: Avebury.

McGregor, J. (2007). Researching wellbeing: From concepts to methodology. In I. Gough & J. McGregor (Eds.), *Wellbeing in Developing Countries: From theory to research.* Cambridge: Cambridge University Press.

McLaughlin, E. (1999). Social security and poverty: Women's business. In J. Ditch (Ed.), *Introduction to Social Security: Policies, benefits and poverty.* London: Routledge.

McQueen, J. (2013). *Guide to Landlord and Tenant Law.* London: Emerald Publishing.

Mead, L. (1997). *From Welfare to Work: Lessons from America.* London: Institute of Economic Affairs (IEA) Health & Welfare Unit.

Meadows, D., Randers, J., & Behrens III, W. (1972). *The Limits to Growth.* London: Pan.

Mehedi, M. (1999, 8 July). *The content of the right to education (A working paper presented to the Sub-Commission on Prevention of Discrimination and Protection of Minorities),* UN Economic and Social Council, New York.

Meiksins-Wood, E. (1995). *Democracy Against Capitalism: Renewing historical materialism.* Cambridge: Cambridge University Press.

Melish, T. (2008). The Inter-American Commission on Human Rights/The Inter-American Court on Human Rights. In M. Langford (Ed.), *Social Rights Jurisprudence: Emerging trends in international and comparative law.* Cambridge: Cambridge University Press.

Menger, C. (1871). *Principles of Economics* (1950 English language edition). Glencoe, IL: The Free Press.

Meyer, J. (2007). Globalization: Theory and trends. *International Journal of Comparative Sociology, 48*(4), 261–273.

Meyer, J., Boli, J., Thomas, G., & Ramirez, F. (1997). World society and the nation state. *American Journal of Sociology, 103*(1), 144–181.

Midgley, J. (1995). *Social Development: The developmental perspective in social welfare.* London: Sage.

Midgley, J. (2013a). Social development and social welfare: Implications for comparative social policy. In P. Kennett (Ed.), *Comparative Social Policy* (2nd edition). Cheltenham: Elgar.

Midgley, J. (2013b). *Social Development: Theory and practice.* London: Sage.

Milanovic, B. (2007). Globalization and inequality. In D. Held & A. Kaya (Eds.), *Global Inequality.* Cambridge: Polity.

Miles, R. (1989). *Racism.* London: Routledge.

Mill, J.S. (1859). *On Liberty* (1972 edition). London: J.M. Dent & Sons.

Mishra, R. (1984). *The Welfare State in Crisis.* Hemel Hempstead: Harvester Wheatsheaf.

Mishra, R. (1990). *The Welfare State in Capitalist Society.* Hemel Hempstead: Harvester Wheatsheaf.

Mishra, R. (1999). *Globalisation and the Welfare State.* Hemel Hempstead: Harvester Wheatsheaf.

Modood, T. (2007). *Multiculturalism.* Cambridge: Polity.

Moore, B. J. (1978). *Injustice: The social bases of obedience and revolt.* New York: Macmillan.

Morabito, C., Vandenbroek, M., & Roose, R. (2013). 'The greatest of equalisers': A critical review of international organisations' views on early childhood care and education. *Journal of Social Policy, 42*(3), 451–467.

Morris, J. (1991). *Pride against Prejudice: Transforming attitudes to disability.* London: Women's Press.

Morris, J. (2003). Community care or independent living? In N. Ellison & C. Pierson (Eds.), *Developments in British Social Policy 2.* Basingstoke: Palgrave.

Morris, L. (2002). *Managing Migration: Civic stratification and migrants' rights.* London: Routledge.

Morris, L. (2006). Social rights, trans-national rights and civic stratification. In L. Morris (Ed.), *Rights: Sociological perspectives.* London: Routledge.

Moss, P. (2005). Learning with other countries. In Daycare Trust (Ed.), *Learning with Other Countries: International models of early education and care.* London: Daycare Trust.

Mulcahy, L., & Lloyd-Bostock, S. (1992). Complaining – What's the use? In R. Dingwall & P. Fenn (Eds.), *Quality and Regulation in Health Care: International experiences.* London: Routledge.

Munck, R. (2005). *Globalization and Social Exclusion.* Bloomfield, CT: Kumarian Press.

Muralidhar, S. (2008). India. In M. Langford (Ed.), *Social Rights Jurisprudence: Emerging trends in international and comparative law.* Cambridge: Cambridge University Press.

Musgrave, R. (1959). *The Theory of Public Finance.* New York: McGraw-Hill.

Naandi Foundation. (2011). *HUNGaMA Survey Report: Fighting hunger and malnutrition.* Hyderbad: Naandi Foundation.

National Consumer Council (NCC). (1977). *The Fourth Right of Citizenship: A review of local advice services.* London: NCC.

Nedelsky, J., & Scott, C. (1992). Constitutional dialogue. In J. Bakan & D. Schneiderman (Eds.), *Social Justice and the Constitution: Perspectives on a social union for Canada.* Ottawa: Carleton University Press.

Neuberger, J. (2010). *The Report of the Advisory Panel on Judicial Diversity.* London: Ministry of Justice.

New Economics Foundation (NEF). (2012). *Happy Planet Index: 2012 report.* London: NEF.

Newby, H. (1996). Citizenship in a green world: Global commons and human stewardship. In M. Bulmer & A. Rees (Eds.), *Citizenship Today: The contemporary relevance of T. H. Marshall.* London: UCL Press.

Newman, B., & Thompson, R. (1989). Economic growth and social development: A longitudinal analysis of causal priority. *World Development, 17*(4), 461–471.

Nissanke, M. (2003). *The Revenue Potential of the Currency Transfer Tax for Development Finance: A critical appraisal (World Institute for Development Economics Research (WIDER) Discussion Paper No. 2003/81).* Helsinki: UN.

Novak, T. (1988). *Poverty and the State.* Milton Keynes: Open University Press.

Nowak, M. (2001). The right to education. In A. Eide, C. Krause & A. Rosas (Eds.), *Economic, Social and Cultural Rights: A textbook* (2nd edition). Dordrecht: Martinus Nijhoff.

Nowak, M. (2011, 19 May). Informal oral presentation to the Road to Global Social Citizenship Co-operation Group, convened at the Center for Interdisciplinary Studies (ZiF), Bielefeld, Germany.

Nozick, R. (1974). *Anarchy, State and Utopia.* Oxford: Blackwell.

Nussbaum, M. (1999). Virtue ethics: A misleading category? *Journal of Ethics, 3*(3), 163–201.

Nussbaum, M. (2011). *Creating Capabilities: The human development approach.* Cambridge, MA: Belknap Press of Harvard University Press.

Nyers, P. (Ed.). (2009). *Securitizations of Citizenship.* Abingdon: Routledge.

O'Connor, J. (1973). *Fiscal Crisis of the State.* New York: St. Martin's Press.

Offe, C. (1972). Advanced capitalism and the welfare state. *Politics and Society, 2*(4), 479–488.

Offe, C. (1984). *Contradictions of the Welfare State.* Cambridge, MA: MIT Press.

Office of the High Commissioner for Human Rights (OHCHR). (2006). *Draft Principles and Guidelines for a Human Rights Approach to Poverty Reduction Strategies.* Geneva: OHCHR.

Office of the High Commissioner for Human Rights (OHCHR). (2012). *Principles and Guidelines for a Human Rights Approach to Poverty Reduction Strategies.* Geneva: OHCHR.

Office of the High Commissioner for Human Rights (OHCHR). (2013). *Directory of Special Procedures Mandate Holders.* Geneva: OHCHR.

Oliver, M. (1990). *The Politics of Disablement: A sociological approach.* Basingstoke: Macmillan.

O'Mathúna, D., Scott, A., McAuley, A., Walsh-Daneshmandi, A., & Daly, B. (2005). *Health Care Rights and Responsibilities: A review of the European Charter of Patients' Rights.* Dublin: Irish Patients' Association.

O'Neill, J. (2001). Building better global economic BRICs. *Goldman Sachs & Co. Global Economic Paper* (66). Retrieved 1 December 2014 from http://www.goldmansachs.com/our-thinking/archive/archive-pdfs/build-better-brics.pdf

O'Neill, O. (1986). *Faces of Hunger: An essay on poverty, justice and development.* London: Allen and Unwin.

O'Neill, O. (2005). The dark side of human rights. *International Affairs* (81), 427–439.

Organisation for Economic Co-operation and Development (OECD). (2010). *PISA 2009 Results: Overcoming social background – Equity in learning opportunities and outcomes* (Vol. II). Paris: OECD.

Organisation for Economic Co-operation and Development (OECD). (2011). *Divided We Stand.* Paris: OECD.

Organisation for Economic Co-operation and Development (OECD). (2013). *How's Life? 2013: Measuring well-being.* Paris: OECD.

Paine, T. (1791). *The Rights of Man* (1984 edition). Harmondsworth: Penguin.

Palmer, E. (2007). *Judicial Review, Socio-Economic Rights and the Human Rights Act.* Oxford: Hart Publishing.

Papadakis, E., & Taylor-Gooby, P. (1987). *The Private Provision of Public Welfare: State, market and community.* Brighton: Wheatsheaf.

Parekh, S. (2008). *Hannah Arendt and the Challenge of Modernity.* Abingdon: Routledge.

Pascall, G. (1986). *Social Policy: A feminist analysis.* London: Tavistock.

Pascall, G. (1997). *Social Policy: A new feminist analysis.* London: Routledge.

Pascall, G. (2012). *Gender Equality in the Welfare State.* Bristol: The Policy Press.

Pashukanis, E. (1978). *General Theory of Law and Marxism.* London: Ink Links.

Patomäki, H., & Teivainen, T. (2004). *A Possible World: Democratic transformation of global institutions.* London: Zed books.

Peck, J. (2001). *Workfare States.* New York: Guilford Press.

Peck, J., & Tickell, A. (2012). Neoliberalism resurgent? Market rule after the great recession. *South Atlantic Quarterly, 111*(2), 265–288.

Pecoud, A., & de Guchteneire, P. (2005). *Migration without Borders: An investigation into the free movement of people (Global Migration Perspectives – Research Paper No. 27).* Paris: UNESCO Global Commission on International Migration.

Pellegrino, E., Schulman, A., & Merrill, T. (Eds.). (2009). *Human Dignity and Bioethics.* Notre Dame, IN: Notre Dame University Press.

Peng, I. (2002). Social care in crisis: Gender, demography, and welfare state restructuring in Japan. *Social Politics, 9*(3), 441–443.

Perry, R. (Ed.). (1964). *Sources of Our Liberties.* New York: McGraw-Hill.

Pfeffer, N., & Coote, A. (1991). *Is Quality Good for You? A critical review of quality assurance in welfare services.* London: Institute for Public Policy Research (IPPR).

Phillips, A. (1999). *Which Equalities Matter?* Cambridge: Polity.

Phillips, A. (2007). *Multiculturalism without Culture.* Princeton, NJ: Princeton University Press.

Piachaud, D. (1981, 10 September). Peter Townsend and the Holy Grail. *New Society, 57,* 419–421.

Pickerill, J., & Krinsky, J. (2012). Why does Occupy matter? *Social Movement Studies: Journal of Social, Cultural and Political Protest, 11*(3–4), 279–287.

Pierson, C. (1998). *Beyond the Welfare State.* Cambridge: Polity

Pierson, C. (2001). *Hard Choices: Social democracy in the 21st century.* Cambridge: Polity.

Piovesan, F. (2008). Brazil: Impact and challenges of social rights in the courts. In M. Langford (Ed.), *Social Rights Jurisprudence: Emerging trends in international and comparative law.* Cambridge: Cambridge University Press.

Piven, F., & Cloward, R. (1977). *Poor People's Movements.* New York: Pantheon Books.

Plant, R. (1992). Citizenship, rights and welfare. In A. Coote (Ed.), *The Welfare of Citizens: Developing new social rights.* London: Institute for Public Policy Research (IPPR)/Rivers Oram Press.

Plant, R., Lesser, H., & Taylor-Gooby, P. (1980). *Political Philosophy and Social Welfare.* London: Routledge & Kegan Paul.

Platt, L. (2011). *Understanding Inequalities.* Cambridge: Polity.

Pogge, T. (2002). *World Poverty and Human Rights.* Cambridge: Polity.

Pogge, T. (Ed.). (2007). *Freedom from Poverty as a Human Right: Who owes what to the very poor?* Oxford: Oxford University Press.

Pointer, F. (1896). *A History of Education* (2006 replica edition). Boston, MA: Elibron Classics.

Polanyi, K. (1944). *The Great Transformation.* New York: Rinehart.

Polis, A., & Schwab, P. (1979). Human rights: A Western concept with limited applicability. In A. Polis & P. Schwab (Eds.), *Human Rights: Cultural and ideological perspectives.* New York: Praeger.

Pollock, A., & Price, D. (2013). *Duty to Care: In defence of universal healthcare.* London: Centre for Labour and Social Studies.

Porter, D., & Craig, D. (2004). The Third Way and the Third World: Poverty reduction and social inclusion in the rise of 'inclusive' liberalism. *Review of International Political Economy, 11*(2), 387–423.

Powell, E. (1972). *Still to Decide.* London: Elliot Right Way Books.

Powell, F. (2007). *The Politics of Civil Society: Neoliberalism or Social Left?* Bristol: The Policy Press.

Powell, M. (Ed.). (2007). *Understanding the Mixed Economy of Welfare.* Bristol: The Policy Press.

Prendergast, R. (2005). The concept of freedom and its relation to economic development – A critical appreciation of the work of Amartya Sen. *Cambridge Journal of Economics, 29*(6), 1145–1170.

Prime Minister's Office. (1991). *The Citizen's Charter: Raising the standard.* Cm. 1599. London: Her Majesty's Stationery Office (HMSO).

Prosser, T. (1983). *Test Cases for the Poor.* London: Child Poverty Action Group.

PSE UK. (2013). *The Impoverishment of the UK – PSE UK first results: Living standards.* Bristol: PSE UK.

Putnam, R. (1993). *Making Democracy Work.* Princeton, NJ: Princeton University Press.

Ramose, M. (2003). Globalisation and ubuntu. In P. Coetzee & A. Roux (Eds.), *The African Philosophy Reader.* London: Routledge.

Raphael, D. (1989). Enlightenment and revolution. In N. MacCormick & Z. Bankowski (Eds.), *Enlightenment, Rights and Revolution.* Aberdeen: Aberdeen University Press.

Rawls, J. (1972). *A Theory of Justice.* Oxford: Oxford University Press.

Reader, S. (2006). Does a basic needs approach need capabilities? *The Journal of Political Philosophy, 14*(3), 337–350.

Reich, C. (1964). The new property. *Yale Law Journal, 73*(5), 733–787.

Ridge, T. (2002). *Childhood poverty and social exclusion: From a child's perspective.* Bristol: The Policy Press.

Rieger, E., & Leibfried, S. (2003). *Limits to Globalization.* Cambridge: Polity.

Roche, M. (1992). *Re-thinking Citizenship.* Cambridge: Polity.

Rodgers, G., Gore, C., & Figueiredo, J. (Eds.). (1995). *Social Exclusion: Rhetoric, reality, responses.* Geneva: International Labour Organisation.

Rolnik, R. (2013, 29 August–11 September). *Report of the Special Rapporteur on Adequate Housing as a Component of the Right to an Adequate Standard of Living, and on the Right to Non-Discrimination in This*

Context on Her Mission to the United Kingdom of Great Britain and Northern Ireland. Geneva: Human Rights Council.

Roosevelt, F.D. (1941). State of the Union address to Congress 6 January. Retrieved 1 December 2014 from http://www.ourdocuments.gov/doc.php?flash=false&doc=70&page=transcript

Roosevelt, F.D. (1944). State of the Union address to Congress 11 January. In S. Rosenman (Ed.), *The Public Papers and Addresses of Franklin D. Roosevelt* (1950 edition, Vol. XIII). New York: Harper.

Rosas, A. (2001). The right to development. In A. Eide, C. Krause & A. Rosas (Eds.), *Economic, Social and Cultural Rights: A textbook* (2nd edition). Dordrecht: Nijhoff.

Rose, N. (1996a). The death of the social? *Economy and Society, 25*(3), 327–356.

Rose, N. (1996b). Governing "advanced" liberal democracies. In A. Barry, T. Osborne & N. Rose (Eds.), *Foucault and Political Reason.* London: UCL Press.

Rose, R. (1988). *Ordinary People in Public Policy.* London: Sage.

Rostow, W. (1971). *The Stages of Economic Growth: A non-communist manifesto.* Cambridge: Cambridge University Press.

Roulstone, A., & Barnes, C. (Eds.). (2005). *Working Futures? Disabled people, policy and social inclusion.* Bristol: The Policy Press.

Roulstone, A., & Prideaux, S. (2012). *Understanding Disability Policy.* Bristol: The Policy Press.

Rousseau, J.-J. (1762). Of the social contract or principles of political right. In V. Gourevitch (Ed.), *Rousseau: The Social Contract and other later political writings* (1997 edition). Cambridge: Cambridge University Press.

Rys, V. (2010). *Reinventing Social Security Worldwide.* Bristol: The Policy Press.

Sachs, A. (2009). *The Strange Alchemy of Life and Law.* Oxford: Oxford University Press.

Sachs, W. (Ed.). (2010). *The Development Dictionary: A guide to knowledge as power* (2nd edition). London: Zed Books.

Sahlins, M. (1974). *Stone Age Economics.* London: Tavistock.

Salomon, M. (Ed.). (2005). *Economic, Social and Cultural Rights: A guide for minorities and indigenous peoples.* London: Minority Rights Group International.

Salomon, M. (2007). *Global Responsibility for Human Rights: World poverty and the development of international law.* Oxford: Oxford University Press.

Salomon, M. (2010). International human rights obligations in context: Structural obstacles and the demands of global justice. In B. Andreassen & S. Marks (Eds.), *Development as a Human Right: Legal, political and economic dimensions.* Antwerp: Intersentia.

Sandel, M. (1982). *Liberalism and the Limits of Justice.* Cambridge: Cambridge University Press.

Sarat, A., & Schiengold, S. (Eds.). (2001). *Cause Lawyering and the State in a Global Era.* Oxford: Oxford University Press.

Saunders, P. (1984). Beyond housing classes: The sociological significance of provate property rights in means of consumption. *International Journal of Urban and Regional Research, 8*(2), 202–227.

Saville, J. (1958). The Welfare State: An historical approach. *New Reasoner, 1*(3), 5–25.

Sawyer, M. (2003). Employer of last resort: Could it deliver full employment and price stability. *Journal of Economic Issues, 37*(4), 881–907.

Scaff, L. (1998). Max Weber. In R. Stones (Ed.), *Key Sociological Thinkers.* Basingstoke: Palgrave Macmillan.

Schiengold, S. (1974/2004). *The Politics of Rights.* Ann Arbor, MI: University of Michigan Press.

Scott, A. (1990). *Ideology and New Social Movements.* London: Unwin Hyman.

Scott, J. (1985). *Weapons of the Weak: Everyday forms of peasant resistance.* New Haven, CT: Yale University Press.

Scruton, R. (Ed.). (1991). *Conservative Texts: An anthology.* Basingstoke: Macmillan.

Sen, A. (1981). *Poverty and Famines: An essay on entitlement and deprivation.* Oxford: Clarendon Press.

Sen, A. (1982a). Equality of What? In A. Sen (Ed.), *Choice, Welfare and Measurement.* Oxford: Blackwell.

Sen, A. (1982b). Rights and agency. *Philosophy and Public Affairs, 11*(1), 3–39.

Sen, A. (1985). *Commodities and Capabilities.* Amsterdam: Elsevier.

Sen, A. (1999). *Development as Freedom.* Oxford: Oxford University Press.

Sen, A. (2004). Elements of a theory of human rights. *Philosophy and Public Affairs, 32*(4), 315–356.

Sengupta, A. (2000). Realizing the right to development. *Development and Change, 31*(3), 553–578.

Sengupta, A. (2010). The human right to development. In B. Andreassen & S. Marks (Eds.), *Development as a Human Right: Legal, political and economic dimensions* (2nd edition, pp. 13–44). Antwerp: Intersentia.

Sevenhuijsen, S. (1998). *Citizenship and the Ethics of Care.* London: Routledge.

Sevenhuijsen, S. (2000). Caring in the Third Way: The relation between obligation, responsibility and care in 'Third Way' discourse. *Critical Social Policy, 20*(1), 5–37.

Shakespeare, T. (2006). *Disability Rights and Wrongs.* London: Routledge.

Shih, S.-J. (2012). Towards Inclusive Citizenship? Rethinking China's social security in the trend towards urban-rural harmonisation. *Journal of Social Policy, 41*(4), 789–810.

Shue, H. (1980). *Basic Rights: Subsistence, affluence and US foreign policy.* Princeton: Princeton University Press.

Sivanandan, A. (1990). *Communities of Resistance: Writings on black struggles for socialism.* London: Verso.

Slote, L. (2001). *Morals from Motives.* Oxford: Oxford University Press.

Smith, A. (1759). *The Theory of Moral Sentiments* (1976 edition). Indianapolis: Liberty Fund.

Smith, A. (1776). *An Inquiry into the Nature and Causes of the Wealth of Nations* (1900 edition). London: George Routledge.

Smith, T., & Noble, M. (1995). *Education Divides: Poverty and schooling in the 1990s.* London: Child Poverty Action Group.

Soper, K. (1981). *On Human Needs.* Brighton: Harvester.

Soper, K. (1993). The thick and thin of human needing. In G. Drover & P. Kerans (Eds.), *New Approaches to Welfare Theory.* Aldershot: Edward Elgar.

Soysal, Y. (1994). *Limits of Citizenship: Migrants and postnational membership in Europe.* Chicago: Chicago University Press.

Spanish Society for International Human Rights Law (SSIHRL). (2010). *Santiago Declaration on the Human Right to Peace.* Retrieved 1 December 2014 from http://www.aedidh.org/sites/default/files/Santiago-Declaration-en.pdf

Stacey, F. (1978). *Ombudsmen Compared.* Oxford: Oxford University Press.

Standing, G. (1996). Social protection in Central and Eastern Europe: A tale of slipping anchors and torn safety-nets. In G. Esping-Andersen (Ed.), *Welfare States in Transition.* London: Sage.

Standing, G. (2009). *Work after Globalization: Building occupational citizenship.* Cheltenham: Edward Elgar.

Standing, G. (2011). *The Precariat: The new dangerous class.* London: Bloomsbury.

Standing, G. (2013). India's experiment in basic income grants. *Global Dialogue, 3*(5), 24–26.

Standing, G. (2014). *A Precariat Charter: From denizens to citizens.* London: Bloomsbury.

Starr, P. (1988). The meaning of privatization. *Yale Law and Policy Review, 6*(1), 6–41.

Steinberg, J. (2011). *Bismark: A life.* Oxford: Oxford University Press.

Stephens, M. (1982). Law centres and citizenship: The way forward. In P. Thomas (Ed.), *Law in the Balance: Legal services in the eighties.* Oxford: Martin Robertson.

Stephenson, S. (2000). Civil society and its agents in the post-communist world: The case of the Russian voluntary sector. In H. Dean, R. Sykes & R. Woods (Eds.), *Social Policy Review 12.* Newcastle: Social Policy Association.

Stewart, J. (2001). *Environmental Health and Housing.* London: Spon Press.

Stiglitz, J. (2003). *Globalization and Its Discontents.* London: Penguin.

Stiglitz, J., Sen, A., & Fitoussi, J.-P. (2009). *Report by the Commission on the Measurement of Economic Performance and Social Progress.* Retrieved 1 December 2014 from http://www.stiglitz-sen-fitoussi.fr/documents/rapport_anglais.pdf

Streeten, P., Burki, S., Ul Haq, M., Hicks, N., & Stewart, F. (1981). *First Things First: Meeting basic needs in developing countries.* Oxford: Oxford University Press.

Sumner, W. (1906). *Folkways: A study of the sociological importance of wages, manners, customs, mores and morals* (1940 edition). Boston, MA: Ginn.

Sunstein, C. (2005). Why does the American constitution lack social and economic guarantees? In M. Ignatieff (Ed.), *American Exceptionalism and Human Rights*. Princeton, NJ: Princeton University Press.

Tawney, R. (1913). Poverty as an industrial problem. In R. Tawney (Ed.), *Memoranda on the Problems of Poverty* (Vol. 2). London: William Morris Press.

Taylor, C. (1992). *The Ethics of Authenticity*. Cambridge, MA: Harvard University Press.

Taylor, D. (1998). Social identity and social policy: Engagements with post-modern theory. *Journal of Social Policy, 27*(3), 329–350.

Taylor-Gooby, P. (1994). Postmodernism and social policy: A great leap backwards? *Journal of Social Policy, 23*(3), 385–404.

Taylor-Gooby, P. (2013). *The Double Crisis of the Welfare State*. Basingstoke: Palgrave Macmillan.

Teubner, G. (Ed.). (1987). *Dilemmas of Law in the Welfare State*. Berlin: Walter de Gruyter.

The Alliance for Legal Aid. (2014). Legal aid today – LAPSO reform. Retrieved 1 April 2014 from http://www.savelegalaid.co.uk/legalaidunderlaspo.html

The Economist. (2012, 21–27 January). Special report: 'State capitalism'. *The Economist.*

Thomas, C., & Genn, H. (2013). *Understanding tribunal decision-making: A foundational empirical study.* London: Nuffield Foundation.

Thompson, C., & Brook, Y. (2011). *Neoconservatism: An obituary for an idea.* Boulder, CO: Paradigm.

Thompson, E. P. (1968). *The Making of the English Working Class.* Harmondsworth: Penguin.

Thompson, E. P. (1975). *Whigs and Hunters.* New York: Parthenon.

Thompson, E. P. (1993). *Customs in Common.* New York: The New Press.

Thomson, G. (1987). *Needs.* London: Routledge & Kegan Paul.

Titmuss, R. (1958). *Essays on the Welfare State.* London: Allen and Unwin.

Titmuss, R. (1968). *Commitment to Welfare.* London: Allen and Unwin.

Titmuss, R. (1970). *The Gift Relationship.* London: Allen and Unwin.

Titmuss, R. (1971). Welfare rights, law and discretion. *Political Quarterly, 42*(2), 113–132.

Toebs, B. (2001). The right to health. In A. Eide, C. Krause & A. Rosas (Eds.), *Economic, Social and Cultural Rights: A textbook.* Dordrecht: Martinus Nijhoff.

Torry, M. (2013). *Money for Everyone: Why we need a citizen's income.* Bristol: The Policy Press.

Townsend, P. (1979). *Poverty in the UK.* Harmondsworth: Penguin.

Townsend, P. (1981). The structured dependency of the elderly: A creation of social policy in the twentieth century. *Ageing and Society, 1*(1), 5–28.

Townsend, P. (1993). *The International Analysis of Poverty.* Hemel Hempstead: Harvester Wheatsheaf.

Townsend, P. (2002). Poverty, social exclusion and social polarisation: The need to construct an international welfare state. In P. Townsend & D. Gordon (Eds.), *World Poverty: New policies to defeat an old enemy.* Bristol: The Policy Press.

Townsend, P. (2007). *The Right to Social Security and National Development: Lessons from OECD experience for low-income countries (Discussion Paper 18).* Geneva: International Labour Organisation.

Townsend, P. (Ed.). (2009). *Building Decent Societies: Rethinking the role of social security in development.* Basingstoke: Palgrave Macmillan/International Labour Organisation.

Townsend, P., & Donkor, K. (1996). *Global Restructuring and Social Policy: An alternative strategy – Establishing an international welfare state.* Bristol: The Policy Press.

Townsend, P., & Gordon, D. (Eds.). (2002). *World Poverty: New policies to defeat an old enemy.* Bristol: The Policy Press.

Townsend, P., & Walker, A. (1981). *Disability in Britain: A manifesto of rights.* Oxford: Martin Robertson.

Tranter, K., Sleep, L., & Stannard, J. (2008). The cohabitation rule: Indeterminacy and oppression in Australian social security law. *Melbourne University Law Review, 32*(2), 698–738.

Travers, M. (2010). A sociological critique of rights. In R. Banakar (Ed.), *Rights in Context: Law and justice in late modern society.* Farnham: Ashgate.

Tronto, J. (1994). *Moral Boundaries: A political argument for an ethic of care.* New York: Routledge.

Tudor-Hart, J. (1971, 27 February). The inverse care law. *Lancet, 405*–412.

Turner, B. (1990). Outline of a theory of citizenship. *Sociology, 24*(2), 189–217.

Turner, B. (1991, 23 February). *Prolegomena to a General Theory of Social Order.* Paper presented at the ESRC workshop: Citizenship, Civil Society and Social Cohesion, London, UK.

Turner, B. (1993). Outline of a theory of human rights. *Sociology, 27*(3), 489–512.

Turner, B. (2006). *Vulnerability and Human Rights.* Pennsylvania: Pennsylvania State University.

Tweedie, J., & Hunt, A. (1994). The future of the welfare state and social rights: Reflections on Habermas. *Journal of Law and Society, 21*(3), 288–316.

Twine, F. (1994). *Citizenship and Social Rights: The interdependence of self and society.* London: Sage.

United Nations. (1993). *Vienna Declaration and Programme of Action Adopted by the World Conference on Human Rights on 25 June.* Vienna: UN.

United Nations. (1995). *The Copenhagen Declaration and Programme of Action: World Summit for Social Development.* New York: UN.

United Nations Committee on Economic Social and Cultural Rights (CESCR). (2001). *Poverty and the International Covenant on Econonomic, Social and Cultural Rights – Statement adopted by the committee, 10 May.* Geneva: ECOSOC.

United Nations Development Programme (UNDP). (1993). *Human Development Report 1993.* New York: Oxford University Press.

United Nations Development Programme (UNDP). (2000). *Human Development Report 2000.* Oxford: Oxford University Press.

United Nations Development Programme (UNDP). (2003). *Human Development Report 2003 – Millennium Development Goals: A compact among nations to end human poverty.* New York: Oxford University Press.

United Nations Development Programme (UNDP). (2006). *Human Development Report 2006: Beyond scarcity: Power, poverty and the global water crisis.* Basingstoke: Palgrave Macmillan.

United Nations Development Programme (UNDP). (2009). *Human Development Report 2009: Overcoming barriers: Human mobility and development.* Basingstoke: Palgrave Macmillan.

United Nations Development Programme (UNDP). (2010). *Human Development Report 2010: The real wealth of nations.* Basingstoke: Palgrave Macmillan.

United Nations Development Programme (UNDP). (2011). *Human Development Report 2011 – Sustainability and equity: A better future for all.* Basingstoke: Palgrave Macmillan.

United Nations Educational Scientific and Cultural Organization (UNESCO). (1994). *Salamanca Statement and Framework for Action on Special Needs Education.* Paris: UNESCO.

United Nations Educational Scientific and Cultural Organization (UNESCO). (2007). *EFA Global Monitroring Report: Strong foundations – Early childhood care and education.* Paris: UNESCO.

United Nations Educational Scientific and Cultural Organization (UNESCO). (2011). *Global Education Digest 2011.* Montreal: UNESCO Institute of Statistics (UIS).

United Nations Educational Scientific and Cultural Organization (UNESCO). (2013). *Education for All Global Monitoring Report Fact Sheet: Girls' education – The facts.* Paris: UNESCO.

United Nations General Assembly. (2000). *United Nations Millennium Declaration (Resolution 2 Session 55).* New York: UN.

United Nations General Assembly. (2012). *Human Rights and Extreme Poverty (Resolution adopted 20 December on report of the Third Committee).* New York: UN.

United Nations Human Settlements Programme (UN-HABITAT). (2003). *The Challenge of Slums – Global report on human settlements 2003.* London: Earthscan.

United Nations Human Settlements Programme (UN-HABITAT). (2009). *Planning Sustainable Cities: Global report on human settlements 2009.* London: Earthscan.

United Nations Secretary General. (2013). *A Life of Dignity for All: Accelerating progress towards the millennium development goals and advancing the United Nations development agenda beyond 2015.* New York: UN.

Vail, J. (1999). Insecure times: Conceptualising insecurity and security. In J. Vail, J. Wheelock & M. Hill (Eds.), *Insecure Times: Living with insecurity in contemporary society.* London: Routledge.

Van Buerren, G. (2002). Including the excluded: The case for an Economic, Social and Cultural Human Rights Act. *Public Law* (Autumn), 456–457.

Van Steenbergen, B. (1994). Towards a global ecological citizen. In B. Van Steenbergen (Ed.), *The Condition of Citizenship*. London: Sage.

Visser, J. (2006). Union membership statistics in 24 countries. *Monthly Labour Review, 129*(1), 38–49.

Vizard, P., & Burchardt, T. (2007). *Developing a Capability List: Final recommendations of the Equalities Review Steering Group on Measurement (CASE Paper 121)*. London: CASE/STICERD.

Vygotsky, L. (1978). *Mind and Society: The development of higher mental processes*. Cambridge, MA: Harvard University Press.

Wainwright, H. (2003). *Reclaim the State: Experiments in popular democracy*. London: Verso.

Walker, A., & Wong, C. (Eds.). (2005). *East Asian Welfare Regimes in Transition: From Confucianism to globalisation*. Bristol: The Policy Press.

Walker, R. (2005). *Social Security and Welfare: Concepts and comparisons*. Maidenhead: Open University Press.

Walker, R., Kyomuhendo, G., Chase, E., Choudry, S., Gubrium, E., Nicola, J., Lødemel, I., Mathew, L., Mwiine, A., Pellisery, S., & Ming, Y. (2013). Poverty in global perspective: Is shame a common denominator? *Journal of Social Policy, 42*(2), 215–233.

Walzer, M. (1983). *Spheres of Justice*. Oxford: Blackwell.

Walzer, M. (1994). *Thick and Thin*. Notre Dame, IN: University of Notre Dame Press.

Warde, A. (1994). Consumers, consumption and post-Fordism. In R. Burrows & B. Loader (Eds.), *Towards a Post-Fordist Welfare State?* London: Routledge.

Warnock, M. (1978). *Special Educational Needs: Report of the Committee of Enquiry into the education of handicapped children and young people*. London: Her Majesty's Stationery Office (HMSO).

Waterman, P. (2001). *Globalization, Social Movements and the New Internationalisms*. London: Continuum.

Waters, M. (1996). Human rights and the universalisation of interests: Towards a social constructionist approach. *Sociology, 30*(3), 593–600.

Watson, A. (1990). Roman law and English law: Two patterns of legal development. *Loyola Law Review, 36*(2), 247–268.

Watson, D. (1980). *Caring for Strangers*. London: Routledge & Kegan Paul.

Watson, P. (Ed.). (2013). *Health Care Reform and Globalisation: The US, China and Europe in comparativep*. London: Routledge.

Watson, T. (1995). *Sociology, Work and Industry* (3rd edition). London: Routledge.

Weaite, M. (2013). The United Kingdom: The right to health in the context of a nationalized health service. In M. Zuniga, S. Marks & L. Gostin (Eds.), *Advancing the Human Right to Health*. Oxford: Oxford University Press.

Webb, B., & Webb, S. (1935). *Soviet Communism: A new civilisation?* London: Longman.

Weber, M. (1978). *Economy and Society*. Berkeley: University of California Press.

White, S. (2003). *The Civic Minimum*. Oxford: Oxford University Press.

Whitworth, A., & Wilkinson, K. (2013). Tackling child poverty in South Africa: Implications of ubuntu for the system of social grants. *Development South Africa, 30*(1), 121–134.

Wikeley, N. (2006). *Child Support: Law and policy*. Portland, OR: Hart Publishing.

Wilensky, H. (1975). *The Welfare State and Equality: Structural and ideological roots of public expenditure*. Berkeley: University of California Press.

Wilkinson, R. (1996). *Unhealthy Societies: The afflictions of inequality*. London: Routledge.

Wilkinson, R. (2005). *The Impact of Inequality: How to make sick societies healthier*. New York: The New Press.

Wilkinson, R., & Pickett, K. (2009). *The Spirit Level: Why more equal societies almost always do better*. London: Allen Lane.

Williams, F. (1989). *Social Policy: A critical introduction*. Cambridge: Polity.

Williams, F. (1999). Good-enough principles of welfare. *Journal of Social Policy, 28*(4), 667–687.

Williams, M. (2007). Non-territorial boudaries of citizenship. In S. Benhabib, I. Shapiro & D. Petrovic (Eds.), *Identities, Affiliations and Allegiances*. Cambridge: Cambridge University Press.

Williamson, J. (1990). What Washington means by policy reform. In J. Williamson (Ed.), *Latin American Adjustment: How much has happened?* Washington, DC: Institute for International Economics.

Winnicott, D. (1953). Transitional objects and transitional phenomena. *International Journal of Psycho-analysis, 34*, 89–87.

Wolfensberger, W. (1972). *The Principle of Normalisation in Human Services.* Toronto: National Institute on Mental Retardation.

Woodiwiss, A. (2005). *Human Rights.* London: Routledge.

World Bank. (1991). *Assistance Strategies to Reduce Poverty.* Washington, DC: World Bank.

World Bank. (1994). *Averting the Old Age Crisis.* Washington, DC: World Bank.

World Bank. (2001). *World Development Report 2000/2001.* Oxford: Oxford University Press.

World Food Programme (WFP). (2013). *WFP Strategic Plan (2014–2017).* Rome: WFP.

World Health Organisation (WHO). (2005). *Resource Book on Mental Health, Human Rights and Legislation.* Geneva: WHO.

World Health Organisation (WHO). (2008). *Commission on Social Determinants of Health – Final report.* Geneva: WHO.

Wraith, R., & Hutchinson, P. (1973). *Administrative Tribunals.* London: Allen and Unwin.

Wright, G., Noble, M., Ntshongwana, P., Neves, D., & Barnes, H. (2014). *The Role of Social Security in Repsecting and Protecting the Dignity of Lone Mothers in South Africa: Final report.* Oxford: Centre for the Analysis of South African Social Policy.

Yan, M. (2014). China's dibao system. In E. Gubrium, S. Pellissery & I. Lodemel (Eds.), *The Shame of It: Global perspectives on anti-poverty policies.* Bristol: The Policy Press.

Yeates, N. (2001). *Globalization and Social Policy.* London: Sage.

Yeates, N. (Ed.). (2008). *Understanding Global Social Policy.* Bristol: The Policy Press.

Younghusband, E. (1964). *Social Work and Social Change.* London: Allen and Unwin.

Zander, M. (1978). *Legal Services for the Community.* London: Temple-Smith.

Zedillo, E. (2001). *Report of the High-level Panel on Financing for Development (to UN General Assembly).* New York: UN.

Žižek, S. (2005). Against human rights. *New Left Review, 34*(July/August), 115–131.

INDEX

Note: Page numbers followed by *b* indicate a box on the corresponding page. Page numbers followed by *f* indicate a figure on the corresponding page. Page numbers followed by *t* indicate a table on the corresponding page.